Immigrant Workers
in Industrial France

Gary S. Cross

Immigrant Workers in Industrial France
The Making of a New Laboring Class

Temple University Press
Philadelphia

Temple University Press, Philadelphia 19122
© 1983 by Temple University. All rights reserved
Published 1983
Printed in the United States of America

Publication of this book has been assisted by a
grant from the Publication Program of the
National Endowment for the Humanities.

Library of Congress Cataloging in Publication Data

Cross, Gary S.
Immigrant workers in industrial France.

Bibliography: p.
Includes index.
1. Alien labor—France—History—20th century.
2. Labor supply—France—History—20th century.
3. France—Emigration and immigration—History—
20th century. I. Title.
HD8438.A2C76 1983   304.8'44   82-19359
ISBN 0-87722-300-9

Contents

Tables

Preface

THIS is a book about the origins of a new social class in industrial societies—the non-citizen alien laborer. Largely because of its contemporaneity, it is a new topic in historical research. The immigrant worker appeared often with industrialization in the nineteenth century not only in the United States but also Britain, Germany and France. Yet the characteristics of the contemporary non-citizen work force emerge only in the twentieth century. It is a distinct product of modern capitalist democracy. While the features of this new society (and the alien working class) become clear after 1945, their origins must be found between 1914 and 1940 and first in France.

This book is not an ethnic history nor a labor history; it may inform the reader about the attitudes, actions and work patterns of immigrant laborers to France. However, it focuses on a different problem—the growing impulse to regulate international migrations. This book attempts to explain the interaction between the social actors which created this new social class. These include French business, labor, and state agencies, on the one hand, and foreign governments, political and cultural organizations, and the immigrants themselves, on the other. Within this broad context of national and international decision-making, this book is about the politics of immigration.

Writing a history is often a solitary act, sometimes too much so. Yet a number of people contributed to this work—in addition to those whose painstaking work is unceremoniously cited in the notes. Harvey Goldberg, whose sensitivity to the urgent questions of modern social history I have learned to respect, suggested this topic to me. Georges Mauco wrote the definitive contemporary work on this subject in 1932 in an exhaustive human geography of the migration of the 1920s,

Les étrangers en France. In an interview, Professor Mauco described how his interest in the social marginality of the immigrants in the early 1930s led him into the study of psychology in the 1940s and beyond. While his perspective is very different from mine, I found that Mauco's work remains extremely useful. Another book, *Les pouvoirs publics francais et l'immigration dans l'entre deux guerres*, published in 1976 by Jean-Charles Bonnet, is basically a parliamentary history of the law on immigration in the interwar period. Like Mauco's work it answers some of the questions that I cannot address.

The historical leftovers of any generation are, from the researcher's point of view, very spotty. My period left a great many theses (for the *doctorat en droit*), basis census statistics, a few surveys, and a widely scattered mine of information in newspapers and archives (largely administrative and police files). Many French librarians and archivists patiently assisted me in finding material for this often elusive topic. The University of Wisconsin supported me during my travels. Helping me to refine my interpretation and writing were historians from Wisconsin (Milwaukee as well as Madison). In particular I must thank Margo Conk, James Cronin, Darryl Holter, and Dominico Sella. Other colleagues who made comments on various parts of the book include Lynn Lees, Christopher Johnson, Gary Freeman, Judy Reardon, Nancy Green, Mark Miller, and Michael Hanagan. Jessica Myers not only typed the manuscript but offered sensible suggestions for improvements.

In my wanderings across the face of industrial France seeking those bits of data buried in the "M" series of departmental archives, I often felt like a migrant worker. Largely out of economic necessity, I stayed mostly in the immigrant quarters where I had the opportunity to get to know a number of immigrant workers. I hope that this book may contribute a little to an understanding of their history.

Immigrant Workers
in Industrial France

I   Introduction

DURING the past decade Europeans have discovered the foreign worker in their midst. Race riots in Britain, shifting policy toward migrants throughout Western Europe, and the plight of immigrants in the bidonvilles of France have attracted the attention of scholars, journalists, and film makers. The Europe that in the nineteenth century was a continent of emigration has today become a region of immigration. Social scientists have seen this wave of immigration as a phenomenon of the post-war world, resulting from the economic renaissance of Western Europe since 1950.[1] Yet a very similar rise of immigration occurred in France a generation earlier, between the World Wars.

Alone in Western Europe, and against a worldwide trend toward restricting migrations, France opened its doors in the 1920s to almost two million foreigners. So important was this wave of immigration that it constituted 75 percent of the population growth in France during the 1920s. Contemporaries usually explained interwar immigration as a temporary phenomenon caused by France's loss of one and a third million young men during the war. Because the influx of foreigners was abruptly cut off in 1931 and because the numbers of immigrants declined during the depression and World War II, the almost three million foreigners in France in 1930 were quickly forgotten. Yet the return of foreign workers after World War II and their contemporary importance in French economic and social life makes the question of the earlier immigration again relevant. Several works which have analyzed contemporary immigration in France have suggested that the immigration of the interwar period was merely a demographic substitution for lost Frenchmen and of little significance to an understanding of the contemporary role of immigrants in the French economy.[2] As we shall demonstrate, the earlier immigration was of major historical importance. It initiated a new labor system in Europe, which was resumed after World War II. The principal features of the foreign labor systems which function in contemporary Western Europe were formed during World War I and the decade thereafter in France.

The unprecedented wave of immigration into France posed the question of whether alien labor should be assimilated into French society or treated as a permanent class of subcitizens whose movements were to be regulated to serve the exigencies of the French economy. Problems which France faced in the 1920s are similar to policy dilemmas more recently debated in other industrial nations, including the United States. The contemporary rise in extralegal Hispanic immigration to the United States has stimulated a discussion of a number of policy options ranging from open borders to exclusion and temporary regulated immigration.[3] In the 1920s France anticipated many of these issues and thus an investigation of the French experience may throw light on the problems facing the United States and other advanced industrial nations.

In order to grasp the significance of this immigration it is necessary to briefly contrast the foreign labor system which emerged in the 1920s from its nineteenth century predecessors—intercontinental migrations (primarily of Europeans to the Americas and Oceania) and continental migrations of Eastern and Southern Europeans to Western Europe. Basically the familiar pattern of transoceanic migrations can be characterized as follows: immigrants were pushed by economic growth inadequate to assure prosperity for a burgeoning European population and pulled by the opportunity of the under-developed frontiers of the Americas and Oceania.[4] It was an unrestricted or liberal migration which corresponded with a laissez-faire capitalist economy. Continental European migration in the nineteenth century stands in sharp contrast: traversing relatively short distances, often merely across one frontier, continental migrants were more likely to be temporary than the transoceanic migrants. Furthermore, these peoples lacked the economic opportunity of their countrymen who made the long journey to the West. The industrializing regions of Europe which offered jobs to foreign migrants sought merely an auxiliary to the labor force. These migrants filled important gaps, often with skilled labor, but did not have the opportunity for social mobility or the possibility of acquiring property which was available for some of the transoceanic migrants. In a word, unlike the massive European settlement of the Americas, the immigration into France and elsewhere in Europe could only supplement an otherwise highly developed workforce.

While we have stressed the differences between these two types of migrations in the nineteenth century, they did share at least one important feature—they were relatively unregulated. Political controls played little role in shaping the migrations. In the receiving countries, labor groups, which favored controls, lacked political power, while business lacked an incentive to press for government intervention. World War I signaled the end of this pattern of liberalism in migration and economics. While the free market on all fronts had been on the defensive since the "Great Depression" of the 1870s and 1880s, the World War was a decisive turn away from the international free market and toward state controls. One of the earliest manifestations of this trend was the restrictions placed on immigration after World War I in a number of countries. Most well-known and important were the exclusions which the United States imposed on immigration in 1921 and 1924, especially from Southern and Eastern Europe. In the United States, but also in Germany, Australia, and elsewhere, the 1920s signaled the end of a dramatic growth in employment opportunities for unskilled workers, necessitating controls on immigration.

In marked contrast, French control of immigration in the 1920s was designed less to exclude eager migrants from jobs and enterprise than to direct an expanded influx of labor into an economy sorrowfully in need of additional hands. Because of the demographic hole created by the war and by declining birth rates, the French faced a unique problem—a shortage of labor. The conditions in France in the 1920s would come to exist in much of Western Europe after 1950, leading to a similar pattern of government-stimulated immigration.

While the French fit the trend away from liberalism, their regulation of the foreign influx in the 1920s has a strikingly contemporary ring. It stimulated and organized immigration, while also channeling and restricting it. The influx was shaped to fit the often contradictory interests of politically articulated groups in France. It was a policy of indirect corporatism—one in which regulatory agencies acknowledged the interests of a number of economic forces, especially labor, agriculture, and heavy industry. The result was a foreign labor system which provided employers with immigrants to assure expansion and economic survival while guaranteeing French labor some protection against a glut of foreigners. It helped to bring prosperity and social peace.

The roots of this system can be found in the two generations before World War I, when realignments of social and political forces in France made the importation of labor necessary. First and most important, through birth control and the tight labor market which resulted, French labor gained social mobility and avoided undesired migration. The slow growth of the labor supply, however, was a drag on capital accumulation. Immigration helped solve this problem without necessarily threatening the improved labor standards of French labor. Secondly, the increasing competition for labor between traditional and modernizing sectors of the economy was partially alleviated through the importation of labor. Thirdly, the French state began to regulate immigration in order to encourage these changes: channeling foreigners into a secondary workforce and expanding the immigrant labor pool.

French laborers dramatically improved their bargaining position on the national job market during the closing decades of the nineteenth century. This occurred because of their success in reducing their fertility rate and because of their use of newly won political rights to avoid the private labor market. The so-called reserve army of labor, that group of propertyless migrants from the countryside, should have, according to Marx, expanded with the development of the market economy. Instead, it largely disappeared in France during the second half of the nineteenth century.

An important factor in explaining this decline in the labor supply is the early drop in the French birth rate. Although the French population rose by nine million between 1801 and 1860, from 1861 to 1913 it increased by only two and one half million. The excess of births over deaths per thousand dropped from a peak of 5.8 in the period 1821–

1830 to a low of 0.7 in the period 1891–1900. France stood alone in this decline of fertility. In contrast, the German rate rose from 9.3 during the decade of 1841 to 1850 to peak at 13.9 in the years 1891–1900.[5] By the turn of the century, the decline in the French birth rate was widely recognized to be a result of deliberate restraint, brought about by the practice of birth control.[6] The demographer Alfred Landry noted that by 1900 the first French child appeared only after five years of marriage on the average, and that the mean number of children per marriage dropped to 2.4 by 1911–1913 as compared with the peak average of 4.5 in 1770.[7] This phenomenon has been attributed to causes as varied as the Napoleonic Code, rationalist attitudes arising out of the French Revolution,[8] the French obsession with saving,[9] deforestation of demographically prolific mountain regions, and the desire to limit the number of children to improve the life chances of offspring.[10] Whatever the causes, the results of this control over reproduction was to reduce the potential size of the labor pool or reserve army of labor.

Unlike other Europeans, many French avoided migration, a fact which seriously threatened French industrialization. The Malthusianism of the French peasant, shopkeeper, and artisan kept families small enough so that few children would be disinherited. As a result, property or skills could be passed from generation to generation with relatively few young people being obliged to migrate in search of work. Family limitation allowed some Frenchmen to avoid proletarianization. Yet, as the demographer Alfred Sauvy notes, demographic stagnation can impede economic growth by making the occupational structure inflexible. Insufficient numbers of young, single, and mobile workers block the development of new and often more productive industries. This was especially true when, as in late nineteenth century France, rural population growth was insufficient to supply enough labor for urban industrial expansion.[11]

Birth control gave French labor not only freedom from job hunting, but the opportunity for social mobility. They began to avoid arduous and socially unacceptable jobs. As early as 1888, the liberal economist Paul Leroy-Beaulieu complained:

The French seldom are willing to be simple laborers or street sweepers, to do certain of the exhausting or painful jobs in the textile mills of the north, in the refineries or olive oil processing plants of the south. ... Belgians, Italians and sometimes Germans are needed for all the infinite and essential tasks of civilization. The French people have become a kind of aristocracy among the more primitive peoples of Europe.[12]

To a large extent what made the French an "aristocracy" was their early control of their fertility, something the more "primitive" people had yet to learn.

The French also avoided the cold chill of the labor market by gaining access to political power and the public budget. Under the Third Republic, labor not only gained the vote but gradually learned how to use their limited access to public power to avoid economic migration. By the turn of the century, both the Socialists and the Radical Socialists promoted public works programs, public job placement, and forms of temporary income maintenance. These measures served as alternatives to migration, especially in hard times. A dramatic increase in the number of public employment opportunities (schoolmasters, postmen, etc.) provided French workers with alternatives to the factory, mine, construction site, or farm.[13] Furthermore, real upward mobility, at least across generations, was a prerequisite for social and political stability. As political scientists have noted, without some degree of upward mobility for individuals, democratic institutions face collective demands that can easily undermine the capitalist social order.[14] By the end of the century, propertied allies of labor recognized this fact in France. As T. H. Marshall notes, with the coming of universal suffrage the masses gradually extended the definition of citizenship to include social rights as well as political ones.[15] These social rights include protections which moved against the worker being a commodity or mobile factor of production.[16]

Obviously these protections conflicted with the interests of employers who were seeking tractable labor at the lowest price possible. As one might have expected, employers combated these trends by encouraging a larger domestic labor supply, through sponsoring an anti-Malthusian movement.[17] Indeed, the issues of Malthusianism became an underlying theme in the social debate in the generation before 1914. The "grève des ventres," as conservatives characterized the practice of birth control by the workers, was commonly associated with socialism and anarchism.[18] Both business and purely Catholic groups sponsored anti–birth control legislation. The Textile Consortium of Roubaix-Tourcoing in 1907, as well as employers in St. Étienne in 1917 actively opposed the Malthusian propaganda that was passed among trade unionists.[19] Although legislation outlawing abortion and limiting access to birth control was passed in 1920, the birth rate remained stagnant in the interwar years.[20]

Business groups also attempted to limit the access to public aid and public employment and thus deny workers alternatives to the private labor market in much the same way as contemporary business leaders seek to restrict the size and cost of government.[21] This effort to assure an adequate supply of workers was limited by the fact that French society, like all relatively advanced industrial societies, demanded an ever-growing number of services which required labor. Furthermore, without denying the vote to the proletariat and lower-middle class, employers had to fight an uphill and ultimately losing battle to control efforts to extend rights of citizenship from the purely political to the social and economic areas. If employers could not meet their demand for labor through encouraging population growth and restricting public alternatives to the private labor market, the only solution was to expand that labor supply through immigration.

Immigration might be understood simply as the replacement of unborn French with foreigners or the international extension of an inadequate internal migration.[22] Yet immigrants did not move into a population vacuum. They filled specific needs of French society for a secondary labor market. This helped to solve the labor shortages which plagued business without necessarily threatening indigenous labor with competition for jobs. As a result of immigration, the rudiments of a dual labor market appeared in France as early as the 1880s: a secondary sector dominated by foreign workers in such trades as construction, seasonal agriculture, and in a variety of relatively arduous jobs; the primary sector dominated by French workers in more agreeable and better paid occupations. As Gaeton Piou noted in 1912 in the *Revue Socialiste*, "foreign workers specialize in the tasks that are the most repugnant, the most difficult, and the least skilled, a situation which happily has freed indigenous labor from the purely unskilled jobs and opened it to the jobs which demand

greater technical and intellectual skills."[23] Immigrants were disproportionately represented in dirty jobs and in the heavy industries. In
1906, while they constituted only 3 percent of the economically-active
population, they represented 10 percent of the workforce employed in
the chemical industry, 18 percent in the metal industries, and 9
percent in the construction industries.[24] As French workers became
less available for low-status jobs, they were also able to acquire the
skills and seniority necessary to gain access to preferred jobs. Immigration provided a relatively simple solution to the economic dilemma
of the slow growth of the French workforce. While French workers
avoided migrating to find jobs and even stayed out of the job market,
immigrants took up the slack. While French citizens began to use the
political process to find alternatives to the private labor market,
politically powerless foreigners took their places. Because this created
a dual job market, immigrants seldom competed directly with French
workers for jobs. This fact tended to mitigate massive opposition of
French labor to immigration.

A second broad social realignment in France, the rise of tensions
between the traditional and modernizing sectors of the economy, was
also mollified by immigration. Traditional sectors of the economy,
including the agriculture, construction, clothing, and food industries,
were characterized by relatively low productivity. They were willing
or able to make only few investments in machines or other improvements which would have increased their productivity; and they sought
to assure a profit through maintaining a customarily low wage and
labor standard. In a tight labor market they had difficulty in luring or
retaining workers. They were forced to compete with the modernizing
sector.[25] By the turn of the century, this group of modernizers included
steel, chemicals, and metal goods. These industries were characterized
by concentrations of capital sufficient to make investments which
increased productivity. They could afford and were willing to pay
higher wages and benefits to lure workers from the traditional sector.
Yet they too had to compete for labor. They sought malleable workers
willing to subject themselves to factory discipline and often unpleasant
working conditions. As Peter Stearns and others have pointed out,
European workers, even in the late nineteenth century, avoided these
types of jobs whenever they had alternatives.[26]

If the French workforce would not sufficiently supply the needs of the labor market, neither would employers pay the price for scarce labor. On the one hand, traditional industries, especially in rural areas, refused to raise wages or sufficiently improve living and working conditions to prevent French workers from seeking alternative jobs in Paris or other large cities.[27] On the other hand, modernizing industries, especially in steel, also failed to lure local peasant labor to the intensive work environment of the factories. Competition for labor between traditional and modernizing sectors resulted. This competition could have produced a serious strain in the ruling classes of France if it were not relieved by an expansion of the labor supply—through immigration.

Immigration provided a kind of safety valve. It gave some traditional industries access to labor at the customary low price, thus allowing them to avoid costly capital improvements to substitute for labor. It also may have made viable some marginal enterprises which otherwise could not have competed for labor. Immigration may have, as it does today, assured the survival of enterprises which lacked the resources or skills to survive in an increasingly concentrated economic system. Rather than improve wages or working conditions, these employers accepted the loss of native workers to more attractive industries or regions (especially Paris) and replaced these French workers with immigrants at pay as close as possible to the traditional level. As the economist Leroy-Beaulieu remarked in 1888, "without this foreign assistance, it would have been necessary to pay workers an exorbitant wage. This would have raised further the costs of hard-pressed enterprises which have contributed so much to improve the financial condition of France."[28] Immigration also provided a relief for modernizing firms, enabling them to expand rapidly with adequate supplies of labor. Thus immigration served to mollify conflicts between sectors of capital, removing tensions which otherwise might have weakened the hegemony of the owning classes of France.

To sum up our argument, immigration seems to have served as a kind of economic and social release. It provided additional hands in the lower levels of the labor market which the French worker was increasingly able to avoid. Thus economic growth became possible in a society in which the native workforce was unwilling to participate fully in its cost. Immigration also assured a labor supply and therefore provided an outlet for competition between the traditional and modernizing sectors of the economy. Employers were thus able to obtain prosperity without fully accepting the responsibility for the modern social costs of labor—citizenship and improved labor standards. In effect, immigration was a means of displacing the tensions inherent in a society which was unwilling to fully bear the burden of capitalism. French workers sought to avoid migrant and arduous labor; French capital, the economic consequences of competition. To a degree, immigration made possible this escape from capitalism.

Yet this happy solution was hardly flawless. Three problems emerged that disturbed the stabilizing impact of immigration. Their solution required governmental action to restore stability. The first problem was that unrestricted access of foreigners to French jobs led to conflicts between French employers and labor over the size and composition of the foreign labor pool. The second dilemma was that shortages of foreign labor threatened to stimulate competition between employers for labor. The third difficulty was that foreign governments began to realize that their emigrating citizens were national assets and that receiving nations, like France, should pay a price for the opportunity to hire them. The French state alone could overcome these problems.

In the first place, immigrants did not always remain in the secondary labor market but rather competed directly with the natives. This occurred whenever the skills of French and foreign workers were similar. Mechanization and advances in the division of labor contributed to a growing trend in the homogenization of skills. As Paul Gemahling observed in 1913, "production has become a series of elementary, simple and automatic acts; the labor market tends to become uniform. The skilled and unskilled increasingly find themselves in the same situation—without any real defense in the battle."[29] Although Gemahling's analysis was probably premature, competition for jobs was becoming more acute during the first half of the Third Republic. Furthermore, expanding the labor supply through immigration without doubt worked against wage increases. This was especially true because French employers usually had to provide immigrants with wages and working conditions only marginally better than what foreigners experienced at home. Most immigrants consumed little in France, and because their cost of living at home was lower, they were willing to accept lower wages than the French would tolerate. More important still, the alternative to migration for many of them was unemployment. Although the French had definite advantages over the foreigner in competing for jobs (e.g., skills, knowledge of the job market, and employment alternatives), direct competition between the two groups was an ever present possibility.

How did the French workers respond to that threat? Often they sought government protection—a labor tariff. However, any attempt to limit this competition was bound to draw French labor into conflict with employers. Business naturally wanted an unrestricted access to cheap foreign labor and generally sought to expand the supply of labor to keep wages down. As the Marxists point out, the size of the potential labor supply (reserve army of labor) is a prime determinant in the price of labor. While the owning classes sought a free labor market, the laboring classes favored government controls in foreign labor.

A second problem, however, also emerged which frustrated the stabilizing influence of immigration. There was no guarantee that sufficient numbers of immigrants would spontaneously appear when the crops were ready or as production was scheduled to begin. Shortages could appear, not only for big employers. Small but strategic gaps could remain unfilled in the thousands of small, marginal, and dispersed enterprises located throughout France. This could easily result in competition between employers for labor, the tendency to bid up the price of workers, and the forcing of marginal employers out of business. Thus, while immigration tended to mollify this competition, competition could easily emerge, since there were no guarantees that the size of immigration would be sufficient. As a result, employers had an incentive to demand more than merely a free labor market. Rather they had reason to violate their own liberal principles by joining together to recruit immigrants and even by seeking governmental support to expand the foreign labor supply.

This brings us to a third factor which frustrated a liberal immigration policy—the change in the conditions under which foreign labor became available to the French market. Traditional and easily accessible sources of immigrant labor (for example, from Belgium) gradually dried up. Conditions at home improved sufficiently to make it no longer necessary to migrate. Moreover, immigrants themselves became more demanding. They eventually adopted the attitudes of the French. As Piou feared, there was no guarantee that the Italians, for example, would "not try to adopt the standard of living of the new milieu in which they moved."[30] Insofar as this occurred, business found immigrants less advantageous. As a result, employers were compelled to recruit labor increasingly distant and peripheral to the French core economy. Swiss, Belgian, and German workers had to be replaced by Spaniards, Portuguese, and eventually Poles, Czechs, and even North Africans.

On top of these problems was the fact that ruling elites in the labor exporting countries gradually came to realize that to allow their citizens to emigrate to France without some kind of compensation was economically unsound. Labor importers reaped the benefits of labor without sharing the costs of raising and training the workers. They received largely young adult workers in their most productive years. Labor exporting nations gained relatively little. As Charles Kindleberger observes in the context of contemporary Europe, emigration is a "capital intensive industry in a capital poor country."[31] It should not be surprising then that labor-supplying nations began to impose conditions and restrictions on migration; they hoped to share some of the productivity of their emigrant citizens as well as to impose a portion of the costs of maintaining and educating those citizens upon the labor importing nations. These trends would develop only gradually and at vastly different rates in the countries of emigration. Yet by the eve of the First World War, the outlines of these trends are clear in countries like Belgium, Switzerland, Germany, and Italy.

What were the consequences of these threats on the unrestricted and ample supply of immigrant labor for the French employers? One response was to band together to improve their chances of obtaining foreign labor on favorable terms. Yet, in the long run, as we shall soon see, they were obliged to call on the French government, in effect, as their bargaining agent, against the demands of the national governments of immigrants.

Because foreign labor did not spontaneously serve the interests of French labor and business, Frenchmen sought to use their access to the state for assistance. French labor wanted a labor tariff to keep foreigners from competing with them for jobs; French business eventually sought governmental support to recruit foreign labor and to reduce the demands of labor-supplying nations.

This brings us to a final factor in the emergence of the modern foreign labor system in France—the appearance of a new class of state functionaries. This group will be committed to the goal of mediating and serving the interests of various social groups in France. At least since the advent of the middle-class revolution of 1789, the French government has served the economic needs of the propertied classes through tariffs, controls over unions, and a commitment to cheap government. Yet by the beginning of the twentieth century, government services began to expand into entirely new areas. These included helping employers find and distribute new sources of foreign labor. It also involved providing diplomatic assistance to business as the political cost of importing foreign labor increased.

Yet we also see a new concern on the part of the state for mediating social conflict—witness the government of 1898, which included the Socialist, A. Millerand. Despite a well-documented history of repressing working-class movements, French governments since the 1890s made efforts to integrate the working classes into capitalist society and to seek means to avoid social conflicts. One example of this trend was governmental efforts to increase labor immigration but, at the same time, to avoid antagonizing native labor. The state, after 1914, will channel and restrict foreign labor so that it would not compete with the citizen worker. State intervention, then, comprised a critical factor in the formation of a foreign labor system in the twentieth century. It served and mediated conflicting French interests. It provided a step toward a corporatist or consensus solution to an outstanding social problem.

We believe that it is these political factors which define the unique pattern of immigration which emerged after 1914. Of course, one could fruitfully study the purely demographic and ethnographic aspects of the interwar migrations, as we hope that others will. Yet what made the foreign influx during this period enduring and innovative was the formation and consequences of a structured or directed immigration. We shall see that immigration into France after the war differed significantly from that influx before the war.

Foreigners as a group became more concentrated in the working classes, more apt to be employed in primary production, and more likely to be concentrated in provincial regions. They were, in a word, more concentrated in regions and occupations which the French worker avoided and in which French employers were unwilling to pay the costs of attracting the French worker. Immigration became rationalized to serve the specific social and economic needs of the French.

At the same time, immigration after the war differed from the influx before 1914 in that it was drawn from more distant nationalities. Fewer Flemish, German, and Swiss workers came across the border and more Poles, Italians, and Greeks were recruited into occupations and regions often separate from the traditional paths of migrants. The new immigration reflected a much higher level of organization and control. While the motives and interests of individual immigrants still played a role in determining the pattern of immigration, the freedom of the foreigner was circumscribed by governmental regulations and the recruitment organizations of employers.

As a result, foreign labor became a radically distinct class in France. Not merely were immigrants predominantly propertyless and unskilled, but they were noncitizens. This lack of political rights became increasingly important as immigration became more controlled by government and private organizations. To a degree the new foreign labor system was a successful attempt to recreate, in a small but by no means marginal portion of the working class, the conditions which had once characterized the native citizen majority of the working class: a migratory workforce under the hegemony of the employers. New means of control in effect reinstituted a labor system under which the French working class labored before it had gained citizenship and attendant social rights.

This new foreign labor system did not emerge automatically out of a new political and social realignment. Rather, it appeared out of a long historical germination, within the context of social conflict and political debate. It would be a rather disjointed compromise between interested parties and would reflect the dominance of employer groups—mine operators and large agriculturalists, especially. The muddiness of the historical record reveals the genesis and dimensions of the directed immigration of the interwar period.

In Chapter II and III we will explain the origins of the new policy and its limits in crystallizing a consensus solution to immigration. Chapters IV through VI will trace the growth of immigration after the war and describe the varieties of foreign labor (for example, Slavic migration into mining and agriculture and Italian influx into construction). We will explain the relationship between employers and the new immigrants within the context of regulation and organized recruitment. Chapters VII and VIII will explore the roles of government in regulating immigration in order to assure that foreigners complemented rather than competed with French labor and to assure its social as well as economic subordination. Finally, in Chapter IX we will investigate the decline of immigration during the economic crisis of the 1930s, and the response of labor, business, and government to the foreign worker who remained. We will see that immigrant labor had become so important to the French economy that even the crisis did not substantially reverse the trends of the twenties. France would never again be able to do without foreign laborers or the machinery used to control, channel, and coordinate them to fit the modern social structure of France. What the French developed in the 1920s would be followed by other advanced capitalist nations after World War II. What we are about to investigate is a telling feature of contemporary European society—the emergence of a noncitizen workforce in democratic capitalist nations.

II   State, Society, and Supplemental Labor, 1880–1918

THE First World War was the great watershed of the modern era. It signaled the beginning of the end of liberal society. No clearer example of this could be offered than that of the transformation of labor migrations into France. Partly in compensation for France's drastic losses during the war, foreign labor flooded the country, doubling the proportion of the non-citizen population (from 2.9 percent in 1911 to 6.6 percent in 1931).[1] Yet postwar immigration was much more than simply a short-term adjustment in French demographic conditions; rather it signified a radical departure from prewar patterns of immigration and of French attitudes and behavior toward foreign labor.

Before the war, immigration was primarily a free movement of populations adjacent to France into border labor markets. After the war, however, immigration became a government-regulated influx of foreign workers who were often recruited in large groups by a monopolistic private labor recruiter and sent to regions and occupations far from the well-worn paths of prewar migration.

What determined the character of the postwar foreign labor system was the introduction of corporatism into the French political economy. Corporatism is a word with many meanings.[2] By using this term we do not mean to suggest that industrial groupings supplanted parliament nor that organized capital controlled French society. We certainly do not imply that French labor joined with management in a regulated capitalist economy. As is well-known, French parliamentary politics survived the dislocations of postwar society far better than elsewhere (Italy, for example); French capital was not nearly so cartelized as in Germany. Class divisions in France clearly precluded the kind of class collaboration which was possible in Sweden from the early 1930s. We do not argue that France experienced a basic change of regime in the 1920s, certainly not a dramatic shift from a liberal to a corporatist state. Our argument is much more modest. While proponents of the economic rationalization advocated a more directed market economy, the liberal character of the Republic remained. In the special area of immigration, however, clearly defined changes occurred in French behavior and policy which can be called corporatist. These include (1) the state (i.e., governmental ministries) began to regulate the foreign work force with the goal of reducing domestic conflict and enhancing economic growth; (2) fractions of capital cooperated in the organization of the foreign labor market; and (3) a portion of French labor joined employers in supporting a program of channeling aliens toward the lower rungs of the occupational ladder. In none of these trends was the pattern purely or completely corporatist. Business resistance to regulation and opposition to direct and equal bargaining with labor as well as divisions within the labor movement prevented a mature corporatist policy. Yet these corporatist trends were crucial and irreversible in the shaping of the foreign labor system in France.

After 1914, the French government expanded but also controlled and channelled the flow of foreign labor into France. The state intervened in the alien labor market in service to specific economic groups: it aided industries whose growth and survival depended upon overcoming a shortage of cheap tractable labor by encouraging massive immigration; the state also attempted to placate indigenous workers by limiting immigration and channelling alien labor into undesirable occupational sectors. As a result French governmental intervention stimulated economic growth, while, at the same time, it fostered social stability.

Not only did interest groups support these governmental efforts, but to an extent they participated in the formation of policy. Although different groups—labor, agriculture and industry—worked through separate governmental agencies, they came close to joining together in a corporatist policy making body—a national immigration office.

This might have contributed to a transformation of French social relations, considerably mollifying tensions in French society and institutionalizing social conflicts. Yet by the mid-1920's overtures toward direct interclass bargaining had failed, leaving the policy of immigration in the hands of separate regulatory agencies and their special interest clients. This created an indirect corporatist policy—immigration shaped in the interests of major social groups—without face-to-face cooperation. We can find the sources of this consensus and the reasons for its partial failure in an analysis of immigration in the generation before the war.

Immigration before 1914

On the eve of the First World War, foreign labor had already begun to play a vital economic role in France. A shortage of French workers, due largely to the decline in the birth rate, had stimulated immigration as early as the 1850s. Almost all of this influx came from spontaneous or loosely organized migrations from border countries. The immigrants located in districts near the frontier or in Paris. Rail transportation and job information seemed to have been sufficient to draw aliens across open frontiers. This unregulated pattern of immigration generally provided French employers with a diverse and flexible addition to their domestic supply of workers with French labor manifesting only a limited opposition to the aliens. Business favored free migration and successfully resisted sporadic demands from labor and xenophobes for controls.

Two problems emerged, however, which modified this rosy picture. First, free individual immigration could not guarantee a sufficient supply of labor to accomodate the diverse demands of employers; second, because there were no political constraints on aliens entering into direct competition with French workers for jobs, the potential for public opposition to foreign workers intensified each year that immigration increased. Thus, by the outbreak of war, both employers and labor had an incentive to organize immigration, both through collective action and state intervention.

Spontaneous Immigration and the French *Patronat*

A largely spontaneous response to the unmet demand for labor resulted in a steadily increasing influx of foreign workers into France from the 1850s until 1914. Census figures (see Table 1) show 379,289 aliens in France as early as 1851, this number rising to 1,159,835 in 1911 (2.9 percent of the population.)[3] As one might expect from a spontaneous immigration, the vast majority came from

Table 1   Foreigners Residing in France, 1851–1911

Year	No. of foreigners	% of total population
1851	379,289	1.1
1866	655,036	1.7
1876	801,754	2.1
1881	1,001,090	2.6
1886	1,126,531	2.9
1891	1,130,211	2.8
1896	1,027,421	2.6
1901	1,037,778	2.6
1906	1,049,051	2.5
1911	1,159,835	2.9

Source: Henri Bunle (Institut national des études économiques), *Mouvements migratoires entre la France et l'étranger, Études et documents*, 4 (Paris: Presses universitaires de France, 1943), p. 67. See also France, *Resultats statistiques du recensement général de la population*, 1, no. 2 (1921), 55.

bordering countries (between 82 percent and 90 percent during the period 1851 to 1911). As Table 2 shows, until the 1880s Belgians (mostly of Flemish origin) and Germans predominated, but thereafter Italians and Spaniards gradually took their place.[4]

These migrations provided employers with small but usually significant additions to the workforce in important occupational sectors and regions. Foreign workers concentrated along the frontiers and in Paris. Although in 1911 foreigners represented 3.2 percent of the economically active population in France, in the southeastern departments of Alpes-Maritimes and Bouches-du-Rhône they constituted 30 percent and 18 percent respectively. In the department of the

Table 2   Foreigners Residing in France, by Nationality, 1851–1911

Nationality	No. of foreigners (in thousands)						
	1851	*1861*	*1871*	*1881*	*1891*	*1901*	*1911*
Italian	63	77	113	241	286	330	419
Belgian	128	204	348	432	466	323	287
German, Austro-Hungarian	57	85	110	94	95	102	117
Spanish, Portuguese	30	35	53	75	79	82	110
Swiss	25	35	43	66	83	72	73
Russian	9	9	9	10	14	16	35
Luxemburger, Dutch	10	13	17	21	40	29	26
Others	59	39	48	62	67	80	93
Total	381	497	741	1,001	1,130	1,034	1,160

Nord, which borders on Belgium, aliens constituted 11 percent of the economically active population while in Paris they represented 7 percent.[5] This pattern of concentration in the frontier districts and in the capital followed from the individual and spontaneous nature of the migrations.

The economic opportunities of aliens were dictated largely by jobs left open by the French. Foreigners concentrated in a variety of traditional and modern industries which offered a large number of unskilled and arduous jobs. Even before the war, immigrants were indispensable in key industries such as metallurgy, chemicals, and construction (see Table 3).[6] Foreign workers also served vital functions as seasonal migrants and commuters, especially in the frontier regions. By 1913, 40,000 Flemish Belgians seasonally migrated to weed, harvest, and refine sugar beets in the north. Twenty thousand Spaniards worked during peak periods in the southern vineyards while about the same number of Italians served as flower cutters and woodsmen in the French southeast. By 1906 about 30,000 Flemish and German commuters, called *frontaliers,* crossed the frontier daily or weekly to work in French textile mills, brickyards, glass works, and mines.[7]

Immigrants who flooded into Paris became vital to numerous industries, especially those requiring skills which the French lacked.

% of total foreign population						
1851	*1861*	*1871*	*1881*	*1891*	*1901*	*1911*
16.5	15.6	15.3	24.1	25.4	31.9	36.3
33.6	41.0	47.0	43.1	41.3	31.2	24.7
15.0	17.2	14.8	9.4	8.4	9.9	10.1
7.9	7.0	7.2	7.5	7.0	7.9	9.5
6.5	7.0	5.8	6.6	7.3	7.0	6.3
2.4	1.8	1.2	1.0	1.2	1.6	3.0
2.6	2.6	2.2	2.1	3.5	2.8	2.2
15.5	7.8	6.5	6.2	5.9	7.7	8.0

Source: Walter Wilcox, *International Migrations*, II (New York: National Bureau of Economic Research, 1931), 223.

A report of April 1907 from the Prefect of Police (Paris) claimed that 40 percent of the demolition workers of the Seine were Italians, that 40–50 percent of the employees of sugar refineries and glassworks

Table 3   Occupational Distribution of Immigrants, 1906

Occupation	% of workers
Metallurgy	17.8
Amusements	11.2
Stone work	10.0
Chemicals	10.0
Construction	9.0
Quarrying	8.7
Goods handling	8.4
Ceramics, glass	8.1
Domestic service	7.0
Mining	6.2
Leather	5.5
Textiles	5.1

Source: France, *Resultats statistiques du recensement général de la population*, 1 (1906), 140.

were foreign, and that 20 percent of the construction workers were Italian and Belgian. Furthermore, a number of craft industries in Paris hired large contingents of immigrants.[8]

This brief survey of the pattern of spontaneous immigration into France before the war indicates that aliens provided employers with a growing, diverse, and often critical supplement to their supplies of native labor. Foreigners mostly took the unskilled, seasonal, low paying and unpleasant jobs that the French avoided. They also served as skilled workers, especially in trades in which insufficient French were trained. Despite the advantages that spontaneous migrations had for French employers, they proved to be inadequate for many enterprises.

Organizing the Foreign Labor Market

Labor shortages appeared for large agriculture as well as mining and metallurgical industries. Large-scale grain producers in the Seine basin and eastern France found it increasingly difficult to retain French laborers or tenants and could no longer draw sufficient numbers of French migrants, particularly from Brittany. Yet these agricultural districts lay beyond the established streams of Flemish, Spanish, and Italian migrations. Substituting French with foreign labor was not easy. Furthermore, as early as 1908, the Syndicat central des agriculteurs en France complained that Flemish seasonal workers had begun "to stop coming and to pass too quickly into industry."[9] Even traditional sources of foreign labor were becoming scarce.

Coal and iron mines, especially in the expanding northern and eastern basins, also experienced shortages of labor which spontaneous migrations failed to overcome. Coal mine operators in the northeast found Belgians unsatisfactory; they tended to leave the mine during the warm months for seasonal farm or construction work.[10] As Philippe Ariès and others have noted, a stable, disciplined coal mining population was formed in France only after several generations of weaning peasants from the land.[11] The mining population could not be renewed with undifferentiated migrant workers, especially those with alternatives to the deadend of underground mining. It is thus not surprising that the Belgians, used to the comparative freedom of construction or even seasonal farm work, would resist the daily drudgery of the mines. Ultimately, mine operators had to recruit seasoned foreign miners who had known no other work culture.

For the iron mines of Briey in French Lorraine, the difficulties were even greater. When this district was seriously exploited after 1895, the Briey basin had no pool of labor upon which to draw. The peasants of the region were generally small land owners, unwilling to quit their independent if modest way of life for the hell of the iron mines. In addition, attempts to lure seasoned miners from other parts of France failed. Operators needed large numbers of workers and were unable to wait for a migratory stream to form spontaneously.[12]

Mining and agricultural enterprises, because of the types of jobs they offered and because of isolation from traditional migratory paths, were obliged to organize in order to recruit fresh pools of foreign labor. Already, in March of 1908, the Syndicat central des agriculteurs en France negotiated a contract with a commercial labor placement company in Warsaw to recruit 400 Polish farm workers for the Meurthe-et-Moselle in eastern France.[13] One year later the Syndicat made a similar arrangement with the Polish Emigration Society of Austrian Poland.[14] Although the Galician Diet subsidized this society and the emigration of Poles was tolerated by the Austrian government, its success was limited.[15] From 1908 to 1914 the Polish Emigration Society placed 20,000 Polish farm workers in northeastern France.[16] Yet, according to a study by the French Ministry of Labor, only 5,000 of these Poles remained on the farms in 1914. A combination of factors, including inadequate organization, alternatives to farm work in France, as well as poor pay and working conditions, contributed to the failure of this effort.[17]

Attempts to recruit and retain Polish miners were no more successful. This was somewhat surprising given the history of the emigration of Polish miners. From the 1890s both the Germans and Americans had drawn extensively upon Polish mining districts in Silesia to meet their growing needs for coal miners. From 1908, French mine operators attempted to follow suit. They used Polish agents to pirate Polish miners working in the Ruhr, appealing to Polish nationalism against the German mine operators. Despite these efforts, by 1912 only about 500 Poles had responded.[18] During the same period the iron mines and steel mills of Briey hired the Polish Emigration Society in Galicia to obtain about 1,000 unskilled laborers.[19] The French found that they could not compete with the nearby German mines and mills in pay or working conditions.[20] In any case, corporate recruitment of Poles was a low-budget pilot project, hardly likely to succeed without better organization and the absence of the German and American alternatives for Polish emigrants.

Only after the war, when Polish labor became a necessity and the cooperation of a new Polish state made recruitment more effective, did large-scale immigration from Poland begin. In the twenties, Polish antipathy to Germany and American restrictions on immigration gave the French an unprecedented bargaining position in procuring Polish labor. Already before the war, however, mining and agricultural associations were able to draw on their international connections to organize, at least, a trickle of migration. These early examples of collective immigration had no French governmental involvement. Indeed, entrepreneurs opposed all governmental interference. This attitude had to change, however, when the intervention of the governments of the labor supplying nations forced French business to seek the assistance of their government.

Italian immigration into the French Lorraine reflects this trend. Although the iron and steel industries had relied on individual migration in the 1890s to fill the ranks of workers, by 1908 rapid expansion of production required an organized immigration. In that year agents from three mines recruited Italians in the frontier towns of Chiasso and Bale. However, they soon realized that they were competing for this labor against each other as well as against German and Luxembourgeois mines. They also found that the Italians were frequently lured away after a short stint on the job by competitors who promised slightly higher pay. As a result, neighboring mines could reap the benefits of the Italian miners without enduring any of the costs of recruitment. Labor discipline also suffered because Italians could easily find work at a nearby mine or mill if they were fired. Therefore, in order to control the Italian labor market, the mine operators authorized their trade association, the Comité des forges et mines de Meurthe-et-Moselle, to organize a recruitment service for all its members. Despite an often voiced commitment to a competitive market, the Comité des forges attempted to eliminate competition between member employers for Italian labor. In 1912, the recruitment service obtained a license from the agency of the Italian government which controlled emigration, the Commissiarato generale dell'emigrazione (CGE), to recruit miners in Italy. In exchange for the privilege of corporate hiring, the CGE demanded that the French do the following: (1) take steps to reduce venereal disease and accidents in the Italian colonies in France, (2) use a model contract which would assure a parity in wages with the French, and (3) provide a mutual aid fund for Italian workers, which would be subsidized by the employers.[21]

At first this arrangement was satisfactory to both parties. Negotiations, however, broke down in 1913 over the CGE's demands that the Italian consul at Nancy be allowed to inspect French mining pits and mills in order to assure safety and health standards. Robert Pinot, president of the Comité des forges, rejected this as an intrusion into French "sovereignty." This disagreement blocked further recruitment of Italian miners and metal workers and led Pinot in 1914 to request the French government to intervene on the behalf of the French employers.

Following the outbreak of war and Italy's entry in May of 1915, the CGE added more restrictions to control the outflow of strategic labor. It prohibited all recruitment in Italy without a license. Not only was detailed information on plant working conditions required of recruiters, but the French employers had to accept the Italian consuls as mediators in disputes between Italian workers and French employers. In response, Pinot stepped up his effort to have the French government exert pressure on the Italian authorities to improve the employers' bargaining position.

Bertrand Nogaro, director of the Service de la main-d'oeuvre étrangère (Foreign Labor Service), at first refused to negotiate under conditions so unfavorable to the French. He feared that because of the acute French shortage of labor, the Italians might be able to set an advantageous precedent in postwar immigration agreements. In spite of these fears, however, the shortages in the war industries were sufficient by March of 1916 to force Nogaro to bargain with the tough-minded Georges de Michelis, chief of the CGE. In May the parties reached an agreement which allowed French employers to obtain Italian workers through the Foreign Labor Service of the French government and the CGE. Italian demands for control over labor relations within France were considerably compromised; an Italian officer could inspect factories if accompanied by a French officer, but the Italian official could not mediate disputes. In exchange for the labor, the French agreed to share a proportion of French munitions and coal (six tons per Italian immigrant). Although only 5,486 Italians entered French factories and mines through this arrangement, this agreement became a model for postwar immigration treaties.[22]

This Franco-Italian agreement signaled the end of liberal immigration. Employers in highly concentrated and well-organized industries, such as iron and steel, represented by the Comité des forges, found the free market in labor to be inadequate to overcome their shortages of manpower. Having chosen to organize a collective demand for Italian labor, the Comité found itself faced with an unsurmountable opponent in the CGE, one who would attempt to control the supply of that labor. As we shall see in Chapter 6, the Italian government would not allow the systematic loss of Italian labor without exacting a cost. By 1914, then, the French employers were obliged to call on their government to obtain any Italian workers. Immigration had become a matter of foreign affairs, linked to commercial and national rights issues. In spite of employer opposition to "bureaucratic" restrictions, especially government involvement in the recruitment process,[23] only the French state could adequately serve the collective interests of the employers vis-à-vis the Italian state.

French Workers React to Protect Labor Standards

Like the French capitalists, the trade unions and socialists of France gradually came to look upon state intervention as a solution to immigration, but for entirely different reasons. Because foreigners often worked at lower pay and under conditions deemed unacceptable to the French, indigenous labor favored controls on immigrant employment. To be sure, aliens were concentrated in frontier regions and in the lower rungs of the occupational ladder. As a result, they were usually isolated from most French workers. In addition, they were concentrated in industries such as metallurgy, as well as road building and other seasonal industries, where French workers were too poorly organized and too unstable to voice any appreciable opposition. Despite the weakness of labor's opposition, however, it was often vocal and even violent in the generation before the war.

In those industries where labor was relatively well-organized and had strong artisan traditions of self-defense, French workers often actively confronted foreign labor. This was especially true in craft trades like tailoring, glass-blowing, woodworking, shoemaking, cabinetmaking and painting, where foreigners could easily be employed in cut-rate or sweat shops.[24] Conflicts emerged also in the dock and construction industries, music halls, and restaurant services. In these seasonal or temporary jobs, local French workers often had to compete with a floating population of foreigners, who often offered superior skills at lower pay.[25] Temporary French workers involved with road and rail construction had to face teams of Spanish or Italian workers led by *marchands d'hommes,* as the unions called foreign labor contractors.[26]

If certain trades seemed especially prone to competition between alien and French workers, a variety of circumstances could cause conflicts in other industries. For example, Flemish *frontaliers,* employed primarily in textiles and construction, were willing to work for as little as half the pay which the French demanded.[27] Naturally, wage differentials encouraged employers to replace French with foreign workers. Immigrants were also used to increase productivity. A parliamentary report of 1903 noted that, in the textiles industries of Lille, employers recruited Flemish workers in order to introduce "modifications in working conditions . . . to discourage the collective action of the other workers and to break their resistance" to mechanization.[28] In 1919, the Congress of Agricultural workers claimed that since 1908, Spanish and Algerian laborers had been responsible for the "general extension of the piece rate" in the viticulture of the Midi and had contributed to unemployment.[29] On numerous occasions employers recruited immigrant labor to break strikes. A strike in 1908, for example, at a quarry in the Yonne, was broken by the use of Dutch replacements, as was a strike of woodcutters in 1910.[30] Dockers at Marseilles in 1903 and at Nantes in 1912 also complained of foreign strike breakers.[31]

How did French workers respond to these varied threats of foreign labor? Just as employers organized to recruit foreign labor, so French labor's concern with an overabundant supply of immigrants led them to collective action. At the level of the trade union, action might include a demand that French be hired first (for example, the dockers of Marseilles in 1903) or that foreigners be excluded from unions (for example, the painters of the Seine in 1894) or even that all foreign workers be expelled (for example, the leather-goods workers in 1895).[32] Occasionally French workers struck to protest foreign labor. This happened in June of 1905 when about 1,000 farm workers from Arles struck briefly to oppose the hiring of Italians.[33]

Competition also led to violence. The army was required to quell a riot at the salt mines of Aigues-Mortes (Gard) in August of 1893, when Italians replaced 100 French workers.[34] Smaller riots between Belgian and French miners broke out in the northern towns of Lievin (1892 and 1897), Lens (1893, 1897, and 1901), St-Pol (1897 and 1899), Billy Montigy (1911), and Ostricourt (1903).[35]

Work-site violence in 1893 was sufficient to lead the minister of the interior to request that the prefects monitor all enterprises which hired foreigners and to take measures to prevent violence.[36] Protests against the employment of foreigners was local, spasmodic, and occasionally violent. It seemed to fit the pattern of traditional social conflict outlined by Charles Tilly.[37] It consisted of spontaneous *rixes*, local outbreaks of violence in which foreigners were pitted against French workers with whom they directly competed. There were reactive demands for the restoration of the local French position in the job market by excluding the immigrant outsider.

Only slowly did French labor adopt a national strategy to respond to immigration. Workers had a basic alternative: either to act through the unions to limit the competition of aliens or to press for political controls. Like the employers, organized labor preferred to rely on corporate action. They did so because of traditions of internationalism and opposition to the bourgeois state. Left labor pinned most of their hopes on unionizing immigrant workers. In 1907, at their national congress in Nancy, French socialists opposed all governmental restrictions on immigration such as those which trade unionists had adopted in the United States, and proposed to organize foreigners around the slogan, "equal pay for equal work." In 1910, at its congress in Lille, the Confédération générale du travail—CGT (General Conferation of Labor) embraced the same tactics in a special meeting on the immigrant question.[38]

But the French labor movement, which had been able to organize no more than one million French workers by 1914, was hardly capable of unionizing the highly unstable and often illiterate foreign workforce.[39] The law of 1884, which legalized unions, also prohibited foreigners from voting for or being elected to leadership positions in unions. Foreign labor organizers, who probably were more effective than French ones, were subject to expulsion. A team of Belgian trade unionists in 1912, for example, was expelled for trying to organize Flemish farm workers in northern France.[40] The difficult job of integrating immigrants into the trade unions was made all the more problematic.

In addition, French workers were certainly not immune to cultural chauvinism. In the working class newspaper *Cri du peuple* in 1884 we find a fear expressed of "the foreign vassals of Catholicism." Michelle Perrot has noted a persistent anxiety beginning in the 1880s about the "Yellow Peril," the fear that French employers might follow the United States and import Chinese labor.[41]

Behind much of this xenophobia was the fear that outsiders— especially those who had a lower labor standard—would deprive natives of the right to a job near home. Whenever French workers acquired any political rights, they immediately attempted to protect their jobs from outsiders. As early as the Revolution of 1848, a workers' delegation from the Paris suburb of Montmartre petitioned the provisional republican government to prohibit Parisian workers from seeking employment in their district.[42] With the coming of the Third Republic, workers demanded priority for local labor, especially in the 1880s and 1890s. Of course, as many contemporary witnesses recognized, this attitude of labor was merely an extension of the point of view of businessmen who demanded protection for local products with tariffs.[43] European and American-born workers in California had already set a precedent by demanding "America for Americans" in the 1880s to prevent the influx of Chinese and Japanese labor.[44] Some of the French would succumb to such nationalist appeals, especially during economic crises. At the same time labor's demand for protecting local jobs was an attempt to defend wage and working standards, often painfully won in France, from outsiders who had lower standards. It was also an assertion of French labor's right of settlement—the right to establish a permanent home or sedentary pattern of work. Priority for national labor could help French workers avoid the status of a floating laborer in constant search for work in an uncertain job market.

Given the organizational weakness of French workers, their tendency to xenophobia, and their desire to protect local job markets, a strictly trade-union strategy for dealing with the problems of immigration was insufficient. Thus French labor would adopt an alternative approach and call on the state for protection. From 1885 to 1895 leftist coalitions in the municipal councils of Paris, Marseilles, Toulouse, and other cities passed laws which limited the percentage of immigrants (usually 5 percent) who could be hired for municipal public works.[45] Jobs, paid for by public funds, it was felt, should be mostly reserved for citizens. Despite success at the municipal level, the central government annulled these restrictions in a series of decrees between 1889 and 1895.[46] Those seeking controls on foreign employment had to shift from the local to the national government.

Both socialists and conservatives proposed legislation to restrict foreign access to the French labor market. Socialists called for limiting foreigners to a fixed proportion of the jobs in each trade. A socialist proposal of 1902 also included the provision of equal pay for equal work; this would have removed the incentive of employers to hire foreigners who could be forced to work for lower pay than the French.[47] All of the bills, however, were repeatedly killed in committee because legislators believed that they restricted the free market. Employers also feared that they would lead to reprisals from foreign countries against French business.[48] Despite numerous parliamentary initiatives before 1914, laissez-faire prevailed.

The only significant law controlling immigration was passed in 1893. It required all foreign laborers to register with the police when they established a residence and whenever they moved thereafter. But this was really only a police measure designed to maintain some supervision over a floating population of foreigners.[49] Besides this law, a decree in 1899 was the only effort to placate those demanding regulation. Promulgated by the reformist socialist leader, Alexandre Millerand, who was then Minister of Commerce, it allowed towns to determine, with the prefect's approval, what percentage of foreigners could be employed in public works. Yet even this mild measure was very seldom put into effect.[50]

Clearly no serious regulation of immigrant labor was tolerated by the dominant political classes in France before 1914. With significant exceptions, spontaneous immigration proved to be sufficient for the needs of employers, while the restrictionism of labor leaders was but a feeble voice. For this pattern of liberal immigration to change, employers would have to suffer from much greater shortages of labor. Labor groups would also have to abandon their protectionist policies and adopt a strategy more consistent with economic expansion. Both of these changes took place during the First World War.

Enter the State: Immigration during the War

Never before had France mobilized more of her human resources than during the First World War. Over seven million Frenchmen were taken out of the economy for the fighting. The war emergency required and also justified government control over and encouragement of immigration to take up the slack. The spirit of patriotism and willingness of all classes and parties to cooperate for the national defense in the Union Sacrée also produced an unprecedented situation: the possibility of agreement and collaboration in developing an immigration policy.

This transformation can be analyzed in two stages: (1) Initially, government involvement was restricted to an ad hoc response of different ministries acting largely independently to serve the needs of well-organized employer groups. However, the mechanisms which these ministries established to recruit, distribute, and control foreign labor became the foundation for the foreign labor system which continues to the present. (2) Beginning in 1916 the state enlisted the cooperation of business and labor groups in several advisory manpower commissions. This participation anticipated postwar cooperation between business and government in formulating French immigration policy. It also provided a model for French labor's goal of a regulated immigration well after the war.

The Government Recruits Foreign Labor

Six months after the outbreak of the war, it was obvious that French manpower was no match for that of Germany. Despite efforts to employ displaced Belgians, French women, and males either too old or too young to fight, the French government still needed more labor[51] to work in the war economy. It was obliged to organize an immigration. In response to the specific needs of employers, the government recruited three separate groups of alien workers: (1) colonial and Chinese laborers, mostly for the docks and military construction, (2) Iberian and Italian farm workers, and (3) southern European industrial workers.

Colonial and Chinese Immigration   Under the direction of the moderate socialist Albert Thomas, the Subministry of Armaments took the lead in procuring colonial workers. Early in 1915, it recruited from the ranks of the 12,000 North Africans (mostly Algerians) already in France for the munition plants. The character of this recruitment changed radically, however, when the War and Colonial Ministries assumed control over colonial labor. These ministries early in 1916 established an agency under military leadership, the *Service d'organisation des travailleurs coloniaux* or SOTC (Colonial Labor Service). Under its chief, Colonel Lucien Wiel, the SOTC abandoned the practice of hiring civilian North Africans in France. Wiel believed that these workers were too contaminated by French life to be productive. Rather he recruited groups of "volunteers" from the colonial army reserve within North Africa who were not only innocent of the knowledge of French society, but were subject to military pay and discipline.[52] In a similar way the SOTC also impressed Indochinese and Madagascarians for labor service in France.[53] The SOTC obtained a number of Chinese laborers from several commercial labor contractors. Ostensibly the Chinese were free labor, but received similar treatment to that of the colonial workers.[54]

Although these nonwhite workers were not part of the army, their situation was virtually identical to militarized labor. The SOTC transported, distributed, and "protected" all nonwhite immigrants, controlling all aspects of their lives at work and leisure. Imported without regard to the availability of jobs, these workers were often billeted for some time in barracks near Marseilles and placed in compounds segregated by nationality. The SOTC distributed each nationality in separate convoys, which, according to Wiel, prevented racial conflicts. The SOTC assigned supervisors, who had often been colonial plantation overseers, to police the colonial workers. These SOTC agents also acted as interpreters and generally helped to maintain the morale of these workers. The SOTC even built a mosque for the North Africans and printed a special newspaper for the Chinese.[55] Whenever possible, the SOTC designated cafés for each nationality, "to assure that the leisure hours of these workers would be spent in harmless pastimes."[56] The SOTC also regulated diets, living conditions, and minimal wage rates.[57]

What was the purpose of this highly regulated movement of nonwhite workers? Obviously, the SOTC system solved many linguistic and cultural problems. It also assured that colonial labor would work under a system which was similar to that experienced back home and to which they would eventually return. French authorities obviously had no interest in introducing colonial labor to French individualism or European labor relations (which often included unions). The SOTC's paternalism was also a product of fears that racial conflicts might emerge between the French and the colonials as well as between the different foreign nationalities. Furthermore, the French authorities also felt that "unprotected" colonial workers might be tempted to adopt the French custom of drinking, to the detriment of their productivity. Perhaps, however, most important in explaining the SOTC's policies was the French desire to keep the colonial workers in compact workteams and restricted to the most onerous jobs. It is probable that only their virtual militarization kept colonial workers from entering the general labor market and drifting into the cities—especially Paris—in search of excitement and better jobs.[58]

Altogether during the war the SOTC imported 78,566 Algerians, 18,244 Tunisians, 35,506 Moroccans, 48,955 Indochinese, 36,941

Chinese, and 4,546 Madagascarians.[59] Most of the nonwhite workers were used in noncombatant military work, primarily in the marine arsenals in dock work. Others were distributed to large farms.[60]

Despite the SOTC's attempts to provide a cheap, docile, and productive workforce, employers and officials were frequently dissatisfied. In fact the SOTC provided only a small number of workers to the French war effort. North Africans failed to volunteer for work during the harvest months of June and July, which coincided with their religious holiday, Ramadan.[61] Ostensibly because of their small size and frailty the Indochinese were viewed by employers as unproductive.[62] Employers also complained about the regulations and charges which the SOTC imposed on those using nonwhite workers.[63] Beyond these problems were the racial tensions engendered between French and nonwhite workers. This was particularly the case with the Chinese. The SOTC, of course, anticipated difficulties and provided employers with special instructions on how to handle these unfamiliar workers.[64] This was insufficient to stop race riots between French and Chinese workers in 1916 at the war plants of Creusot and the gasworks of St. Denis in late 1917.[65] French officials feared that the presence of single male Chinese and colonial workers near the civilian populations might give rise to fears of sexual attacks on the wives and daughters of soldiers at the front. The Chinese, who were not French colonial subjects, apparently proved to be less tractable than the other nonwhite workers on the job. Employers in Bordeaux, Rennes, Nantes, and Brest complained of the insolence of the Chinese and of their pay, which was six times as high (at three francs a day) as the cost of prisoners of war.[66]

The use of nonwhite labor in France during the war was largely a failure. While they may have been crucial when the forced labor of the POW's was not available, employers resisted hiring them. From the standpoint of the French employer, nonwhite labor was unproductive, cumbersome to utilize, and much more expensive than forced labor. In addition, French society was hardly ready to tolerate non-European workers in their midst. As a result of this experiment, the French discontinued most nonwhite immigration after the war and did not resume it until an even more grave shortage of labor after World War II obliged them to import non-European workers.

Iberian-Italian Farm Workers In stark contrast with colonial immigration, the government played a facilitating rather than a controlling role in recruiting European farm workers. The state merely provided subsidies and technical aid to farm groups that jealously guarded their entrepreneurial rights. While widening well-established migratory streams from southern Europe, agriculture laid the groundwork for a separate farm labor program after the war.

The French Ministry of Agriculture did not create a public agency to recruit farm workers abroad. It simply subsidized and gave official status to a private organization created in 1912 by the Societé des agriculteurs en France. From April of 1915, this organization, the Office national de la main-d'oeuvre agricole—ONMA (National Farm Labor Office) not only researched sources of labor in Italy and Spain, but it organized recruitment and placement on the farms.[67] By the spring of 1915, the need for southern European labor had become obvious. Efforts to mobilize women, youth, prisoners of war, and garrisoned soldiers were insufficient.[68] In a conference in Toulouse in April of 1915, 300 representatives of French agricultural societies approved the ONMA's plan to recruit Spanish farm workers. Departmental farm societies established contracts which set wage and working conditions for all immigrants sent into that department. ONMA agents then filled requests for labor in sixteen immigration offices strung along the Spanish and later the Italian frontiers.[69] Altogether 146,446 Spanish and Portuguese as well as 2,225 Italians crossed the frontier to work on French farms.[70] Furthermore, the ONMA obtained colonial workers for large wheat growers and even Chinese laborers were occasionally sent to farms.[71] Large-scale sugar beet growers also received 7,580 North Africans and one thousand Indochinese by war's end.[72]

Despite the efforts of the ONMA, its success was modest. While 5.2 million French workers were employed in agriculture in 1911 and some 3.28 million of them had been mobilized by the end of the war, barely 160,000 foreigners had been imported to replace them.[73] Why was so little foreign agricultural labor used? First, farmers had access to other forms of cheap labor, and secondly, they had difficulties in recruiting and retaining immigrants. Farmers often used soldiers and POW's for critical seasonal work because they cost far less than immigrants.[74] As a result, hardly one-fourth of the French farm associations utilized the services of the ONMA and these were located largely in the south, where farmers already had experience with southern European workers.[75] Small farmers were generally reluctant to hire unseen workers even on approval of the agents of their own associations.[76]

Even if farmers did hire immigrants, unacceptably low wages and poor working conditions deterred immigrants from returning or staying. In a study of the Spanish farm workers placed in Loir-et-Cher, the ONMA found that wide differences in pay (from three to six francs daily) led to rapid turnover. Many farmers offered wages as low as seventy-five francs a month, which inevitably resulted in broken labor contracts and flight to the war factories.[77] For many reasons,[78] farmers could not easily compete with the higher paying urban industries. Realizing this fact, the ONMA tried to maintain its labor service for the exclusive use of farmers and thus channel labor into the rural job market. Yet the Ministry of Labor, seeking to control the entire placement of labor, repeatedly blocked the Ministry of Agriculture and its attempts to protect the ONMA's separate channel of labor. By 1917, the government forced the frontier offices of the ONMA to open their doors to industrial as well as farm immigrants.[79] In effect, agriculture had to share its mine of labor. These patterns of failure to retain foreign labor as well as the struggle to maintain a separate stream of immigrants would be repeated throughout the interwar period.

European Industrial Labor   Although the war industries were able to supplement their workforces with French women and noncombatant male workers, they too experienced shortages of labor. To help fill the gap, the Ministry of Armaments (after 1917, the Ministry of Labor) sought immigrants. It looked first to Italy and sent Bertrand Nogaro to Rome to negotiate. As we have seen, Italian restrictions on recruiting workers led the French government to search elsewhere.[80] Providing France with an alternative in June of 1916, the French consul at Rhodes suggested recruiting Greek refugees. Nogaro arranged at once to transport them to Marseilles. The Ministry of Armaments established an agency, the Service central de la main-d'oeuvre étrangère (Central Foreign Labor Service) to administer these immigrants. In August of 1916, Nogaro added Portuguese construction workers and in February of 1917, Spanish industrial workers to the labor pool after negotiations with their respective governments.[81] By the war's end, nearly 81,000 European immigrants entered French industry, including 22,849 Portuguese, 15,212 Spaniards, 24,274 Greeks, 5,486 Italians and 12,770 other nationalities.[82]

Initially, European industrial workers were distributed like the colonials out of temporary labor depots near Marseilles or various frontier placement offices where they were billeted.[83] However, unlike the nonwhite workers, the European received six-month contracts with their employers and were not placed in convoys.[84] European workers had to be treated like "free" labor and yet they were to be strongly encouraged to serve the immediate needs of the war economy.

This fact becomes obvious when we examine how the government attempted to control the mobility of the European immigrants. Government officials feared that European immigrants had a propensity for high rates of turnover and instability, both of which would lead to higher labor costs and social problems.[85] Nogaro, for example, noted that immigrants lacked personal ties to any single locality, and thus were more likely than indigenous labor to migrate at the slightest opportunity for an increase in wages. This tended "to provoke a general rise in wages, while the cost of living in the regions where this rise takes place has not yet required such an increase." More specifically, Nogaro believed, unstable foreign workers tended to equalize wages between Paris, where immigrants often went in search of higher pay, and the labor-starved provinces. This pattern of movement to the cities, he feared, also led to concentrations of uprooted and often unemployed foreigners in Paris and other large cities.[86]

To counteract this development, Nogaro's Foreign Labor Service attempted to minimize competition for labor between provincial and Parisian employers. The key to this policy was to encourage the immigrant to remain in the provinces and thus provide employers with needed labor and also maintain traditional low wages. At the same time this policy would avoid the social costs of masses of presumably dangerous foreigners in the cities. How did the government encourage immigrants to remain in the provincial industries, often when this must have been contrary to their own interests? First, unemployed immigrants were sent to regional labor depots located in towns like Lyons and Nantes, where they were pooled and sent into jobs in low-wage regions. In Paris, however, there was no depot but simply a placement office which immediately employed the immigrant or directed him to a provincial depot for a work assignment. Another device was to give workers who completed their contract a bonus. The Foreign Labor Service also concentrated each nationality in specific industries and regions. These practices were designed to give the immigrant a stable cultural environment and thus prevent anomie and excessive migration. Immigrant work groups were also aided by interpreters. Like the agents used by the SOTC, interpreters came from older members of the military auxiliary who had experience in foreign countries. These interpreters were not only to mediate and anticipate any disputes but also to help weed out and expel "troublemakers," especially those complaining about wages and working conditions.[87]

Besides these economic and cultural means of controlling the mobility of the immigrants, the government also forced immigrants to carry an identification card in order to survey their movements. Beginning in June of 1916, all European immigrant workers were issued cards which designated the geographical limits within which they could travel and whether they were farm or industrial workers. Whenever the worker moved, a copy of his card was forwarded to the police nearest to his next workplace (where he would pick up his card); if he were unemployed, the card was sent to the nearest placement depot. By these means the government discouraged job hopping and controlled necessary employment changes. Resourceful immigrants did break their work contracts and skip off to Gay Paris, but a host of government measures attempted to reduce this to a minimum.[88]

According to a circular from the Ministry of the Interior of June 1916, the identification card was designed to "restrain the unjustified migration [of immigrants] which could easily become a general trend." The circular instructed police to threaten to expel workers who broke their contracts, which was defined as failure to produce up to their capacity or refusal to accept a job offered by the government.[89] The Association national d'expansion économique, representing major industrial groups, proposed in March of 1917 that the identification cards become permanent and be centrally administered by the Ministry of the Interior.[90] One month later this was done by government decree. In a report which accompanied that decree, the government claimed that the cards would enable the state to "maintain an absolutely indispensable surveillance over the movements" of the immigrants so that they would "not become unproductive at the expense of France which shelters them, or fall into idleness which is often dangerous to the public order," and so that they could "be sent as soon as possible to enterprises which serve the national defense or the economy."[91]

The identification cards were designed to help police supervise a foreign population which lacked roots in France, was unknown to local authorities, and was presumed to be irresponsible or even dangerous. In this sense the cards were simply an extension of the requirement, in force since 1893, that immigrants register with the local police. More important, however, the cards helped to create an unfree labor force since immigrants were compelled to sell their services to buyers favored by the state. Often these were employers who could not find willing French workers.

European immigrants were slightly more free than were nonwhite foreign workers. Colonial laborers were treated as hardly more than paid slaves, hauled in gangs by military personnel wherever they were needed. European workers, however, were constrained by bureaucratic regulations designed to impede their mobility as much as possible. These procedures were, of course, established in time of war, which partly explains their illiberality. But they also show that French employers had come to rely on the state as a recruiter of supplemental labor and as a tool to constrain that labor in the immediate interests of French capital.

These governmental services, however, did not solve all of the problems of employers. The three immigration services, created in an ad hoc manner to serve the immediate needs of special economic interests, failed to provide several vital functions: they did not rationally allocate scarce foreign labor among the various economic sectors, nor did they channel the immigrant to avoid conflicts with the French worker. These tasks would be addressed by two additional institutions, both organized along corporatist lines.

Corporatism: Business and Government as partners

In March of 1916, the government created the first of these corporatist bodies, the Conference interministerielle de la main-d'oeuvre —CIMO (Interministerial Labor Commission). Including representatives from the key employer groups and the trade unions, it was an exemplary product of the Union Sacreé.[92] Although formally both labor and management were represented, it primarily served as a clearinghouse for the employers' needs for labor in the war economy.[93] At first business funneled their needs for labor through the appropriate ministerial official on the commission (for example, F. H. Brancher of the ONMA for agricultural employers) who attempted to fill the order with supplies secured by the recruiting ministries (for example, Ministries of War and Colonial Affairs). In an attempt to rationalize this procedure, in October of 1917, the Commission gave the Ministry of Labor the task of collecting the data on the supply and demand of labor and of apportioning the limited supply.[94]

The commission distributed immigrants in ways which reflected racial discrimination. Whenever lodging was "unsuitable for Frenchmen," it used nonwhite workers (or POW's).[95] For construction work near the front which was unsuited for POW's for security reasons, and for which it was impossible to find civilian French labor, the Ministry of War asked for unemployed Algerians from Paris.[96] Agriculture was willing to take anybody, even to accept Indochinese in exchange for POW's who were needed for skilled metal work.[97] Finally, Nogaro tried to reserve his European immigrants for industrial work rather than to allow their skills to be wasted in agriculture or construction.[98] The state distributed foreign workers into the job hierarchy in accordance to the racial or social hierarchy.

The Interministerial Labor Commission not only distributed foreign manpower but gave employers and government officials invaluable experience in cooperating with each other and in sharing ideas about immigrant labor policy. It surely helped employers discard laissez-faire notions that government should stay out of the labor market. From now on business and government would be partners in manipulating the flow of foreign labor into France.

The Other Corporatism: Labor Joins Management and Government

Although French trade unions had only a nominal role in the operations of the Interministerial Labor Commission, they were not used merely as a window dressing in the Union Sacrée. Because of their general support for the war effort and recognition of the critical need for additional hands, few trade unionists sought to exclude foreign labor as they sometimes advocated before the war. Rather, they wished to insure the priority of French workers in the distribution of jobs. Having little influence at the ministerial level of government, they attempted to control the job market at the local departmental level. A second corporatist institution, the Offices départmentals du placement (ODP) was created to fill this need.

Like the Interministerial Labor Commission, the departmental placement offices were administered by corporatist bodies, called parity commissions, which included representatives of business, labor, and administration at the departmental level. Although the public employment office had existed in France since 1904, and the idea of a parity commission had been advocated by the government since 1910, only the war and the Union Sacrée induced employers and labor to cooperate.[99] In December of 1915, the Labor Ministry urged the prefects to organize departmental placement offices with parity commissions, hoping to minimize irrational migrations of unemployed labor and to give priority for jobs to local French workers.[100] By December 1916, there were eighty-six such offices, thirty-seven with parity commissions.[101] In some of the urban departments, the ODP's gave labor some voice in the distribution of jobs on the local level. For example, in Paris private placement services of both management and labor coalesced into subsections of the ODP of the Seine.[102] In some cases, especially in departments where dock workers were important, these offices were created to placate workers' fears of foreign competition. In 1916, for example, the ODP of Bouches-du-Rhône (Marseilles) created a special section for dock workers because of complaints that immigrants were hired in preference to the French. Similar anger, when the docks hired Chinese, Moroccan, and other nonwhite stevedores, led to the formation of special placement offices in Le Havre, Dunkerque, and Rouen.[103] When employers chose to use these offices, the ODP's could stop employers from hiring outsiders—especially immigrants—when unemployed French were available.

These goals of the ODP's conflicted with the activities of the Interministerial Labor Commission. A two-track system appears to have regulated the labor market during the war. One was dominated by the employer associations and was oriented towards the expansion on the national level of cheap, docile, and constrained pool of labor. The other was dominated by local interests and was restricted to the major towns: it included real participation by labor, and attempted to rationalize the labor market with the least displacement of native workers. Efforts by the Office central de placement, which coordinated the ODP's, to gain control over the employment of all foreign workers was rejected by the Labor Ministry's Arthur Fontaine.[104] He claimed that labor was already represented in the Commission at the national level and that local ODP's lacked the requisite information on the needs of national defense to decide on the employment of foreign or colonial workers.[105] As a result, a poorly coordinated system resulted; one that would continue after the war and remain a source of conflict.

Despite the inherent conflicts between these two institutions and their approaches to the problem of manpower, they both represented a significant depature from pre-war patterns. For employers it was a sharp turn away from the liberalism of prewar immigration; for unions, an equally significant shift from the simple advocacy of ceilings on the employment of foreign workers. Both groups discovered a new role for the state through the corporatist advisory committee. This experience was a powerful impetus for the development of a national policy on immigration after the war. However, as this analysis of the history of French attitudes toward foreign manpower suggests, serious divisions between agricultural and industrial employers limited a solid front of business in the formation of immigration policy. Strongly divergent interests between employers and labor likewise impeded consensus.

III Organizing Immigration after the First World War

BY the end of the war immigration was no longer free and spontaneous, but regulated and organized. Because of the war experience, all groups (except the communists, who opposed all forms of class collaboration) shared important expectations about immigration in postwar France. They recognized that if France was to capitalize on its military victory through economic expansion, additional labor was needed to replace the young workers slaughtered in the war. Heavy industry, big agriculture, and noncommunist labor all accepted the need for a large increase in immigration. They all agreed that this immigration must be regulated as well as expanded: the government must eliminate the undesirable foreigner—principally the colonial and Chinese worker, whom the French had found unacceptable during the war. The government must also secure regular streams of selected European workers. Finally, a regulated immigration would result in a reduction of spontaneous immigration and the free movement of immigrants within the French economy and, produce instead, a channeling of the foreign workers into jobs in which there was a shortage of indigenous labor. The war experience, then, had created the possibility of consensus on immigration.

Yet, by 1924, a corporatist solution was left stillborn. It was blocked by the conflicting goals with which each group accepted government intervention. Employers sought government aid to increase their access to foreign workers; labor groups, to assure natives' priority in a regulated job market. Furthermore, during the reconstruction period, 1919–24, employers succeeded in utilizing the diplomatic and police powers of the state to shape immigration. At the same time, labor interests were largely excluded from policy making. In addition, an alternative to state-managed immigration emerged in a commercial labor contractor, the Societé générale d'immigration—SGI. This powerful company, owned and operated by a consortium of coal mining and agricultural associations, obtained a monopoly over eastern European immigration. In the SGI employers obtained an agency able, like the French state, to prevail over weak states—especially Poland—and thus control immigration. Yet the SGI was free from the critical political pressures which were imposed on the French government. Thus it was a nearly perfect vehicle for business. In effect, employer groups were able to exclude labor from a policy role both by dominating government decision-making and by establishing a private alternative to government. While there was surely an opportunity for compromise and consensus, employer dominance made a multi-class immigration policy impossible.

Preparing for the Foreign Worker, 1917–1919

In 1917, a major federation of French employer groups, the Association national d'expansion économique, laid the basis for a common program on immigration. It affirmed the necessity of a drastically enlarged immigration after the war.[1] Participants noted that hopes to capitalize on France's expected military victory through economic expansion required foreign manpower to make up for French losses due to the war. Not just any workers would do, however. The Association agreed that colonial and Chinese workers were poor producers and sources for racial tensions.[2] The Association also recognized that unregulated European immigration, which had prevailed before the war, allowed foreigners with inappropriate skills or uncooperative attitudes to enter France. This employers' group advocated that the government continue to require immigrants to obtain identity cards. Because these cards could be denied the unemployed or those having nonauthorized jobs, the state could exclude the undesirables and channel acceptable foreigners into jobs offered by politically powerful employers.[3]

Moreover, French failure before the war in priming new streams of immigration showed employers that only the state could assure the flow of desired foreign workers, especially in the face of foreign political pressures.[4] As the administrator of the National Farm Labor Office, F. L. Brancher, pointed out in 1919,

> the nations . . . capable of sending us labor consider it as a kind of capital. They will allow workers to immigrate only if France gives them something in return. It follows that this problem can be solved only through governmental negotiation rather than through the professional associations. As long as this is the case, the cooperation of the state will be indispensable for agriculture.[5]

An important representative of industry, Paul de Rousiers, president of the Shippers Committee, agreed at the Association d'expansion meeting when he noted that because private agencies had failed to recruit sufficient numbers of Polish workers for French mines and farms before the war, an "organization with an official authority" would be required after the war.[6] In order to fill their demanding specifications for labor, French employers expected the government both to restrict and channel foreign manpower as well as to encourage migrations from desirable populations.

This unity of French employers, however, failed when farm interests broke rank and demanded special treatment. Because farmers believed that they could not compete with industry for foreign labor,[7] agriculture demanded that it maintain the separate foreign labor service which was established during the war.[8] The old problem of the exodus of farm workers to urban industry, which was greatly exacerbated by the war, lay at the heart of this attitude.[9] Another reason for the separatism of the farmers was their suspicion of government. While industry accepted foreign workers recruited by the placement offices of the Labor Ministry, farmers preferred that their agents control all recruitment as they had during the war.[10] Agricultural groups also disliked the parity commissions, which administered some of the departmental placement offices. A former minister of agriculture,

J. Meline, objected that unionized industrial workers would inevitably represent unorganized farm workers on these commissions; trade unionism might spread to agriculture and wage differentials between agriculture and industry would decrease.[11] In order to isolate themselves from the wage competition of industry and the more modern labor relations which the parity commissions represented, farm associations stuck fast to their separate immigrant labor system. This policy was to fragment control of immigration.

Still, by 1917, both industry and agriculture had abandoned their prewar commitment to the free labor market and embraced government intervention as a solution to their needs for foreign manpower. Just as the growth sectors of the industrial economy demanded specific pools of foreign workers to break the labor bottlenecks which they anticipated would occur during the period of postwar growth, so the relatively stagnant agricultural sector pressed for immigrants to avoid competing for labor with industry and to provide a substitute for modernization. Only through state intervention could both of these broad needs be served.

Labor groups also reversed their prewar position on immigration. Key labor officials, after joining the Union Sacrée in 1914, came under the influence of corporatist ideas on immigration. They were especially impressed by the positions of the Association française pour la lutte contre le chômage, which included important officials from the Labor Ministry, especially in the placement offices.[12] The association advocated a rationally organized labor market. This involved not only government-assisted expansion of immigration as the business community demanded, but also the effective allocation of available labor within France.[13] These objectives alone would assure social peace as well as prosperity. The association believed that French labor's hostility to immigration might lead to violence if the state did not regulate the internal labor market to prevent excessive foreign competition. Foreign labor depots and departmental placement offices should direct immigrants into jobs left by the French and away from urban or frontier areas where foreigners might compete with native labor. In March of 1918 an article in the *Bulletin de l'Association française pour la lutte contre le chômage* makes the rationale for this policy very clear:

If foreign labor were employed only in the most unpleasant work, in the jobs which our citizens mostly avoid, there would be scarcely any reason to fear that their low pay would effect French wages. But for several years in Paris, luxury goods industries, such as wood, leather, and fur goods, in which workers earn rather high wages, have been flooded by foreigners, who earn a lower rate. If this prevails, it will produce lower wages in all these professions.[14]

The solution to this potential for social malaise was to prevent large numbers of immigrants from entering these attractive trades, especially at wage levels below the standard. Thus, in addition to helping French industry obtain supplemental labor, the governmental regulation of foreign labor should also assure that immigrant manpower complemented rather than competed with citizen labor.

The noncommunist wing of the French labor movement embraced this position wholeheartedly. For example, Léon Jouhaux, chief of the CGT, wrote in August of 1917: "After the war it will be necessary to enlist foreign workers. We will need to fill the vacuum caused by the war and to prepare ourselves for a new attempt to develop our national industries." Again, up to this point, the CGT had reversed its protectionist attitude of the pre-1914 period, and now shared with business a commitment to prosperity through an expanded labor supply. But Jouhaux goes on and says:

> But the recruitment of foreign labor must be made in a methodical way. . . . In a word it must be organized . . . to include the interests of the working class, which has so well served the general interests of the nation. . . . If the workers return from the front to find themselves faced with foreign workers, who, because there are no guarantees against their exploitation, may cause wage decreases, the discontent will be widespread and violent.[15]

In 1916, the CGT demanded that employers "not be allowed to import foreign workers en masse when the local workforce is sufficient. . . . it would be better to channel [already] imported labor where it may be needed," especially into new heavy industries. The CGT advocated that parity commissions for the departmental placement offices investigate whether "the recruitment of foreign workers for an industry or region corresponds to a real need," and that they place a "ceiling on this recruitment."[16]

When one compares the expectations of industry, agriculture, the CGT and its allies in the placement offices, obvious points of agreement emerge which had not existed before the war. Employers favored government intervention which it opposed before the war and unions accepted an expanded immigration which they had formerly fought. Yet business sought government intervention primarily to improve its access to desired foreign labor supplies; French labor accepted this on condition that it had a veto over foreign employment in competitive job markets. This concession, however, employers were generally unwilling to accept.

The political complexion of postwar France was a critical factor determining the outcome of this conflict of interests. This is not to suggest that immigration policy was fashioned in parliamentary debate and legislation. Immigration was not an important issue in either elections or the Chamber of Deputies. The topics which dominated parliamentary politics between 1919 and 1926 were foreign policy (especially war reparations), economic concerns revolving around inflation and taxation, as well as the social issues of labor unions and Bolshevism. Immigration was largely irrelevant to party politics.[17] Yet toward the end of the war and in the five years of reconstruction, political power swung broadly to the right, while labor and the socialist left split in two. This situation destroyed the political climate of the Union Sacrée and ended the possibility of a direct bargaining between labor and business over immigration policy.

As early as the spring of 1917, growing opposition to the Union Sacrée was shown in strikes against the war in munition factories.[18] When the socialists left the government in September of 1917 in the midst of mounting leftwing antiwar pressure, the national coalition ended. The policy of cooperation between labor and management, which the socialist minister of armaments Albert Thomas had instituted, was reversed by his replacement, the industrialist Louis Loucheur. The labor and socialist leadership which had supported the war alienated a large share of the rank-and-file; many split off in unauthorized local strikes (for example by metalworkers in the spring of 1918) and rallied to the cause of Bolshevism. Following the Armistice and the threat of massive strikes, the French parliament hurriedly passed a bill for the eight-hour day in April of 1919—one of the few significant concessions to labor after the war. In the midst of this apparent upsurge of militant labor, conservatives were able to organize a Bloc National, an electoral coalition of the right, which successfully appealed to voters on the themes of order, anticommunism, and national honor. In the elections of November of 1919 the Bloc National won a smashing victory: they sat 338 supporters to the Socialists' 68 with most of the rest of the 610 seats going to the centrist radicals and small parties who generally supported the Bloc National. During the following year, the socialists and the Confédération générale du travail (CGT) divided into bitter factions over the question of support for the Bolshevik's Third International. The split of the socialist party in December of 1920, with a majority forming the communist party, further undercut the political strength of labor's position. Finally, the division of the CGT, with the expulsion of the generally procommunist wing in 1921 and its formation of the Confédération générale du travail unitaire (CGTU) in December, assured the impotence of the labor movement in the 1920s.

With a conservative government in office there was little room for compromise with French labor. Following the outbreak of a general strike in support of a walkout of railway workers (May 1920), the government of the ex-socialist Alexandre Millerand succeeded briefly in winning parliamentary approval for the suppression of the CGT. The split of the left and the unions not only weakened their bargaining power but split the voice of labor on the question of immigration as on many other issues: the moderate and larger wing led by Léon Jouhaux, who retained control of the CGT, continued to advocate cooperation with management as it had during the war; the communist-led CGTU opposed any collaboration with the bourgeoisie and generally opposed any regulation of foreign labor. This assured business control over immigration policy during the precedent-setting years of reconstruction. For example, in 1920 a Conseil national de la main-d'oeuvre, was chartered by the government to give labor and management advisory roles in shaping immigration policy. Yet business representatives frustrated its promulgation until 1925 by objecting to the CGT's claim to represent all of French labor.[19] Furthermore, the Bloc National governments between 1919 and 1924 reversed the etatist trends of the war period by refusing to back Etienne Clemental's plan for a national economic council (modeled after the Germans) and returning to a policy of liberalism.

However, labor's interests were not entirely ignored. The Bloc National feared labor unrest, rising from the experience of the strikes in 1919 and 1920 and the haunting example of the Bolshevik Revolution. The government could not afford to undertake an entirely pro-business policy of providing an unlimited supply of foreign workers without considering the threat of competition with native workers. Nor could the Bloc National governments simply return to the free foreign labor market. Business groups, who supported these governments, still required the coordination of certain governmental agencies—especially the Foreign Ministry, the Agricultural Ministry, and the Foreign Labor Service of the Labor Ministry—to assure the flow of foreign labor.

Of equal importance is the fact that employers of immigrants did not use the parliamentary process to advance their goals. No legislation concerning immigration was passed by the French parliament during these crucial four years of the Bloc National period. This may have been in part because of the reluctance of this conservative parliament to endow the state with additional powers. More likely the beneficiaries of government assistance preferred to deal directly with the Ministries as they had done during the war in order to develop a policy without explicit parliamentary sanction. The politics of immigration were fashioned between 1919 and 1924 largely by the French executive in collaboration with powerful employers of immigrants.

The Government Organizes Immigration, 1919–1924

During the five years of postwar reconstruction, the government played a decisive role in organizing and regulating the influx of foreign labor. Anticipating large-scale unemployment of French workers and fearful of Jouhaux's predictions of "discontent and violence," the Ministry of Labor closed the frontier to further immigration immediately after the signing of the armistice. The Interior Ministry also repatriated as many of the colonial and Chinese workers as it could lay hands on.[20] Yet, with the loss of 1.3 million young men in the war and the expectation of economic growth following the victory, labor shortages rather than unemployment were soon to be the problem. At first, the government anticipated labor shortages in industries where prisoners of war had been heavily used and where housing, wages, and working conditions compared unfavorably with alternative occupations. For these reasons, dock work, as well as construction, quarrying, mining, and the glass industries were opened to immigrants during the spring of 1919.[21] These two general policies—emergency priority for French labor and funneling foreign workers into labor-short sectors—were to become the hallmarks of postwar immigration policy.

While fears of French labor unrest entered the policy-making equation, employers' interests dominated. The government recognized that a long-term solution to French business' need for acceptable foreign workers required an aggressive research and development program. Drawing on its war-time experience, the government in March of 1919 established a Conférence permanente de la main-d'oeuvre étrangère. The Conference was a carry-over from the Interministerial Labor Commission and included key governmental functionaries.[22] It established priorities for recruiting various nationalities.[23] While rejecting out of hand any further experimentation with colonial labor, it determined that to gain access to prized nationalities, especially the Italians, Poles, and Czechs, subtle diplomatic action was required. The Conference realized that nationalistic governments of these countries would demand a quid pro quo for any workers which the French were allowed to recruit.[24] Consequently, France negotiated a series of bilateral treaties with Poland, Italy, and Czechoslovakia to assure a regular flow of immigrant labor. Signed in September 1919 and March 1920, these treaties established bilateral commissions to determine the number and occupational categories of immigrants who could be recruited under labor contracts. The supplying nations were to control where and in what occupations the French were allowed to recruit workers, although these nations were to have no formal authority over the working conditions or pay of their emigrating citizens.[25]

The bilateral immigration treaties prepared the way for a large-scale flow of foreign labor into France. On January 19, 1920, all foreign manual workers under work contracts as authorized by the treaties were allowed to enter France.[26] The opening of the sluices coincided with a major labor shortage in France, resulting from the reconstruction of war-damaged regions. As many as 400,000 workers were needed from 1919 to 1924 to fill trenches and level bomb-scarred land, to rebuild towns and factories, and to repair flooded mines in the war zones of the northeast.[27]

Not only had many potential workers been killed or maimed in the war, but the population had been scattered by the fighting. Even if sufficient numbers of French workers were available, very poor living and working conditions deterred French applicants for these construction jobs. At the same time, opportunities in construction threatened to draw some native labor from important mining and agricultural industries which already faced labor shortages. This could result only in general wage increases, a prospect which employers resisted.

Large-scale immigration was an inevitable solution to these problems. Not only did it alleviate the immediate labor shortage but it provided a malleable workforce: because the immigrants were single or left their families at home, they accepted barracks life more readily than did the French worker. Furthermore, employers had greater control over the foreigner than the French worker: none could enter France without a work contract nor could they remain without an identity card which specified their work assignment. These controls filtered the immigrants exclusively into reconstruction jobs, often those rejected by the French, and discouraged them from breaking their contracts (see chapter VII). Immigrants were also an advantage to the employer because they could be imported to fit specific skill requirements.

In the reconstruction zones, the state continued to dominate the immigration process as it had during the war. A Ministry for the Liberated Regions was created in 1919 to organize the reconstruction. The Office of Industrial Reconstitution, a joint government-employer agency, served as a liaison, funneling employers' requests for labor to the Ministry for the Liberated Zones who then filled them with foreign workers recruited at government-run job offices. This whole process bypassed the departmental placement offices, which in principle were to be consulted in order to give priority to local labor. In 1920, about

200,000 Belgian workers were recruited at frontier hiring offices, mostly for the unskilled work of leveling and clearing land.[28]

This first flow of immigrants from Belgium was relatively simple. However, as soon as masons, bricklayers, and other skilled construction workers were needed, the French were obliged to go further afield.[29] In 1920–1921 employers sought Czech labor from an estimated pool of 16,000 unemployed construction workers. Yet, despite French government efforts to pursuade the new Czech government to allow French recruiters to tap this labor pool, the Czechs resisted these entreaties, fearing that an exodus of skilled workers would compromise their economic development.[30]

The French were more successful with a traditional source of skilled building workers—the Italians. Following the ratification of the bilateral immigration treaties with Italy in 1920, the Italian government allowed French employers to recruit Italian construction workers (see chapter V). The French also imported Portuguese and Spanish laborers, mostly for less skilled work. By September of 1922 there were 135,044 immigrants working in the reconstruction (44 percent of the total labor force of 307,615). Fifty-seven percent of these immigrants were skilled.[31]

As it had during the war, the government also assisted employers by attempting to prevent turnover and competition between employers for foreign labor. The state expelled immigrants who broke their contracts and threatened to withdraw government contracts from firms who pirated immigrants under work contracts. The government took a direct interest in the problem of labor instability, for it was presumed that turnover and competition for labor raised the cost of workers and thus the expense of the reconstruction.[32]

Between the end of 1919 and 1924, the French state had facilitated the entry of over one million foreign workers into France.[33] This huge influx of labor was probably decisive in France's post-war economic recovery.

Commercial Recruiters of Foreign Labor: The General Immigration Society (SGI)

The demand for immigrant labor was hardly restricted to the reconstruction industries. Coal mines and a variety of agricultural enterprises in the northeast also desperately needed foreign workers. Even before the war these industries had difficulties obtaining French workers and even nearby Flemish labor. Their situation was worsened in the tight postwar labor market, and further exacerbated by the demand for labor for the nearby reconstruction projects. They sought an alternative to the nationalities recruited for the reconstruction (Italians, Spanish, and Belgians) in order to avoid competing for workers. Their natural choice was Polish labor: not only had these industries already experimented with importing Poles before the war, but they correctly saw an opportunity to tap the labor supply of a new, relatively weak state in which the French were to have great influence.

Unlike foreign labor sent to the reconstruction projects, the government played little role in bringing Polish workers to the mines and farms of France. Rather, a commercial immigration company, the Societé générale d'immigration (SGI), controlled by coal and farm interests, imported the Poles. In general, employers resented government interference in this important prerogative of management—recruiting labor. Government intervention was tolerable in the reconstruction primarily because it was temporary, state-financed, and otherwise government controlled. Not so for the coal and agricultural industries, who were less willing to see a permanent government control over the foreign labor market, especially in the private sector. Furthermore, the coal and farm employers, who needed Polish labor, were well organized and capable of establishing a foreign labor service largely outside government control. The prospects of profit also provided an incentive to create a private commercial recruitment service.

The SGI constituted a new factor in the foreign labor system of France: a profit-making foreign labor recruiter with a near monopoly oversupplying France with eastern European workers. It supplied 541,594 workers or 28 percent of the foreign labor entering France in the 1920s.[34] Moreover, the SGI was an important example of organized capitalism: it was owned and operated by the trade associations of the coal industry, the Comité des houillères (Coal Committee) and a consortium of farm groups from the northeast (the Confédération des associations agricoles des régions devastées (CARD). The SGI eliminated competition for labor between these industries and channeled eastern European workers into these labor-starved sectors. Finally, the SGI operated almost independently of the states of France or eastern Europe as a supranational corporation. The emergence and success of the SGI would help frustrate a national immigration policy in France in the 1920s. Thus we must investigate its origins and development with some care.

In 1919, Polish immigration began, as did the organized immigrations of the war period, under the control of the French state. Within two years, however, the government turned over its Polish labor service to the Coal Committee and CARD. In October 1919, immediately after the signing of the bilateral immigration treaty with Poland, the Ministry of the Liberated Regions established a mission in Warsaw to recruit Polish workers. A depot at Toul in eastern France was established to distribute these workers to worksites in northeastern France.[35] Almost immediately, however, employers resisted this government service. For example, farmers complained that the Poles sent to them were unqualified.[36] Government officials also reflected private interests' reluctance to accept government recruiters. J. Baches, the director of the Toul depot, stated in October 1920 that "it would be best to eliminate the administrative character of the immigration," which ought to be "a purely commercial activity" with "a unified management with responsible field agents."[37] This sentiment was shared by the Minister of the Liberated Regions, G. Ogier, who in July 1920 advocated that the state "gradually allow more private action and initiative" in labor recruiting.[38] His successor, Louis Loucheur, followed his advice. Late in 1920, Loucheur arranged a visit to Poland for representatives of the Coal Committee and CARD to study how to set up their own recruitment services.[39]

At first both employer groups worked independently to serve the particular interests of their members. CARD agents found ready supplies of both farm hands and skilled workers in Western Galicia, Posen, Carpathia, and the Warsaw region. CARD insisted on recruiting only farm workers still uncontaminated by urban and industrial wage expectations. They intended not only to select workers in their native villages (rather than at regional or national placement depots), but also to isolate their recruits from immigrants bound for French industry. As a CARD representative explained:

It was necessary to form convoys composed exclusively of farm
workers; the contact between agricultural and industrial workers is
dangerous. They may make comparisons between their wages. . . .
[As a result, farm workers may be] tempted to desert the land for
the factory.[40]

Also to avoid turnover, workers from the same region in Poland were
to be sent to the same area in France. CARD hoped to recruit whole
families, both to utilize female as well as male labor, and to preserve
the stabilizing influence of traditional peasant culture.[41]

Gradually the CARD mission in Poland gained nearly total control
over labor recruited for French farms. In January 1921, with the
support of the French Ministry of Agriculture, CARD established in
Paris the Office central de la main-d'oeuvre agricole (Central
Agricultural Labor Office). It served as a liaison between departmental farm associations, through which farmers requested Polish
workers, and the CARD recruitment mission in Poland. By August
1921 this network had replaced the foreign labor service of the
Ministry of the Liberated Regions in Poland.[42] Soon this private
group would send Polish workers throughout France and greatly
expand the number of Polish immigrants.[43] Although only 5,167 Poles
entered French agriculture in 1920–1921, when the government
controlled recruitment, the number rose to 33,416 in 1922–1923, after
the employers took over the process.[44] It became the agency of the
most powerful farm interests (e.g., sugar-beet producers and large
wheat farmers in the Paris region).[45]

The Coal Committee followed a similar path. From January 1921 it
began to recruit skilled Polish miners at missions in Upper Silesia,
which were near Polish mining centers; it also sought to draw Polish
miners from Westphalia in Germany at its mission at Duisburg.[46]

In June 1924 CARD's missions coalesced with those of the Coal
Committee to form the Societé générale d'immigration (SGI). This
alliance was possible because the labor needs of the two groups were
distinct and noncompetitive. It allowed these groups to form a united
front in Poland and to gain a near monopoly over immigration to
France. Soon the SGI expanded its operations, winning contracts
from iron mine operators to recruit Poles into the Lorraine basin.[47]
The sugar beet and distillery cartels paid the SGI to recruit Poles to

supplement declining numbers of Belgian workers.[48] Farm associations from southwestern France requested Polish peasants to become sharecroppers in the depopulated regions of Gascony. By 1925, the SGI had contracts with sixty industrial groups through France for Polish immigrants.[49]

The SGI did not restrict itself to the Polish labor market. Edouard de Warren, a deputy from eastern France, president of CARD, and a director of the SGI, proposed that the company find alternatives to Polish labor for "reasons of economics as well as politics."[50] Despite their entrenched position in Poland, SGI officials sought leverage by freeing themselves of dependence on the Poles. By 1928, Jean Duhamel, a representative of the Coal Committee and executive director of the SGI, expanded SGI missions to other eastern European nations including Hungary, Czechoslovakia, Yugoslavia, Austria, and Lithuania, as well as Switzerland, Belgium, and the Netherlands; these offices enjoyed varying degrees of success and official French support.[51]

During the 1920s the SGI controlled a significant and increasingly large share of the immigration, rising to nearly half of total labor immigration in 1926 and 1929 (see Table 4).[52] 76 percent (or 308,506) of the workers recruited between 1921 and 1931 by the SGI (or its predecessors) were Polish. 43 percent of the Poles recruited in the 1920s were hired in agriculture. 53 percent of the Poles sent to French industry were hired by coal mines (103,472), and 19 percent were hired by iron mines (37,733).[53] The SGI successfully channeled a sizeable portion of the Poles into economic sectors which could not attract Frenchmen and other foreign workers.

Why was it possible for the SGI to import large numbers of Poles in the 1920s when similar efforts had failed before the war? Severe unemployment in Poland plus restrictions on emigration to the Americas and Germany gave the French immigration company a great advantage. Especially between 1922 and 1926, the Poles were heavily dependent upon France as an outlet (see Table 5).[54] As a result, the Polish government made important concessions in amendments made to the bilateral immigration treaty in 1924 which allowed the Polish government only token control over the immigration process. The SGI gained access to one hundred public labor exchanges in Poland. Local officials could only observe the recruitment and all

Table 4   The Role of SGI-Controlled Immigration in the 1920s

Year	Total labor immigration (no. of foreigners)*	RL-CH-SGI-controlled immigration† No.		%
1920	201,935	17,040		8.4
1921	80,412	8,654	(RL—25,694)	10.6
1922	181,652	48,197		24.7
1923	262,877	86,567	(CH—134,764)	31.8
1924	239,365	75,837		28.8
1925	176,261	49,776		28.2
1926	162,900	70,615		43.6
1927	64,325	13,746		21.4
1928	97,743	29,082		29.8
1929	179,321	82,639		46.1
1930	221,619	85,235	(SGI—406,950)	38.5
Total	1,915,957	567,388		29.6

* The category of "total labor immigration" includes all immigrants under work contracts made either prior to entry into France or at frontier placement bureaus.

† RL (Ministry of Liberated Regions) immigration includes only the eastern European immigration, and the CH (Coal Committee) immigrants include farm and industrial workers as well as coal miners.

Source: Henri Bunle (Institut national des études economiques), *Mouvements migratoires entre la France et l'étranger, Études et documents,* 4 (Paris: Presses universitaires de France, 1943), p. 91 and *Revue d'immigration,* 6 (April 1932), 26.

Polish grievances had to be forwarded to Warsaw for uncertain redress.[55]

Although theoretically Polish workers could migrate to France as individuals, few could afford the train fare, which was advanced by the SGI to its recruits. Also, in order to enter France, visas were required from the French consuls. They were granted only if the Polish worker had a work contract, which was difficult to obtain outside the SGI network.[56] As a result, from 1919 to 1931 only 10 percent of the Poles emigrating to France did so as individuals outside the system controlled by the SGI (or its predecessors).[57]

How did the SGI operate? Both sympathetic and critical accounts of their procedures give a similar picture: "company agents posted notices of hiring in areas of desperate unemployment, attracting

Table 5 The Role of France in Polish Emigration, 1920–1930

Year	Emigration to France	Emigration to Germany	Emigration to other European nations	Total European migration No.	% to France	Trans-oceanic	Total emigration No.	% to France
1920	13,398		785	14,183	93	74,121	88,304	15
1921	9,306	180	1,659	11,145	86	108,544	119,689	8
1922	31,750	41	1,593	33,384	81	41,151	74,535	43
1923	70,898	35	1,185	72,118	98	54,341	126,459	56
1924	50,884	80	3,090	54,054	94	24,279	78,333	65
1925	40,880	266	3,129	44,275	92	39,441	83,716	49
1926	68,704	43,706	5,206	117,616	58	50,421	168,037	41
1927	16,211	68,779	4,437	89,427	28	58,187	147,614	11
1928	32,145	85,375	5,239	122,759	29	64,581	187,340	18
1929	81,508	87,247	9,387	178,142	46	65,310	243,452	33
1930	86,500	77,540	7,092	171,132	51	48,534	219,666	39
Total	502,184	363,249	42,802	908,235	55	628,910	1,537,145	33

Source: *Revue d'immigration*, 6 (April 1932), 17.

crowds of up to 1,200 who fought to get in the door of the office" of the labor exchange.[58] Company agents herded the workers through a cursory selection process (involving an examination of the eyes and the size of the hands and neck), accepting from 10 to 50 percent of the applicants. Although they did receive contracts, Poles complained that they were incomplete and had insufficient time to study them. They were then sent to Posen or Myslenice (usually within twenty-four hours) for medical screening, with another 50 percent rejected and then hauled by train to Toul, where they were distributed to employers.[59] According to one Polish farm worker they were shipped in cattle cars without windows or light for three days across Germany.[60]

A Polish miner recalled twenty-five years after coming to France that the "condition of the voyage was deplorable. . . . Upon arrival at Toul the emigrants were packed into old infected barracks; they slept on straw, were poorly fed and had to wait for some time for the recruiters from the French mines." Another miner claimed that the SGI had treated the Poles "like human cattle."[61] This procedure minimized SGI costs while it maximized Polish competition for work. No doubt it also had a humbling effect on those who passed the gate. In obvious ways this process was similar to a slave trade. Like the "black cargoes" to America, the Poles were treated as merchandise and, if they were not owned by the French employers who received them, they clearly were not freely entering a free labor market.

The efficiency of this operation allowed the SGI to amass large profits from its fees. In 1926 the cost per adult immigrant worker was 445 francs, which produced a profit of about 145 francs. This yielded 4,280,472 francs in profit in 1926.[62] The SGI used its capital not to improve the recruitment procedure, but to make highly diversified investments in Poland (e.g., timber and loans) as well as founding a holding company to undertake various immigration and land colonization schemes in North Africa and South America.[63]

Not surprisingly, the SGI encountered criticism from customers as well as government officials. Farmers' complaints about high fees in 1929 prompted the French government to pressure the SGI into a vague promise to set aside "excess" profits for "projects in the general interest."[64] By 1929, the head of the French Agricultural Ministry's labor service, Marcel Paon, began to plot with the Polish government to break the SGI monopoly over seasonal farm labor. They made an abortive effort to shift this immigration to another organization.[65] French public health officials in 1926 complained of the perfunctory screening of Polish immigrants for medical disabilities which increased French welfare costs.[66]

Nevertheless, the SGI was hardly isolated. It enjoyed the cooperation of most of the great industrial associations who channelled requests for Polish labor to the SGI. It vigorously promoted immigration. Its director, Jean Duhamel, for example, declared that France's declining birth rate was not a passport to decadence but rather gave the French an opportunity to become a "nation of supervisors" with manual labor being imported "whenever necessary, i.e., neither too soon nor too late, but on the precise day they are needed."[67] Far from being weakened by a dependence on immigrants, French employers could tailor, through immigration, the labor supply to the business cycle.

Yet, despite its claims to serve the French economy, the General Immigration Society was essentially a transnational corporation, responsible ultimately to no nation but only to profitable international exchange. The SGI was an autonomous agency, virtually sovereign, whose impact was parallel to that of the French state in shaping immigration in the 1920s. In effect, the pro-business governments of France in the early twenties ceded to the private interests controlling the SGI an important component of national immigration policy. The consortium of mining and farm interests behind the SGI were assured of a labor supply without having to compete with other industries or make costly compromises with social policy makers (e.g., public health). Yet very quickly the SGI broke from its roots in the French economy to become a business with diverse international investments and ambiguous loyalty to France's economic and social well-being. Clearly, the SGI was an obstacle to an integrated and consensus immigration policy.

Movements for Reforming Immigration Policy

During the reconstruction period, the state concerned itself almost exclusively with serving employers' immediate need for supplemental labor. Wartime trends toward a corporatist development of policy failed to develop. The government took little interest in managing the social and political problems which the large-scale influx of foreigners engendered. In fact, it encouraged the commercialization of eastern European immigration.

It became apparent, however, that immigration was not a temporary phenomenon, but rather a permanent feature of French capitalism. It also became clear that the demand for foreign labor was not confined to a few industries and regions as it had been during the reconstruction, but rather permeated the economy and directly confronted French labor and the general public. Indeed, by 1924, right-wing deputies had resurrected the xenophobic appeals against the foreign peril which had peppered the parliamentary debates of the 1880s and 1890s. For example, a bill sponsored by members of the rightist coalitions of the Entente republicaine and Republicains de gauche denounced the "plethora of foreigners of all types in our country" and made a vague demand to limit their entry and movement in France. Groups like the *Action française* and far right journals like *Revue de Paris* attacked the notion of equality of economic and civil rights for immigrants, which the migration treaties were to protect, as unjust to French workers.[68] Although this xenophobic response would remain marginal until the 1930s, it was a potential threat to the government's immigration policy. It indicates also that conservative opinion, which obviously included many businessmen who did not use foreign labor, was not unanimously in favor of the government's immigration policy.

More important during the mid-twenties was the opposition from the left. By 1924, the Bloc National was a spent political force. Divisions within this broad coalition had led to the typical parade of governments (led by Millerand and Leygues in 1920, A. Briand in 1921, and Poincaré in 1922 and 1923). Poincaré's invasion of the Ruhr in January of 1923 was a disaster, leading to an inflationary budget to pay for an occupation which alienated French allies. The Bloc's uninspired record and deflationary proposals for economic recovery gave the left an opportunity for victory in the May 1924 elections. The Cartel des Gauches (which included the Socialists as well as the Radicals) won 266 seats to 229 for the members of the former Bloc National. This victory could have led to a new immigration policy if the Cartel had a clear policy. However, not only did it lack a cohesive program on this or most other economic and social issues, but its electoral victory became meaningless in Parliament: the Socialists remained true to their long-established policy of abstaining from participation in bourgeois governments—which included those made by their erstwhile Radical allies. Even if they had joined with the Radicals, ideological differences would have prevented an effective government. The Socialists, of course, favored nationalizations and higher taxes, while the Radicals with their small business and farmer constituency supported economic liberalism and weak government. The Cartel faced a hostile banking community while its own unwillingness to raise taxes led to uncontrolled inflation. The result was two short Ministries of E. Herriot and Paul Painlevé between 1924 and July of 1926, when President Doumergue succeeded in placing the conservative Raymond Poincaré at the head of government. Again, as during the Bloc National period, the Parliament failed to take action on the immigration or almost any other issue.[69] This guaranteed the continuation of an immigration policy dominated by employers.

This, of course, did not mean that there were no proposals to reorganize immigration policy. In fact, by 1924, labor, urban, and public service interests and even business groups offered comprehensive solutions to the immigration problem. Each claimed to encompass the interests of all and included a tripartite policy-making body. Yet they represented clearly conflicting economic and social goals which, in the context of parliamentary stalemate, prevented any solution.

During the reconstruction, organized labor was surprisingly restrained in its criticism of immigration despite the large influx of aliens and the fact that labor had little direct impact on policy. There were a few isolated strikes in which foreign reconstruction workers were an issue.[70] Yet labor showed none of the hostility that one might have expected from the experience of the much smaller immigration during the prewar period.

How can this be explained? The union offensives of 1919–1920, followed by defeat and schism, hardly allowed time or energy to be focused on the question of immigration. For example, the trade union congresses of miners and construction workers ignored the issue of immigration until 1922. More importantly, the state accommodated French labor by limiting immigration at precisely the moments (December 1918 to June 1919 and 1921) when the economy was disrupted and in recession (see chapter VII). Furthermore, from 1922 to 1924, the government channeled immigrants into a few low-status jobs which were concentrated in the reconstruction zone, while French workers were allowed to move freely within the job market. Surely if French workers had not received this favored treatment, opposition to immigrants would have been greater than it had been before the war. While the reformist leadership of the CGT believed that immigration was necessary for French economic growth, the rank-and-file workers could hardly expect to have this view; they would support the government's immigration policy only if aliens were not allowed to compete with French labor—especially in the skilled and urban job markets.

Another explanation for the muted response of French labor to the influx of foreign labor was the immigration policy of the CGT (or reformist) leadership. The CGT had chosen not to fight immigration but instead to participate in its regulation. Since 1917, the CGT had pressed the government for a role in the decision-making process of the French immigration authorities. Yet while the employers in 1920 were served by the Conférence permenente de la main-d'oeuvre étrangère, the trade unions were left out in the cold. The CGT leadership could do little but regularly repeat Jouhaux's demand that immigration be regulated by the public placement offices, in which the CGT would have had a share of power.[71] However, the trade unions played only a small role in these offices outside of the Seine and other large urban areas in the early 1920s (see chapter VII). Rather than abandon their support of regulation, the CGT was eager to enhance their impact on government control of immigration.

A variety of groups and individuals not directly involved in the economic aspect of immigration also began to take an interest in the foreign influx of the early 1920s. Public health officials, the police, parliamentary representatives from urban areas, and various publicists became concerned that the strictly business-oriented policy ignored the social costs of immigration. For example, public health specialists were alarmed by the nearly nonexistent medical screening of immigrants. Police feared that the concentrations of Polish miners which had formed in 1923 in the north, harbored criminals and communists. They advocated their strict control.[72]

Politicians from the Cartel des Gauches (especially Edouard Herriot and his Radical colleague from Lyons, Charles Lambert), stated that the new immigration would require a revision of naturalization laws to encourage the "better" foreign element to settle permanently in France.[73] Educational and other groups demanded that measures be taken to provide immigrant children with French schooling in order to assure their acculturation.[74] Concerns about immigrant assimilation, strikingly similar to those of American opinion, appeared in the press in the mid-1920s. Thus disparate interests sought an immigration policy which would control the social costs (see chapter VIII).

Finally, despite the fact that business groups were the primary beneficiaries of immigration during the reconstruction, they too sought a permanent and improved immigration service. As it became clear that immigration was to be a long-term source of labor, employers realized that they faced a permanent problem of procuring foreign labor in the face of formidable obstacles. These included increasingly demanding nationalistic governments—led by Fascist Italy—who threatened to cut off labor if pay and working conditions of their emigrating citizens were not improved.[75] Continued state negotiation with supplier nations and research into alternative sources proved necessary (see chapter V). French labor and a potential xenophobic opposition to unlimited recruitment of foreign labor created another threat. Thus business groups also sought to establish a national immigration service to serve their complex interests.

Indeed, business interests were the first to propose a plan. In March of 1921, Edouard de Warren, president of CARD and deputy from Meurthe-et-Moselle, sponsored a bill to create an immigration service. The key provision in de Warren's proposal was to make the immigration office a part of the Ministry of Foreign Affairs and have it financially independent of the government: operating revenues were to be generated by user fees and employers' subsidies. These provisions were designed to limit "political" influence on the office and to maximize its financial dependence upon the employer associations who used foreign labor. They were also guaranteed to weaken the influence of the Labor Ministry and the public placement system. Labor organizations were to have unequal representation in the administrative committee overseeing the office's operations. Under the Ministry of Foreign Affairs, de Warren's immigration office would have helped to overcome the diplomatic impediments to the availability of foreign labor and to counteract the interference of foreign governments in the working lives of their citizens in France.[76] This approach, however, was apparently too flagrantly one-sided to ever reach a vote.

In response, the CGT and its Socialist allies proposed their own plan to reform immigration control. They sought the creation of a national labor office under which both the departmental placement offices and the Foreign Labor Service would be subsumed. Their national labor office would be directed by a parity commission. Through the coordination of the national labor office, the departmental placement offices could distribute labor already in France according to changing economic conditions. Only after all available French workers had been offered jobs would the Foreign Labor Service be allowed to bring in immigrants. This arrangement would have restricted the entry of immigrants beyond the needs of local labor markets and given French workers a priority for any job in the country over immigrants.[77] The CGT's wartime allies in the Labor Ministry and the French Association for the Struggle Against Unemployment favored this proposal as the best means of preventing a massive influx of immigrants, which might have led to lower wages and thus weakened the internal consumer market. Yet, even after the victory of the Cartel des Gauches in November of 1924, the CGT-Left proposal also failed to get through Parliament.[78]

The former head of the Foreign Labor Service, and Radical deputy, Bertrand Nogaro, offered a compromise in 1924. His bill represented the concerns of the third group, those interested in social controls over immigration. Nogaro's immigration office was to coordinate all the problems of immigration, including those of hygiene, education, and naturalization. Its objectives were not only to protect French workers and to recruit and distribute needed foreign labor but also to study and act on all the social problems relating to immigration.[79] Yet this bill was also quickly killed, this time by deputies representing agriculture who opposed placing the farm labor service, still run by the Agricultural Ministry, within the immigration office. Industrial interests also opposed the state's control over recruitment and distribution, which Nogaro's bill included. Finally, the CGT feared that a centralized office would simply serve as a recruitment agency for the employers.[80] Divisions within the Cartel prevented either the socialist-labor bill or Nogaro's Radical bill from becoming law.

Conclusion: Immigration and the
Corporatisme Manqué

The failure of a parliamentary solution to the problem of immigration was a major defeat for corporatist politics in the 1920s. Social conflicts, which were articulated in the political system, prevented a corporatist policy. Significantly, clashes over the immigration program were not uncompromising conflicts between the advocates of lassèz-faire and exclusion as had been the case before the war. Rather, all sides clamored for governmental regulation of the foreign labor supply. Difficulties arose over whether governmental action would be primarily directed toward expanding or controlling immigration. Finally, in these critical years of 1921–1924, a powerful coalition of farm and mining interests was forming the SGI. This private immigration service was soon capable of serving disparate needs of employers for eastern European labor without any of the social constraints of a government immigration office, organized on corporatist principles.

This defeat of corporatist politics had an especially profound impact upon the reformist or non-communist wing of French labor. During the war, the leadership of the CGT had abandoned a confrontational stance toward capitalism. An important manifestation of this change was its acceptance of an expanded labor market through immigration. Reformists, such as Léon Jouhaux, were willing to forego the "class struggle" in exchange for a role in regulating capitalism, including the control of the domestic and international labor market. These labor leaders acknowledged that immigration was necessary for victory and after the war, for economic growth. They simply wished to have a part in policy making to protect their members, primarily in the skilled sectors of the work force, from competition with foreigners. This effort failed in the 1920s; it was symptomatic of the impossibility of a political resolution to social conflict in France. Ultimately, the refusal of the French elite to admit the reformist wing of labor into the inner circle of policy makers led to the defeat of the CGT's corporatist policy in the 1930s.

When the French parliament failed to establish a corporatist immigration policy, this did not mean that France lacked a policy. Instead it was ceded to the government ministries, each working within the limits of its own powers and serving different constituencies. For example, the Ministry of Foreign Affairs continued to negotiate immigration treaties with foreign nations to supply new sources of foreign labor to French employers; the Ministry of Agriculture remained, until 1935, a willing servant of French farm interests, providing them with foreign workers through a separate distribution system. Furthermore, the bureaucracies did not leave French labor entirely out of the picture. In fact, the Ministry of Labor restricted immigration into France during recessions in 1921 and 1927, and, through the departmental placement offices, it exercised some control over immigration into the skilled trades in major urban markets. In a sense, then, the corporatism which failed at the parliamentary level was practiced by the bureaucracy.

The functionaries recognized that state regulation of foreign labor was an important tool for promoting both prosperity and social peace. Although the foreign labor system of the 1920s was an ad hoc and poorly coordinated construct, it did serve all the relevant interests. It allowed employers to obtain foreign workers on favorable terms, mollifying in the process potential competition between different economic sectors for scarce labor. The importation of labor became a critical factor in the reconstruction of the northeastern war zones and in the development of French mining and metallurgical industries. Politically articulate sections of French labor, especially skilled urban labor, were also appeased when the government directed foreign labor into unskilled sectors.

Yet the failure to establish a national immigration office clearly affected the shape of immigration in the interwar years. The fragmented and partially ineffective policy which resulted produced an environment where organized business, foreign states, and the free labor market could play decisive roles in determining the foreign labor system. In the next three chapters we will explore the patterns of immigration from different parts of Europe. Each of these migrations will be shaped in differing degrees at the hands of the French state, organized business, foreign states, nationalist organizations, and the labor market. The following analyses of the Polish, Italian, and other European migrations will stress these exogenous factors as keys to an understanding of the new immigration of the interwar years.

IV   Farms, Mines, and Poles

FRANCE in the 1920s entered the modern social and economic world.[1] By numerous indicators she experienced an unprecedented boom: rates of economic growth were similar to what France would realize in the 1950s. Heavy industry, especially iron and steel, nearly doubled output over prewar levels, stimulating the demand for French coal. New technologically advanced industries such as electricity, chemicals, and hydroelectricity grew even faster. Throughout the 1920s France was Europe's leading automobile manufacturer and entered other mass production industries. By the end of the 1920s, France even lost her status as a nation of peasants, becoming an urban nation. Further, despite France's reputation as a nation of small producers, labor was increasingly concentrated in large establishments: the proportion of the workforce in establishments of over fifty employees grew from 42 to 66 percent between 1906 and 1931. France was beginning slowly to adopt the pattern of heavy industrialization that was common in Germany, Britain, and the United States.

Yet, unlike those nations, French economic development was threatened by a shortage of labor. In addition to the losses of men during the war (which will be discussed presently), the net rate of natural increase in population in France was a low two per 1,000 per year. This created very low rates of unemployment (from a high of 2.7 percent during the recession of 1921 to 1.2 percent during the boom year of 1926). This could have produced serious bottlenecks in production and caused wage increases, which could have been inflationary and impeded investment.

Furthermore, French economic growth was uneven. Heavy and new scientific-based industries blossomed but textiles, construction, and most important, agriculture, lagged behind. French coal output was never sufficient for her industrial needs. Besides, a substantial small-scale sector survived in the fashion garment, leather, and building industries. This sector required a skilled, artisan workforce at low wages. This phenomenon of uneven development exacerbated the manpower problem.

Not only were employers obliged to compete for labor, but they required a highly diverse workforce which prevented a smooth flow between labor markets. Furthermore, many industries—especially coal and agriculture—could not easily compete for labor nor find sufficient supplies of native workers willing to remain at these jobs when other positions, especially in the service sector, were available.

While capital shifted to mass production industries and to heavy industry, the primary sector of farming and mining remained important. Although portions of the primary sector rationalized and even mechanized production (for example, the coal and sugar beet industries), most primary industries still required a workforce similar to that of the nineteenth century. Farmers and mine operators found that the labor standards and working conditions which they offered could not compete with the newer industrial and service sectors. Farmers and mine operators tried to recreate the traditional workforce which they had lost—one which would accept labor standards and working conditions that no longer were the norm, and which would reproduce itself for the future labor needs of the farms and mines. Some French employers sought to fill this tall order by importing foreign workers.

Only an immigration which was organized by employers could fit these labor needs of primary industries. As we have already seen, the General Immigration Society successfully gained control over a valuable new source of labor in Poland and elsewhere in eastern Europe. This labor pool proved to be particularly useful for the primary sector because it came from a relatively backward region of Europe and had no experience with liberal patterns of migration, as had the Italians before 1914. Thus the Poles were not yet infected with modern labor expectations. An investigation of the Polish migration into the farms and mines of France will reveal a nearly pure effort of employers to create a workforce to fit their needs. The success and failures of this effort may indicate some of the possibilities of modern capitalist hegemony over labor.

French Agriculture and the Foreign Farm Worker

Although foreign farm workers were hardly unknown before the war, in the 1920s they became an integral part of French agriculture. While in 1931, foreigners constituted only 125,000 of the two million farmworkers in France,[2] during the 1920s some 830,484 immigrants had filtered into and often out of agricultural employment.[3] French farming had a need for a small but constantly replenished supply of foreign workers.[4]

Representatives of agriculture usually attributed immigration to the demographic gap left by the war and the rural exodus caused by the attractions of the easy life of the city.[5] The war deeply drained the pools of indigenous rural labor. Not only were 673,500 peasants killed and about 350,000 incapacitated but agriculture suffered more than industry, whose labor was often spared combat duty.[6] To make matters worse, veterans often could not be kept down on the farm after they had seen Paris. They abandoned farms both to fill the shoes of those who had not returned from the war as well as to enter expanding factories.[7]

Despite the rural exodus, farm labor standards did not improve enough to attract workers. Wages continued to lag behind those offered by industry and even got worse.[8] Farm labor continued to suffer from underemployment,[9] while agricultural workers gained nothing from the law which reduced the workday in industry to eight hours in 1919.[10] Living conditions for farm wage-earners remained inferior: even a mild proposal to prohibit lodging farm workers in barns on straw beds was repeatedly stalled in the 1920s by rural deputies.[11] Low farm labor standards might be explained by the decline of commodity prices and low productivity as well as weak labor unions. Yet, for whatever reasons, agriculture clearly succeeded in preserving the traditional standards, despite their uncompetiveness with industry. In many cases the cost of this success was a shortage of French labor and the need to recruit foreign workers.

The Widening Sphere of Immigration

Farmers sought the labor of Spaniards, Italians, Belgians, and increasingly, Poles, in the 1920s. An annual average of 69,207 immigrants officially entered France under farm work contracts between 1919 and 1930. Table 6 shows[12] a substantial annual variation in the demand for foreign labor, which reflects cyclic patterns (for example, the 1921 and 1927 recessions). It also indicates that most of these immigrants came from the bordering nations of Belgium, Spain, and Italy. Census data also reveal that almost half worked on farms near the frontiers.[13] This suggests that farmers continued, as they had before the war, to hire immigrants across short distances and without significant organization. Yet Table 6 also indicates a new pattern of immigration from eastern Europe, mostly of Poles. Although still representing a minority of immigrants, this trend indicated that employers increasingly had to seek labor beyond the traditional sources nearby and to organize collectively to recruit that labor.

Foreign farm workers were channeled into two broad but distinct labor markets: (1) seasonal migratory farm workers often hired en masse by large semi-industrial agribusinesses and (2) farm hands usually employed singly or in small groups by peasant farmers. Sixty-one percent of the immigrant farm workers were hired for seasonal jobs between 1928–1930 (years when data is available).[14]

The use of large numbers of immigrants for seasonal farm labor began in the 1890s. From that time traditional French sources of seasonal labor from Brittany, the Pyrénées, and the Ariège began to dry up. As a result of the labor shortage, the black cloud of higher wages loomed over the wheat-producing areas of the Brie-Beauce, the vineyards of the Hérault and the Var, and the sugar beet regions of the North.[15] Workers attempted to organize unions in the southern vineyards in the 1900s and in the wheat fields of the Brie in 1920. But French agriculture easily found Spaniards, Belgians, and Italians to

Table 6   Controlled Agricultural Immigration, by Nationality, 1919–1930

Year	Italian	Iberian	Belgian	Polish	Czecho-slovak	Other	Total
1919	1,720	55,084	5,313				62,117
1920	10,564	41,442	15,213	3,693			70,912
1921	4,682	28,162	20,737	2,241			55,822
1922	7,704	41,851	14,344	9,077			72,976
1923	10,542	27,386	10,122	25,797	3,224		77,071
1924	15,274	32,265	16,477	17,749	5,939	223	87,927
1925	13,263	17,941	21,354	13,080	3,313	2,833	71,784
1926	11,317	7,837	21,945	19,177	1,654	1,240	63,170
1927	5,783	8,728	22,513	6,773	583	1,169	45,549
1928	10,512	12,324	24,100	11,701	1,402	1,642	61,681
1929	11,854	18,450	15,127	16,087	3,529	3,403	68,450
1930	18,502	18,896	13,649	26,586	6,523	8,672	92,828
Total	121,717	310,366	200,894	151,961	26,167	19,182	830,287

Source: *Bulletin du Ministère du travail* (1920–1931).

supplement French migrants and to stem wage increases. In the 1920s, during the August to September season, about 14,000 Spaniards (mostly from Catalonia) harvested grapes throughout southern France.[16] In the North at least 10,000 Belgians (mostly Flemish) travelled in workteams on six-month circuits through northern France. They cut wood in the Ardennes forests in winter, weeded sugar beets in May, worked in vegetable gardens and orchards in summer, and harvested wheat or sugar beets in the fall. A subcontract system was common for most foreign farm labor.[17]

Demand for seasonal foreign labor changed with variations in production. Stagnation in wine production in the mid-1920s along with an unfavorable rate of exchange led to a temporary decline in the number of Spanish vineyard migrants.[18] On the other hand, sugar beet production increased dramatically in the 1920s, requiring more foreign labor.[19] By the mid-twenties, this growth made it necessary to employ Poles to supplement the Belgians. Finally, in 1927, due to a drop in wheat prices and thus wages, Poles and Slovaks were hired in wheat farms near Paris to underbid migrants from Belgium as well as

Brittany.[20] By the early 1920s, French agriculture had become dependent upon foreigners for its needs of seasonal labor: as many as 85,000 to 100,000 immigrated to France to do migratory farm work, while scarcely 35,000 French continued to do this arduous work.[21] These foreign workers made an indispensable contribution to large sugar beet growers and wheat producers in northern France, to the grape growers of the southwest, as well as to a variety of fruit and vegetable producers throughout eastern France.

In the generation before the 1920s, French agriculture had to attract labor from increasingly distant regions. At first, French migrants from the overpopulated fringes of the country sufficed; but soon migrants from across the frontiers were necessary, and by the midtwenties, these groups had to be supplemented with new migratory streams from eastern Europe. Each shift of labor involved greater cost and higher levels of organization, culminating in the relatively rationalized recruitment of the General Immigration Society, who provided the eastern Europeans. With the rise of the labor standards of the French and then of the Belgian, Spanish, and Italian workers, the growers had to draw on labor ever further from the modernized regions of western Europe.

A similar pattern characterized a second type of agricultural labor, the farm hand. Hired usually on an annual basis, he or she worked closely with the peasant family in general field work, did domestic service as well as specialized tasks such as milking and shepherding. Like the employers of seasonal labor, French farmers, especially in the region northeast of Paris, had to rely increasingly upon immigrants. In fact, compared to seasonal workers, shortages of farm hands were even greater and finding replacements even more difficult.

Typical working conditions on the farm may explain the problem: peasants often hired male farm hands (servants de ferme) on annual contracts. They were expected to work ten hours a day in the winter and twelve in the summer. They were often the only employee of the farmer. Farmers sometimes lodged them in the hay loft. Not only did the farm hand work long hard hours, but he lacked the rudiments of privacy, leisure, and social contact.[22] Female farm hands (bonnes de ferme), if anything, had it worse: they often worked six and a half days a week for up to fifteen hours a day in broken shifts; they tended the chickens, pigs, and cows and did general domestic and farmyard work. Milk maids, who worked similar hours, also had to be skilled and strong. Specialists in herding sheep and cattle also had an arduous life; few workers were willing to accept the long lonely hours of work.[23]

Traditionally these jobs were filled by unmarried French youth, who usually had families and friends in the vicinity. Perhaps they also expected to inherit property in the area. These factors often balanced the unattractive aspects of farm work. Yet local French labor became increasingly scarce as the poor rural population reduced the size of their families and young workers fled to the factory.[24]

Naturally farmers sought replacements in seasonal immigrant workers, especially from Flemish Belgium and Spain. Yet, despite the long hours of work and difficulties of constant migration, the seasonal laborers seldom preferred employment as farm hands. After all, as immigrants they had greater freedom, higher wages, and often months of leisure during the winter.[25] Families of seasonal workers sometimes had small plots at home in Spain or Italy and sent family members to France only on a temporary basis to earn savings necessary for accumulating more property.[26] These people were hardly candidates for the deadend job of farm hand. Unlike the local French, they had no social or economic ties to rural France. As a result, farmers sought new sources of labor; increasingly in the 1920s they found them in eastern Europe.

Polish Peasants on French Farms

Since 1920 French farm associations from the northeast had banded together in CARD to recruit workers from eastern Europe; after 1924 these efforts were further rationalized under the aegis of the General Immigration Society or SGI (see p. 58). Through these agencies, farmers received not only a new source of labor, but workers who generally suited their specific requirements for docile, skilled, and inexpensive manpower. Most of these workers were Polish (87 percent in 1926 with Yugoslavs and Czechoslovaks making up the balance).[27] Given the impetus of CARD, it is not surprising that 69 percent of these Poles were concentrated in the fourteen departments of the northeast by 1931. They became significant competitors to the traditional source of foreign farm labor, the Flemish Belgians. By 1931, Poles comprised 45 per cent of the foreign farm workers in the four departments which bordered Belgium, while the Belgians remained only 47 percent; in the Seine region, they outnumbered the Belgians (44 percent to 30 percent).[28] During the 1920s sugar beet growers and wheat producers in the northeast increasingly supplemented their use of Flemish seasonal labor with Poles. Yet most (77 percent in 1926) of those imported by the SGI were hired as farm hands on small farms.[29] Poles seem to have taken the permanent farm jobs which were abandoned or passed over by the Belgians, who usually preferred seasonal farm employment.

Despite the obvious complexities of recruiting Polish workers, their use did have some advantages over hiring other immigrants or the French: Poles were more likely to be stable employees, fulfilling their annual work contracts and even remaining for several years. Because of the relatively greater distance from their homelands, they were less likely to make visits to their native villages, something which was common among the immigrants from the bordering countries. Lack of knowledge of job opportunities in France probably also made them more stable than others. Furthermore, French farmers generally appreciated them, if not for their speed at work (something more important in seasonal farmwork) then, at least, for their docility and capacity for heavy labor. The French were especially impressed with Polish female workers, whom they considered to be "more docile, stronger and more energetic" than their French counterparts. The French also found skilled Polish farm hands, especially for milking and cattle tending.[30]

The greatest advantage of Polish farm workers, however, was their low wages. While the immigration treaties guaranteed that foreign workers were to receive the prevailing local wages, they frequently were paid much less than French workers of similar skills or even foreign workers who were hired on the spot. Louis Powzma, a Polish priest from Amiens, claimed that the immigrant farmhand was paid only 300 francs per month while the starting rate offered at the departmental farm labor office was 350; the immigrant specialist earned only 350, while the local rate was 550 to 600. Furthermore, Polish immigrants were obliged to sign blank work contracts, which omitted both wage rates and job descriptions. As Powzma declared, the Poles "have only the meaningless freedom to accept the contract such as it is or rather such as it is imposed on them or to accept unemployment and misery for themselves and their families." Ultimately, work contracts were determined not by the state of the labor market in France, but rather by conditions in Poland.[31]

Naturally the result of the influx of Polish workers was a stagnation of local wages and a displacement of French farm workers. In 1927, for example, local farm workers, who had been trying to organize unions in the cereal-producing areas of Beauce and Brie, complained that immigrants undercut the wage standards of seasonal workers from Brittany and local farmhands.[32]

French farmers found Polish workers to be very advantageous employees: they were relatively docile, often skilled and hard working, and cheap. Nevertheless, there were some drawbacks. Language barriers were troublesome, since most of the Poles could only be directed in German or by gestures.[33] Farmers also had to hire immigrants sight unseen, a considerable problem when farmers had little choice but to accept whoever the SGI recruited. Yet even this difficulty was partially solved when many farmers began to hire close relatives of farm hands whose work was already known.[34]

The main problem, however, from the farmers' viewpoint, was the tendency of the Poles to do what French and Flemish farmworkers had done before them—to break their contracts and head for the factory. M. Augé-Laribé, one of the best informed advocates of French agriculture during this period, aptly described the situation of all farm laborers when he wrote: "the rural exodus in France is similar to the strike, except that it is permanent and individual . . . ; more exactly it replaces the strike."[35] French farmers hired the Poles not only to replace the departed French but in hopes that the Poles might be more stable. French employers in the Brie region preferred the Poles because their ignorance of the French labor market made them less likely than the French to abandon their low paying farm jobs.[36] Yet the Poles quickly learned to follow their French predecessors down the road to the city. M. Pairault, an official of the SGI, claimed that only 30 to 40 percent of the Polish farm workers remained on the job after completing their contracts.[37] The Polish ambassador in 1927 noted that only 29,500 Poles remained in farm work from the 68,357 who had been recruited by the SGI between 1920 and 1926.[38] Many also broke their contracts, a fact which obsessed French officials.

The social as well as economic disadvantages of farm life explain this disloyalty to the land. A report from the farm labor service (Ministry of Agriculture) claimed that 25 percent of the Poles broke their contracts over pay disputes, another 18 percent, over excessive hours of work, while 11 percent left their employers because of complaints of inadequate housing; only 30 percent were said to have broken their contracts simply out of "caprice." In addition to these job-related motives, René Martial, a public health official and first hand witness of Polish immigration, declared that the simple loneliness of Polish workers, isolated on farms with little contact with Polish-speaking people, contributed sizably to contract-breaking.[39]

Poles also had alternatives to farm work, especially those placed in the departments near mining and industrial areas where many Poles worked. An analysis of sixty-two police reports of contract breakers in the Pas-de-Calais (1929) reveals the pull of the mines. Half of these cases were women. Police reported that 40 percent of these contract breakers left to seek an industrial or mining job; 23 percent fled the farm to seek husbands in the mining district; 14 percent left to join their families elsewhere in France, while 23 percent found wage and working conditions to be unbearable; only 2 percent of these contract breakers were said to be incapable of doing the work.[40]

Naturally, landowners, officials of the SGI, and the government attempted to stem this exodus of foreign labor. In some cases, farmers could mitigate the social isolation of their Polish workers by importing relatives. By 1931, 54 percent of the Polish farm workers were hired by name on the request of relatives in France.[41]

Yet, despite these efforts of employers and the cooperation of the state to stem the tide of instability (see p. 55), small scale farmers had little that they could do. Rather, they tended to rely on the good offices of the Polish elite to stabilize their compatriots who worked in France. Realizing that many of these Poles would eventually return to their homeland, the conservative Polish government was concerned that they be sheltered from pernicious radical ideas or excessive economic expectations. Toward these ends, Polish consuls mediated disputes between Polish farm workers and French farmers. Probably more important was the influence of the Polish clergy. Farm labor recruiters favored Polish missions, for religion, especially in "the first several years" of an immigrant's stay in France, provided a moral ballast to counterbalance the threat of cultural shock and Bolshevism.[42] Polish Catholic missions followed the Polish farm workers to several departments (Aisne and Somme, especially). These missionaries, organized under the revealing name of Protection polonaise (or Opieka Polska), not only provided traditional religious services to the farm workers but also mediated labor grievances and helped Poles find farm jobs.[43]

While it is impossible to determine the exact impact of these efforts of the Polish elite, they were probably not very effective. The Polish farm workers were simply too widely dispersed across the countryside for a few priests to have much influence. Without substantial material incentives to remain on the land, their spiritual influence would have had limited value. The French also recognized this problem. *Le Temps* and *Moniteur des intérêts materiels* advocated in addition that immigrants be encouraged to acquire small plots of land in order to root them in French soil.[44] Of course this was unrealistic given the immigrants' lack of capital or possibility of inheriting French land. While some Belgians gained rural property, few Poles were able to do so.[45] Sharecropping in southwest France became a well-publicized alternative to land ownership for immigrants (see chapter VIII), but it hardly touched the Polish farm worker.

In the Polish immigrant French farmers gained a relatively docile, skilled, and cheap worker. They were able, to a degree, to recreate their traditional workforce without making accomodations to the expectations of the modern French laborer. Yet, despite the hegemony which agriculturalists exercised over the Poles, they lacked an ability to prevent the Poles from following the French and Belgian to the city. The French mine operators were somewhat more successful.

French Coal and Polish Miners

Perhaps the best example of employers' collectively organizing an immigrant workforce was the SGI's recruitment of Poles for the coal mines of the Nord and Pas-de-Calais in northeastern France. Because of their extraordinary need for manpower after the war, the coal operators recruited exceptionally large numbers of

Poles. The mines sought not only labor to replace French miners who did not return from the war but also the creation of a stable workforce, isolated from the radical movements of the French miners. Toward these ends, the French developed a policy of social control which was designed not only to reduce turnover but also to maintain traditional Polish culture. This policy drew on long-established tradition—the use of company housing and subsidized cultural programs, for example. Yet, because it was tailored to isolate the Poles and thus encouraged Polish nationalism, the results often conflicted with French interests. Nevertheless, the coal companies were successful in utilizing the Polish immigration to create a new stable pool of labor to replace the French and to exacerbate divisions within the mining community, thus enhancing the hegemony of the mine operators over the workforce.

In the generally tight labor market of 1919 the coal mines were particularly desperate. Not only was labor scarce because of war losses, but the prewar labor pool from which miners were drawn had been scattered during the mobilization and the German occupation.[46] As late as January 1923, only 64 percent of the prewar workforce had returned to the department of the Pas-de-Calais, where coal mining was the dominant industry.[47] Former French miners tended to flow into relatively high-paying jobs in the reconstruction of railroads and buildings in the war zones.[48] Thus, when the mines lost their complements of prisoners of war and militarized French workers six months after the armistice, insufficient numbers of Frenchmen were willing to take their places. Workers employed in the mines actually dropped from 207,000 at the end of 1918 to 163,000 in July of 1919.[49] The coming of the eight hour day to the coal mines in June of 1919 exacerbated the labor shortage. It required the expansion of the workforce in surface jobs up to 37 percent precisely at a time of acute scarcity of labor.[50] This shortage of miners plus strikes drastically reduced output. In 1920 French mines produced only 25.3 million tons of coal (44 percent of France's needs). By contrast, in 1913, the mines had an output of 40.8 milion tons (61 percent of French coal consumption). In the northern mines tonnage of coal produced per miner dropped from 700 tons in 1913 to 475 in 1920.[51] This declining productivity threatened the profits of the coal operators. Cost per ton rose from 20.3 francs in 1918 to 27.2 in 1919. Labor shortages also

frustrated French efforts to exploit their new resources in the iron and
steel mills of Lorraine, which the French had just won back from the
Germans. Throughout 1920, the French steel industry complained of
coal shortages and called for increased production of up to 40 per
cent.[52]

In the short run, increased production required more labor. But the
solution was not simply to hire unskilled workers off the street.
Underground mining, in particular, demanded dexterity and
strength which the general worker often lacked. More important,
mine operators had traditionally relied on a self-perpetuating and
largely isolated pool of mining families to replenish the ranks of coal
miners. As Philippe Ariès observes, the mine company towns had
created an isolated work culture in the generation before the war.
Operators encouraged miners to produce large families and to
preserve community loyalties by establishing an elaborate system of
subsidized housing and social welfare. This system, however, could
not be restored after the war. This is shown by the fact that the birth
rate of mining towns decreased and members of mining families
abandoned their parents' occupation for jobs in Paris and other
growing industrial regions.[53] Thus the mine owners sought not only a
new supply of seasoned miners, but also a substitute for its traditional
pool of mining families.

Polish Miners Fill Manpower Needs

The coal industry found this replacement in Poland. Even
before the war, Polish miners had an international reputation for their
skill and docility. German mines in Westphalia successfully recruited
Poles in the 1890s and many a Polish family emigrated to the United
States to work the mines.[54] The French also had attempted to recruit
Poles before the war without, however, much success. When, in 1919,
Poland became a state, many of the impediments to French recruitment were eliminated. As described in Chapter 3, from mid-1919
until 1922, the French government used its friendly relations with the
new Polish state to organize an emigration of Poles into the mining
regions of the French North. In 1922, the French Coal committee took
over their recruitment and in 1924, helped form the General

Table 7   Collective Immigration into the French Coal Industry, 1919–1929

Year	No. of miners	Total, including families	Family members as % of total
1919 –1920	9,269	13,231	30
1921	6,107	8,392	27
1922	19,763	37,037	47
1923	29,104	58,462	45
1924	21,870	45,052	51
1925	10,788	20,850	48
1926	15,611	22,183	30
1927	231		
1928	1,148		
1929	22,127		
Total	136,018		

Sources: C. Kaczmarek, *L'émigration polonaise en France après la guerre* (Paris: Berger, 1928), p. 131, and Robert Lafitte-Laplace, *L'économie charbonniere de la France* (Paris: 1933), pp. 197–198.

Immigration Society which hired almost all of the Polish miners. Between 1919 and 1929, the French imported 135,206 miners, some 100,380 of whom were Polish (see Table 7).[55] The French wasted no time recruiting over 100,000 miners within five years. The recessions of 1921 and 1927–1928 slowed the process but immigration was clearly critical to the manpower plans of the mines. Unlike the immigrant farm workers, these Polish miners brought their families and were thus expected to become a permanent part of the mine workforce.

Largely as a result of immigration, by December 1924 the workforce had been restored to prewar levels, allowing the mines of the North to extract 91 percent of the coal mined in 1913.[56] But the coal industry had much more ambitious goals than this: in 1923 M. Georges, the *Ingénieur en chef au corps des mines,* proposed to increase total French production up to fifty million tons. He calculated that the mines needed a total of 100,000 foreign miners to reach this goal.[57] As a result of continued massive immigration, by 1926 coal output surpassed Georges' target (52.5 million tons of coal).[58] In 1927 immigrants constituted over one-third of the total workforce of 320,000 in the coal mines. In contrast, in 1913, only 11 per cent of the 221,000 coal miners were foreign. In fact, between 1913 and 1927, 86 percent of the growth of the coal mining workforce was due to immigration.[59] It is difficult to imagine how the mine operators would have so rapidly expanded their manpower and thus production without the aid of the Poles.

While immigration helped raise production, further economic progress could not be made simply by adding more immigrant miners. The key to profitable mining was to increase labor productivity. During the war there had been a drop in productivity just as there had been a decline in the labor supply. According to an industry report, veterans returning from the war had been "uprooted from their natural milieu" and were "a little less productive than their normal rate."[60] Miners produced an average of 740 tons each in 1919, compared with 945 tons in 1913.[61] Key to this decline of productivity was the trend toward French miners abandoning the basic production task of underground mining for cleaner surface jobs. Jean Condevaux, a French mining engineer, wrote in 1928 that the French miner returned from the war wishing to "imitate the bourgeois, personified in his eyes by the auxiliary employee and in particular the clerk." The influx of foreign labor tended only to accelerate this trend: "Employing the foreign miner has caused a decline in the prestige of the indigenous miner, who thinks that the foreigner is an inferior."[62] This attitude hardly encouraged the native miner to remain or to send his son to the mine.

One solution to the problem of productivity was to channel the immigrant into the underground work. By 1932, 86 percent of the foreign mine workers were employed as underground miners, compared with only 54 percent of the French.[63] Not only did immigrants fill the manpower needs of the mines, but they probably were more adaptable than the French to efforts to increase productivity. Some Poles had already worked in the more modernized mines of Westphalia and were thus less opposed to the rationalization of the work process than the French. Others, direct from the farm, had no experience in traditional work methods and were therefore more willing than the French to accept attempts to increase their productivity. The mines also readily exploited their susceptibility to tighter controls and more productive methods. In 1924 Georges linked "the increase of productivity and the intensive utilization of foreign personnel."[64]

Finally, immigrants aided efforts to increase productivity simply because they could be more easily laid off, while standards of production were maintained. After eight years of massive immigration a period of contraction began in 1927. This decline paralleled the beginning of a long upward swing in mine productivity. Until 1927 productivity in the northern coal region continued to lag behind the levels of 1913; it was only 78 percent of the 1913 rate in the Nord and 84 percent in the Pas-de-Calais. By the second half of 1928, however, productivity rose to 101 percent of the 1913 rate in the Nord and to 93 percent in the Pas-de-Calais.[65] The engineer of the Arras mining district attributed this improved productivity to layoffs, especially of immigrants.[66]

As an additional bonus to the mines, immigrants hired by the SGI were much cheaper than the French. In 1928 skilled Polish coal miners earned between 23 and 26 francs a day compared with the average of 40 francs earned by the French. This discrepancy resulted from the fact that Poles entered the mines under contract at the lowest pay level within each job classification without regard to their skill or experience.[67] Thus immigrants, especially of Polish origin, became an important tool in the reconstruction and rationalization of the coal industry in the 1920s.

This huge influx of foreign workers gave mine owners a bargaining advantage over the miners; immigration probably weakened the ability of miners to successfully press for higher wages or impose other demands. The Polish miners gave the operators a much more flexible labor supply than they had with a mostly French workforce. Because of their lack of French citizenship, and thus their lack of rights to remain in France without government-sanctioned employment, the Poles could easily be dispensed with. This became very important during the economic downturns of 1927 and much of the 1930s.

Managing the Polish Mining Community

Although the mines dominated their foreign workforce, the employers found the Poles unsatisfactory in two ways: their high turnover rates and their social or cultural independence. Like all immigrants, the Poles tended to job hop. Having no incentive from ties of family or sentiment to remain in one spot or job, as was the case with indigenous workers, immigrants were notorious for breaking their labor contracts in order to seek new jobs or a change in scenery. Because signing a work contract with a coal mine was an easy and costless way of entering France, some Poles gained access to France in this way only to immediately quit the mine in favor of a better job elsewhere. And jobs were plentiful, especially in the labor-starved building industry during the period of reconstruction (1920–1924) and during the boom years of 1928 and 1929. The chief engineer at the mines of Ostricourt, for example, complained in 1929 that 10 percent of its newly hired Poles had been pirated by other companies before even reporting for work.[68]

The mines obtained the support of the state to reduce turnover. In November 1921 the minister of the Liberated Regions threatened to withhold government contracts from any company which hired immigrants who had been recruited by another company. Throughout the 1920s prefects and a local police helped employers find absconding immigrant miners and forced them to return to work.[69] Despite these efforts, few of the contract breakers were ever found for they easily disappeared in immigrant neighborhoods. Also, because there was no special police force assigned to control the immigrants, the state was an ineffective tool for coercing the immigrant into remaining on the job.[70] Employers had to find other ways of making the immigrant workforce more stable.

Mine operators and French police feared that the immigrants would be independent of French employer control and thus would engender social problems. The rapid influx of a population, foreign in language and culture, into the confines of the mining regions of the Pas-de-Calais and Nord seemed to threaten social stability. Police reports in 1922 complained that they had few trustworthy translators and lacked confidence that security officers had sufficient knowledge of the movements and mentality of the Polish miners.[71] Police believed that the Polish mining community harbored criminals and illegal aliens. One report expressed anxiety that young Polish miners, unlike farm workers with their "many tasks" to prevent "boredom," lacked sufficient "distractions" to keep them out of trouble when their "short" workday was completed. This report advised that employers especially seek to control the leisure of unmarried immigrants, suggesting that they form sports teams for these youth "in the most dangerous period of life with respect to the inclination toward crime."[72]

French authorities also feared the influence of the communists and their union, the CGTU. They were shocked when communists led a strike on February 22, 1923, in which immigrants predominated (comprising two-thirds of the 14,000 participants in the Pas-de-Calais).[73] According to the prefect of the Nord, writing shortly after this strike, the Poles were "still uprooted, poorly adapted to our traditions" and thus "prey to pernicious influences."[74] From the standpoint of the French authorities, immigrant communities not only harbored criminals and germinated criminality, but were susceptible to wholesale subversion.

Coal mine operators naturally hoped to counteract foreign labor turnover and to eliminate "pernicious influences" in the immigrant community. They sought also to duplicate in the Polish mining population the characteristics which they had cultivated in the French mining families before World War One—an isolated, docile, stable, and prolific population, able to assure the mines a steady source of mine labor for the future.

To meet these challenges, the operators and French authorities had some well-established tools, modified somewhat to fit the peculiarities of the Polish community. These included: (1) company housing; (2) family immigration; (3) ethnically segregated residences; (4) company-subsidized cultural and religious activities, and (5) toleration and often support of Polish nationalist activity.

Long before World War One mine owners endeavored to create a stable and fertile population of mining families through building and subsidizing housing grouped near the pits. As Rolande Trempé has pointed out, company housing provided an alternative to the peasant villages from which many miners were drawn. Company towns eliminated the lure of the traditional peasant life to which many miners held tenaciously. Company housing became a major means of social control. The housing was often large enough for sizable families and usually included land for family gardens. It was designed to provide a surrogate for the farm, lower labor costs, and most importantly, to reduce turnover. Companies limited the number of taverns, provided meeting halls for cultural activities, and built churches. Thus mine owners hoped to minimize crime and drunkenness, while also encouraging a stable family and work-oriented life among the miners.[75]

What was a well-established policy before the war, and before the influx of Polish immigrants, was greatly expanded. While in 1913, 47 percent of the miners in the north were already lodged in company towns, by the end of 1924, 73 percent lived in mine-owned housing.[76] Although there are no aggregate data indicating the number of Poles lodged in company towns, it was probably a much greater proportion than that of the French. Unlike many of the French, who traveled by train to the mines from peasant villages, Poles were forced to accept company housing for lack of an alternative.

Furthermore, most mine companies confined the Poles to newly-built housing compounds which were separate if not distant from French-dominated quarters. The prefect of the Nord claimed in 1923 that the Mines of Anzin grouped the Poles into separate "colonies" to make sure that they "as families do not speak French. . . . They are accustomed to live among us as if they were in Poland. . . . and only communicate to the French whenever it cannot be avoided."[77] This isolation was further assured because the Poles were highly concentrated in the mining department of the Pas-de-Calais (25 percent of all Poles in France by 1933). Nearly 82 percent of this number lived in the mining district of Béthune. Some eight communes each contained over 5,000 Poles.[78] In sharp contrast to the Polish farm workers, Polish miners lived in tight familiar communities; mine operators encouraged this pattern as a means of fostering a stable workforce.

As another way of promoting stability, mine operators and the government generally encouraged Polish miners to bring their families. Often with six or more children, most or all unable to work, a miner could hardly afford to tour France looking for a higher paid or less boring job. In addition, the coal operators expected married foreign miners to produce more than coal: they would also procreate future coal miners. As we have noted, the mine owners had long been concerned with the formation of a steady supply of young miners brought up in the mining milieu and kept as isolated as possible from alternative employment.

As part of this family policy, the French government, in December of 1921, eliminated all restrictions on the entry of close relatives of miners, and automatically granted miners' wives and children authorizations to work. As a further means to encourage family immigration, a French-Polish Convention of March 1982 required that employers pay 60 percent of the costs of transporting the families of their Polish employees to France.[79] The success of the family policy is evident from the fact that only 27 percent of adult male immigrants in the Pas-de-Calais were unmarried in 1931, compared with 42 percent in the foreign population in France. Furthermore, 41 percent of the immigrant population in the Pas-de-Calais in 1931 were children (under 20 years old), while only 27 percent were so in all of France.[80] Polish-dominated communes also had relatively high birth rates.[81]

Along with a mine-controlled residential milieu and the encouragement of family life, mine owners employed other techniques of social control. They subsidized and even helped to establish cultural and social organizations for the Polish community. French authorities favored distinctly Polish groups, to make the Poles "calm and docile" as one subprefect put it.[82] Separate organizations were to help young Polish miners remain rooted in their own culture and thus prevent the formation of a criminal society or other manifestations of anomie. These organizations were also to impede assimilation into the French mining culture, particularly radical miner unionism and communism. In fact, the prefect of the Nord, Alfred Morain, advocated that mine owners establish "various activities" for the Poles in order to forestall the growing influence of the CGTU. These activities were to include "musical and sports groups to be organized in the spirit of emulation with local French groups." Morain hoped that the French authorities would control the leadership of these organizations, thus leading the Poles gradually into conservative French groups which paralleled the Polish ones. This task, however, involved certain problems. As Morain noted, the mines must act so that the Polish organizations "not appear in the public eye as emanations of the employers"[83]— which, of course, would discredit them.

The mine owners and the French government clearly had to rely on Polish leadership. Generally, this was readily available in the Polish government (principally the consuls), the Polish Catholic hierarchy, and various nationalist organizations. Like the French authorities, these Polish interests had no intention of seeing often temporary emigrants attend schools of communism in France, nor lose their religious and moral beliefs in the brutal atmosphere of a foreign mining town. Furthermore, because the French authorities had the inexpensive recourse to expelling "undesirables," the ultimate responsibility for socializing the Polish immigrants was placed upon the Poles themselves who would, of course, have to control most of these "deviants" upon repatriation. Finally, Polish authorities shared an ideological goal of preserving and thus isolating the Polish community abroad.

The Stabilizing Influence of Polish Nationalism

The French and Polish elite were natural allies in a drive to stabilize and isolate the immigrants in the mining regions. For example, Alfred Morain joined with the Polish consul in Lille to create "all kinds of projects" in the mining districts to keep the Poles from communism.[84] Labor and interior ministers of Poland and France met in November of 1924 for the same purpose.[85] A French parliamentary report claimed that the General Immigration Society received from the Polish government twelve francs per Polish immigrant "for projects to encourage the Poles to remember their fatherland and their national culture."[86] There is also some evidence that the French police employed nationalist Polish journalists as anticommunist spies and agitators.[87]

The work of the French and Polish elites would have borne no fruit without the help of Poles living in the mining community. This assistance came from the Polish church, including lay and clerical elements, as well as from nationalist groups which migrated to France primarily from the Westphalian mines of Germany. Although most Poles were Catholic like the French, the Polish church had distinct national ritualistic qualities which sharply distinguished it from French Catholicism. Polish religion was infused with national costume, traditional songs, and numerous festivals and pilgrimages. It was imported *in toto* to the French mining towns and was subsidized by the mining companies. At least sixteen Polish priests worked in the mining fields of the North in 1927 in complete independence of the French hierarchy. One informed Polish observer claimed that Polish religion was the linchpin of Polish stability; if any aspect of it were missing its absence would "unloose all their inhibitions." Catholic influence also spread throughout the Polish community through church involvement in Boy Scouts, sports, music, and other Polish associations.[88]

The conservative goals of the elite were also fostered by a nationalist core of Polish miners from Westphalia. These miners brought stable families, mine experience, and social conservatism nurtured during a generation defending their Polish identity in Germany. In sharp contrast to the largely unmarried, young, and inexperienced miners imported directly from Poland,[89] the Westphalian Poles formed a stable core of closely knit coal-mining families. Since the 1890s Polish miners in Germany had developed an autonomous ethnic culture bound together with an all-encompassing religious nationalism. "Having had practice at emigration and having adopted the habit of grouping themselves to defend their common interests," one witness wrote, they "resist the influence of their environment." Indeed, they came to France to avoid German citizenship and to preserve their Polish nationality.[90] Although in the interwar years the Westphalian Poles comprised only 19,700 of the 139,000 Poles who entered French coal mines,[91] they were a core of seasoned miners who dominated the emigrant community.[92]

This cultural influence was assured by a communications network which the Westphalian Poles brought with them from Germany. In fact, the most important nationalist organization of the Westphalian Poles, the Polish Workers Association (Societé des ouvriers polonais or Zwiazek Rabotników Polskich—ZRP) persuaded Polish miners to abandon Germany for France in the early 1920s.[93] In 1923, the ZRP, along with two important nationalist newspapers, *Wiarus Polski* and *Narodowiec,* moved from Westphalia to the mining regions of the French North. Few newspapers or organizations, however, originated in Poland, where the vast majority of the miners actually originated.[94] So important were the Westphalian Poles to the employers for creating a stable conservative community of immigrant miners that they were the last to be laid off and repatriated during the depression years of 1933 to 1936.[95]

Some measure of the influence of Polish cultural nationalism may be found in the following statistics. In the key mining district of

Béthune in 1924 there were already eighteen musical, eleven religious, ten sports, six mutual-aid, and eight theatrical societies.[96] In Douai, about 700 Poles belonged to fifteen gymnastic clubs, 670 to eleven devotional groups, and 6,000 to eight choral societies. A congress of Polish associations claimed that 25,000 Poles or about 20 percent of the Polish population had joined 402 Polish organizations in France in 1924.[97] Whatever the impact of these associations on the lives of the miners, they did provide an important alternative to assimilation into the culture of the French miner.

This point can be put into focus when we consider the functions of the largest Polish organization, the Polish Workers Association (ZRP). Officially, it was a federation of mutual aid societies, providing emergency assistance and death benefits to its members. Its central office also furnished legal advice regarding immigration regulations and even job-related grievances. The ZRP also supported Polish cultural and educational events. Beginning with a claimed membership in 1924 of 4,200, by 1930 it reached about 25,000, mostly in the northern coal mining region.[98]

Despite its non-political goals the Polish Workers Association was a source of anti-communist and even anti-union propaganda. Although legally it was only a mutual-aid society, police considered it a "disguised union" which attempted "to prevent Poles from joining the old miners' union."[99] Because of its nationalist and conservative politics, the Polish government openly supported it, giving free passports to its members and sending representatives of the Polish Labor and Education Ministries to its conventions.[100]

In June 1924, two months after its arrival in France, the CGT miners' union complained to the French Ministry of Labor that the ZRP was operating illegally as a trade union. The CGT claimed that the Polish consuls intervened in union activities, through their partiality toward the ZRP. The French union also objected to "Polish exclusiveness, which threatens to incite an incident similar to the anti-Belgian riots in the mines in the late 1890s." The CGT was particularly incensed with the sharp attacks on the CGT in the newspaper, *Wiarus Polski*, which was closely linked to the ZRP.[101] In January 1926, the CGT weekly, *La Tribune des mineurs*, departed from its usual dry discourse to call the ZRP "agents provocateurs of international fascism who wanted to deliver the Poles bound hand

and foot to the French capitalists." *Wiarus Polski* returned the insult by labeling the leaders of the CGT, "communist bandits." Although there is no direct evidence of support for the ZRP from French mining interests or the state, neither were the demands of the CGT to prohibit this foreign-run union carried out. Only after this particularly heated exchange between the CGT and *Wiarus Polski* in 1926 did the prefect of the Nord ask the Poles to be "less aggressive" in their opposition to the French unions.[102] Clearly, French authorities had few reason for limiting the divisiveness caused by Polish nationalism.

The CGT, of course, attempted to neutralize the influence of the ZRP leadership. They worked with the more moderate chapters of the ZRP and advocated that ZRP members as individuals join CGT locals.[103] However, the ZRP remained throughout the 1920s a vital organization; only in 1936 did it merge with the French unions. Unlike their French counterparts, they could provide Polish miners with support in areas specifically relating to their status as immigrants: aid in handling regulations, support of Polish cultural identity, and access to leadership positions. In none of these areas were the French unions able or willing to provide assistance. As a result, the mine operators enjoyed a situation in which the mining community was divided not only between communist and socialist but between French and Polish. The mine companies also gained invaluable assistance from Polish religious and nationalist organizations in stabilizing the immigrant community, allowing the companies to keep a relatively low profile.

The mine owners' policy achieved results: turnover was quickly reduced. While 30 percent of the foreign coal miners in 1920 broke their work contracts, by 1922 only 9 percent did so. By the mid-1920s the immigrants were as stable as the French.[104] Furthermore, 95,744 of the Poles remained as miners in 1931 from the 103,475 who entered coal mining in the 1920s. Compare this admittedly rough indication of stability with the figures for agriculture: only 46,083 Poles were farm workers in 1931 despite the fact that 151,961 Poles entered France as agricultural workers in the 1920s.[105] Unlike the farmers, mine operators had the resources to carry out a policy of stabilization. Because the Polish miners were concentrated in quasi-urbanized communities, whereas the farm workers were not, the mines also had the opportunity to make such a policy work.

Limits of Employer Hegemony over Polish Miners

For the French, this policy was not entirely a blessing, however. By favoring slow or minimal assimilation of the Polish miner, French authorities opened the possibility of losing control over the socialization of the Polish community. Polish nationalism had tendencies which conflicted with the goals and interests of important elements of the French community. In the first place, Polish nationalism had to defend the immigrants' interests, if not as workers, then as expatriated members of the Polish nation. Secondly, Polish leaders had an ideological incentive to encourage Polish social mobility in France. Without upward individual mobility, miners might be tempted to adopt collective or class modes of social advancement. The competent had to climb the social ladder, either in France or upon return to Poland. France could not be a human dump for the unwanted but rather had to provide opportunities for the hard-working family. France also had to be a market for Polish commerce, banking, and journalism. For the Polish nationalist, France was a substitute for a colony. These goals clashed with those of the French, who naturally wanted merely a tractable, stable, and permanent immigrant proletariat.

The mainstays of Polish nationalism in France were the small but influential service and commercial classes—petty merchants, journalists, and the clergy. As a large concentration of Poles developed in the northern mining regions, so did a number of grocers, butchers, tavern-keepers, and other small business people who catered to Polish tastes. Many of these merchants entered France disguised as miners; others, as was common among the French, graduated into petty commerce after being miners. Another important current of Polish capitalism was savings banks. Because many Poles sent home money or saved for their return, Polish money merchants found a ready market. At first money changers, often doubling as booksellers of nationalist literature, appeared in small mining towns. By 1928 Polish banks had infiltrated the mining regions in the hope of draining off some of the small savings of these hard-working immigrants. By 1930 three Polish banks formed a savings bank which gathered about 11 million francs from about 16,000 small savers.[106]

In spite of the growth of the Polish business class in the mining regions, it remained weak relative to the French—only 2.7 percent of the Polish population in the Pas-de-Calais in 1931 compared with 6 percent of the French who were engaged in commerce.[107] Without a nationalist Polish culture in France these Polish merchants could not easily have survived. They depended upon a closed Polish market which would be dissipated if the Poles assimilated. As a result, they were key promoters of the ideology of Polish solidarity. As a police report noted in 1929, the Polish petty bourgeoisie "are involved constantly in the lives of their compatriots. . . . They serve as their lawyers, business agents, etc., pressuring them and imposing their viewpoint which is opposed to assimilation."[108]

Polish journalists clearly expressed the petty bourgeois nationalism of these merchants. An editorial in *Narodowiec* (1926) claimed: "American Poles lived also in barracks at first, but all that is over now and it will be the same for us too. We must act together to aid each other. Our prosperity in France depends upon our initiative, our desire to work, and our intelligence."[109] *Narodowiec* proposed that Poles send their children to mine school to become foremen and even to trade and agricultural schools to escape the pits. Above all, they should save in Polish banks and establish businesses as in America.

These service and commercial groups naturally were thorns in the side of their French counterparts. A French tradesman from Lens (1925) probably expressed a common opinion when he declared that the Poles "ought to stay in the mines or get out. In having them come here, France has not asked for grocers, etc., but help to rebuild destroyed houses and mines." In the same year the commercial association of the Pas-de-Calais demanded that no immigrant be allowed into business before completing a two year work contract. French commerce had no interest in seeing a Polish nation form in its midst if this nation included a business class. Poles were supposed to be workers and consumers, not competitors in business.[110]

Polish clergy posed similar threats to French interests. In their zeal to preserve their flock (an effort that the mine operators generally supported) they often overstepped the bounds. True to the social ideology of Pope Leo XIII and Pius XI, some priests condemned lack of social progress in France. To the irritation of the companies, some "intervened between the workers and employers with too much authority and with too many demands."[111] The chief of the Polish

Religious Mission in France was not above complaining in a Warsaw newspaper that Poles were left destitute—"on the streets"—during the recession of 1927.[112] The mines of Aniche found "their Polish priest's intransigent defense of the interests of his compatriots" so intolerable that he was dropped from the payroll.[113] The French church hierarchy also complained that the Poles were too independent. The archbishop of Cambrai demanded in 1925 that Polish priests give their salaries from the mines directly to the French church.[114] French clergy chafed not only at Polish nationalism but also at their paternalistic social activism. The Poles also threatened the monopoly and authority of the French Catholic hierarchy.

Finally, the Polish Workers Association and its journalistic allies were a constant irritation to the French elite. In 1926 a police agent from Lille observed that the ZRP had increasingly "interfered directly in favor of Poles in grievances with farm and industrial employers," so much so that the public placement office of the Nord warned it to leave these matters to the French authorities. Repeatedly, the ZRP and *Wiarus Polski* offered Polish miners in France information about jobs available in the mines of Holland and Belgium. This led the French Interior Ministry to threaten to ban the newspaper in 1927. Because of its attacks on the Polish and French governments the Polish state outlawed the circulation of *Wiarus Polski* in Poland in 1929. With the help of Polish newspapers, the ZRP did in fact act as a trade union, much to the annoyance of the employers and French authorities. It intervened in labor relations between Polish workers and French employers, attempted to limit the Polish labor supply to improve the bargaining position of Poles already in France, and tried to impose the principles of seniority and job security on the mine operators.[115]

In spite of their acceptance and often direct support of Polish nationalism, French authorities inevitably clashed with the agents of this nationalism. Yet, although Polish nationalist organizations were not completely under the sway of French authorities, they did form a useful alternative agency of socialization to the socialists and communists.

The migration of Polish labor to the coal basins of the French northeast was a clear example of an effort of organized capital to shape a workforce to suit its specific needs. This migration not only filled a critical shortage of manpower, but provided employers with a flexible and generally skilled workforce. Moreover, unlike the farmers, the mine operators were able to manipulate the social and cultural environment of its foreign workforce. With the support of the government they fostered a stable, conservative, and culturally isolated class of Polish miners. This policy helped to create a new demographic well from which the mine operators could draw future generations of miners, nurtured in an exclusively mining environment. This policy also produced a class of anti-left Catholic miners organized around a paternalistic cultural nationalism, profoundly divided from the radical French milieu. As we have seen, the mines had to rely on Polish agents of social control to carry out this policy. This could only lead to conflicts with those members of the French elite who favored assimilation. Polish nationalism also backfired for the mine operators when it became the vehicle whereby Polish miners defended their economic interests. Yet on balance the mines gained unprecedented advantages through the organized immigration of Poles: it not only efficiently solved the need for productive labor but assured employers a divided and thus powerless community of miners.

V   The Fascist State and Italian Emigration

THE ease with which organized business was able to dominate Polish immigration was not possible with the largest migration—the Italians. Employers from the iron and steel, construction, chemical, and agricultural industries, who used Italian labor, did not, like their colleagues in the Coal Committee and CARD, create an inter-industrial organization to recruit Italian workers. Not only did these industries lack the necessary cohesion to form a SGI, but faced a relatively strong Italian state with interests very different from their own. It was the Italian government's Commissariato generale dell'emigrazione (CGE) which dominated the flow of Italians into France. Unlike Poland, which had only in 1919 become a state, lacked a rationalized bureaucracy, and was under the influence of French interests, the Italian state was relatively strong and independent. Italy's elite also had a clear understanding of the importance of emigration for national economic development. The result was a nationalist emigration program which combined public regulation with private encouragement. While the religious nationalism of the Poles protected them from cultural disintegration in France, it poorly defended the economic interests of Polish workers. By contrast, the Italian state was more successful in advancing the economic position of its emigrants but less effective in maintaining the cultural cohesiveness of the Italian community in France.

Mussolini's fascist regime inherited a well-developed emigration policy from his predecessors. Besides modifying this program somewhat to fit ideological concerns, he essentially continued the CGE's policy. Elements of this nationalist program would be imitated by other governments in the late 1920s, frustrating French business's desire for an unimpeded access to European labor. Immigration became increasingly less a matter of individual choice, a personal response to the market and demographic conditions, and more an affair of state.

The CGE Regulates Italian Labor Emigration

The powerful position of the Italian state vis-à-vis the French capitalist can be explained by France's dependence upon Italian labor. Despite Italy's need for an outlet for unemployed labor, Italian workers were well integrated into the French occupational structure and difficult to replace. Already in 1911, 256,811 Italians worked in France.[1] While southern Italians migrated primarily to the United States and Latin America, northern Italians, especially from Piedmont, Lombardy, and Venetia, took the short trek north to Switzerland, Germany, Austria, and France.[2] During the 1920s France's share of continental Italian emigration increased sharply. While in the decade 1901–1910 France received an annual average of 57,262 or 22.8 percent of continental emigrants, in the period 1921–30 France's annual share rose to 101,609 or 74.6 percent. Emigration to France was particularly important during the reconstruction period of 1922–25 as indicated in Table 8.[3]

Of course, Italian emigration was an indication of sluggish economic growth and population pressure. Throughout this period, workers from Italy's often erratic metallurgical industry, as well as from the building trades, regularly migrated to France. There, many hoped to improve skills and to earn working capital in order to found small businesses upon their return to Italy. Temporary or seasonal jobs in France of wood cutters, gardeners, and orchard workers produced a necessary supplement to the income of many Italian families.[4] Also, Italians in the 1920s had fewer options for emigration: German, Swiss, and Austrian demand for foreign labor greatly decreased in the 1920s thanks to relatively high rates of unemployment.[5] Immigration

Table 8   The Role of France in Italian Emigration, 1921–1930

Year	Emigration to France	Total European emigration		Total emigration	
		No.	*% to France*	*No.*	*% to France*
1921	44,782	79,002	56.7	201,291	22.2
1922	99,464	150,555	66.1	281,270	35.6
1923	167,982	199,674	84.1	389,957	43.1
1924	201,715	232,403	86.8	364,614	55.3
1925	145,529	171,630	84.8	280,081	51.9
1926	111,252	134,484	82.7	262,396	42.4
1927	59,784	81,801	73.1	218,934	27.3
1928	40,048	62,471	64.1	140,856	28.4
1929	53,186	94,342	56.4	174,802	31.0
1930	99,346	155,157	64.0	236,438	42.0

Source: Istituto centrale de statistica, *Sommario di statistische storio dell'Italia, 1861–1965* (Rome: ISSN, 1966), pp. 28–29.

restrictions in the United States, however, implemented in 1921 and 1924, had little impact upon the continental emigration. In 1925 southern Italians constituted only 10.6 percent of the continental emigration, scarcely more than the 7.8 percent at the peak of trans-continental emigration in 1910.[6]

While Italy needed an outlet for underutilized labor, the French also found that manpower indispensible. Italian wood cutters, masons, and other skilled construction workers were irreplaceable.[7] Attempts to supplement Italian construction workers with Czechs in the early 1920s had failed when, in 1924, the Czech government placed prohibitive restrictions on their export.[8] The electrochemical and metallurgical industries in the French Alps relied upon a steady supply of seasonal laborers from Piedmont.[9] Poles or other immigrants were no substitute. While the iron and steel industries of the Lorraine attempted to replace Italians with Poles from 1924, the Italian migration into this district remained important.[10] By 1926, Italians constituted 9.4 percent of the basic metal workers, 14 per cent of construction laborers, and 8.5 percent of glass and stone workers in France.[11] Furthermore, French employers had few options for immigrant labor, especially from neighbouring countries which required little organized recruitment. The German and Belgian populations in France actually declined in the 1920s: the number of Germans dropped from 75,625 in 1921 to 71,729 in 1931 and the number of Belgians from 253,694 to 238,986.[12]

As a result of this reliance on Italian labor, the Italian state was in a favorable position to demand a quid pro quo from the French for any labor exported. The Italian state acted as a kind of trade union for its emigrants; it attempted to bargain with France for the best jobs and wages for its citizens. The demand for their labor and the threat of withdrawal yielded bargaining power. This policy hardly reflected a deep commitment to the amelioration of Italian labor. More important was a desire to secure a profitable return on the Italian investment in the emigrant laborer. Italy lacked the political and economic resources for a genuine colonial policy of exporting capital and goods. As a result, it had to rely on its major asset, labor, for export. While Italian emigrants might have been a social and economic burden had they remained at home, through their emigration they became a potential economic benefit to Italy. They could repatriate earnings and return with new skills.

From 1901 to 1927, the CGE carried out a nationalist emigration policy. Led by Georges de Michelis from 1919, the CGE endeavored to improve the value of Italian emigration. As de Michelis claimed in 1924: "The CGE is directed toward treating the human element as an essential factor in the production of foreign exchange. . . ." The CGE became an active proponent of an imperialism through emigration in which the "interests of the emigrant coincides with the national interest."[13]

In 1913 the Italian parliament granted the CGE the authority to prohibit any emigration which did not improve Italy's position on the world labor market. In that same year, after having temporarily suspended emigration, the CGE forced a model work contract on the French Comité des forges and the German Feldarbeiterzentrum (Farm Labor Office). This contract compelled employers to specify wages and provide job descriptions prior to recruiting labor in Italy. During 1915, in negotiations with the French Armaments Ministry, the CGE obtained specific guarantees for the wages, housing, and food of Italians imported into French war industries.[14] In 1919, in anticipation of a "disorderly exodus of our best workers," the CGE demanded that passports be granted to workers only if they had obtained "contracts advantageous economically and morally" to Italian labor. For this purpose, in November 1919 the Italian government gave to the CGE the authority to suspend emigration in any specific geographic area or occupation.[15]

Armed with these sweeping powers the CGE made a systematic effort to improve the wages and skills of what it hoped would be Italy's temporary emigrants. The CGE gathered detailed information about the wages and working-living conditions of workers in various French industries and regions. It strongly favored channeling Italian workers into building trades, especially in the reconstruction zone in the early 1920s. An Italian mason hired for the reconstruction in 1922 could average forty-five francs per day compared with the twenty to twenty-five francs offered to experienced miners and laborers in the Lorraine iron and steel industry, which had been an important zone of emigration before the war. The construction industry offered unusual opportunities for on-the-job training and promotion. The CGE claimed (1922) that many Italians progressed from the status of low-skilled laborers to specialists in the reconstruction zones in France. Some even became small contractors and hired Italian labor. Both the rapid growth of the construction industry in France from 1922 to 1924 and the relatively low capital needed to establish a business in this industry seemed to offer social mobility that the unskilled jobs in the large-scale metals and mining industries did not provide. "Our workers," the CGE boasted, "found in the work of the war-torn regions a school of professional advancement."[16]

Even in trades where advancement was more difficult, the CGE attempted to secure the highest possible wages. The CGE negotiated an agreement with the French railways in 1922 for Italian labor to lay rail beds and repair exchanges. Although workers were paid only 1.8 to 2 francs an hour, they soon earned 2.5 to 3 francs as skilled repairmen. More importantly they were housed and fed on isolated rail cars which prevented them from spending their earnings in France. Finally, these jobs provided an outlet for some of the pressure of unemployment among unskilled Italians. In a similar vein, while the wages and opportunities for advancement in the mining and metal-lurgical industries were limited, the Commissariato saw the advantage of subsidized housing, free gardens, family bonuses, and recreation which some of the companies provided. These benefits reduced living costs, made low wages more bearable, and gave some the opportunity to save. Even so, the disadvantages of the iron and steel industries were such that the CGE resisted the appeals of the Comité des forges for additional Italian labor, obliging them to turn to the SGI and the Polish worker in 1924. The CGE also favored emigration into industries which violated or obtained exemptions from the eight-hour day law. For example, in the early 1920s the CGE encouraged Italian emigration into the hydroelectric chemical and metallurgical centers of the French Alps because they could work ten hours a day, seven days a week, thus earning more money to return to Italy.[17]

The Italian government was concerned about neither the length and quality of the work day nor the living conditions which the emigrants experienced (as long as these conditions did not cause the repatriation of sick citizens). Instead, it wanted Italians to earn as much as possible in the shortest period of time and to minimize their living costs during their stay in France. Italian emigration was to be temporary; it was to improve the Italian balance of payments through wage repatriation.

In order to carry out this policy, the CGE carefully used its powers to review and veto work contracts which French employers submitted. In 1924, for example, of 37,945 contracts from French employers (some of which were requests for many workers—collective contracts), 12 per cent were rejected; in 1925, 13 per cent of the 30,339 contracts requested were refused, in both cases mostly because of the low wages offered. For instance, on account of substandard pay, the CGE rejected contracts for shipwrights, iron miners, and forestry workers. The CGE vetoed the emigration of general farm hands for the Nord, because these farms offered only 120–180 francs monthly; instead it encouraged emigration into the French southwest where there was a demand for sharecroppers. The CGE saw this as a step toward land ownership, something that the farmers of the Nord could not provide. These farmers were obliged to draw on the less protected Poles for their manpower needs.[18]

Finally, the CGE attempted to improve the marketability of Italian labor in France (and elsewhere). As early as 1912, the CGE stationed agents in Paris and other areas of potential emigration to investigate job openings and to publicize the advantages of Italian labor to French employers. The CGE dispersed this job information and offers of employment through a complex network of provincial and communal emigration committees and state-administered labor offices. This effort had become increasingly necessary, the CGE admitted in 1913, because of shrinking job opportunities abroad, economic crises at home, and the danger of general "disillusionment from extended unemployment."[19]

The CGE also subsidized private placement offices within France. These offices found work both for those Italians who entered France as tourists and those who were temporarily unemployed. In 1924 these Comitati per l'assistanti dei lavoratori italiani (Committees to Aid Italian Workers) were established under private Italian auspices and administration in a number of centers of Italian emigration. Comitati located in Paris, Briey, Mulhouse, St. Auventin, and Modane helped to find work for Italians. The CGE had as little use for idle Italians in France as did the French government. The Comitato in Paris set up a placement office at the Gare de Lyon to find jobs for emigrants as soon as they stepped off the train from Italy as well as for construction workers as they drifted into Paris after rebuilding the war zones. During the first ten months of 1924 this office placed 4,000 Italians. In particular, it attempted to locate them outside Paris, where the high cost of living and the temptation to spend discouraged savings. The Paris and provincial Comitati also helped Italians with workers' compensation and pension claims. The Briey Comitato assisted about 500 victims of industrial injuries in filing insurance claims in the first half of 1924 alone.[20] The Italian state did not want the side-effects of working in France to fall ultimately on Italy; rather, it sought to receive the full benefits of the work of its citizens in France.

The CGE also attempted to improve the skills of prospective Italian emigrants. By 1922 the CGE operated nineteen schools which trained 1,084 workers in cement, masonry, mosaic work, and other building trades in great demand in France. These programs, however, touched relatively few, since in September of 1922 almost 80,000 Italians were already working in the reconstruction of French war zones.[21] Yet the CGE's training programs were at least symbols of its policy of upgrading the skills of Italians. Its social services and quasi-trade union activities were designed to maintain the Italians' identification with their homeland and thus to encourage their eventual return to Italy with their skills and savings.

Beyond this, the CGE served Italian business by discouraging any exodus of labor which might raise wages in Italy. In order to assure that only surplus labor was recruited in Italy, the CGE allowed French employers to individually select workers only in regions of high unemployment. The CGE also recruited batches of workers for French employers in "collective contracts" from these same areas. The CGE occasionally denied passports and thus the right of emigration to workers whom it considered crucial to local economic interests. For example, when Italian farm employers complained in 1924 and 1925 of excessive emigration to the French southwest, where Italian day laborers were recruited as sharecroppers, the CGE responded by prohibiting migration to this region.[22] Through these discretionary powers the CGE helped to drain saturated labor markets in Italy, while still protecting the Italian employer from the foreign competitor.

The Italian state and employers expected a substantial return on the investment in emigrant labor. Government controls over expatriation helped but this did not necessarily guarantee that Italian emigrants would continue to identify with their homeland, avoid assimilation into the foreign society, and eventually return to Italy with capital and skills. Thus an integral part of Italian policy was a cultural program, which attempted to wed Italians abroad to the goals of this nationalist emigration policy. It was equally important that emigrants returned to Italy uncontaminated by French radicalism and that Italian socialists and communists did not gain influence over Italian workers in France. Thus the Italian state tried to control the leadership of the Italian community in France in much the same way as the Polish state attempted to infiltrate the Polish mining communities. The Italian elite had a very clear intention of dominating the political and cultural life of Italian expatriates. According to the Chamber of Commerce in Padua in 1922 emigration should:

> develop peaceful expansion of Italian power, eliminate germs of social discontent, contribute individually to improving labor and collectively to enriching the country . . . [It should] encourage the desire to save and especially to raise the standard of living, thus

improving the individual. If, however, emigration is not properly controlled, there will be corruption and subversion, a state of affairs which can and ought to be eliminated.[23]

This control of the emigration was, of course, to be delegated to the public powers. In an age of growing class consciousness, employers could not attempt to control the expatriate workers directly. In turn, the state and the CGE delegated this role to supposedly neutral religious and philanthropic agencies.

This policy, already well-established before World War I, was adopted and extended by Mussolini after the fascist takeover in October 1922. Ever since the fascists began their attack on the left and the trade unions in 1920, and especially after they suppressed the unions and left parties in 1925, socialist and communist activists fled Italy, many migrating to France.[24] The fascist state certainly would not tolerate Italian contact with radicalism in France after it had been uprooted in Italy.

Even before the fascist victory, the CGE subsidized twenty-eight private agencies abroad and fifty-eight similar groups in Italy that were devoted to placing Italians in jobs outside the country and to perpetuating conservative and nationalist ideas among emigrants. These offices recruited workers without the stigma of government, much less that of the employers. Most of these welfare societies were linked either to the Opera Bonomelli, established in 1900 by the Catholic church, or to the secular group, Umanitaria (organized in 1901).[25]

Although the Umanitaria was present in France, it was stronger in Switzerland and Germany. Furthermore, Mussolini destroyed it in 1924 to the temporary advantage of its rival, the Opera Bonomelli. This clerical organization, created in 1900 by a Turin priest to preserve the Catholicism of the continental emigrants, had the Vatican's strong support. It was influential in the French Lorraine, especially in the iron and coal basins of Briey and Longwy, where it established offices in 1907, soon after Italian miners appeared. In 1909 the Opera Bonomelli spread to Marseilles and Lyons. By 1927 there were sixty-six offices in Europe (fifteen located in Italy and seventeen in France). It provided hostels in northern Italy for immigrants in route to France. Its services included clinics, nursery schools, and Italian language and cultural classes. The Opera Bonomelli had two publications, a mass weekly, *La Patria*, and a house organ, *Opera Bonomelli*, as well as almanacs and assorted brochures.[26]

As an indication of how valuable the CGE considered the Opera Bonomelli, the CGE in 1920 paid it 183,000 lire in subsidies, or 30 percent of its budget of 599,715 lire.[27] Although obviously catering to Catholic emigrants, the Opera Bonomelli was hardly distinguishable from the Italian consuls. In the Lorraine, for example, it served as an intermediary between emigrants and the Italian diplomatic services.[28] The consuls helped to form Opera Bonomelli mutual-aid societies.[29] The Opera Bonomelli also helped to place temporarily unemployed Italian emigrants and performed functions of social amelioration that would otherwise have fallen on the consuls. Most important, the CGE and Opera Bonomelli shared an ideology. This Catholic organization fostered not only religion and the cult of the family but that of the nation as well. It did not question the state's attempt to organize Italian emigrant workers abroad under Italian "technical chiefs and leaders."[30]

Unlike other labor exporting states, Italy clearly recognized the economic consequences of emigration and undertook a systematic program to realize the greatest benefits. Yet what was the impact of this policy on Italians in France and how successful was it? This aggressive involvement of the Italian state and private groups may be reflected in the relatively advantageous economic position of Italians in France. If one compares the occupational and class distribution of Italians with Polish immigrants in 1931, one finds that the Italian population had gained a relatively large degree of economic mobility. As Table 9 indicates,[31] while the Poles were heavily concentrated in primary industries (into which the SGI recruited them), the Italians realized a wide penetration of the occupations. The class distribution of the Italians was also closer to the pattern of French society as a whole than was that of the Poles, who were heavily proletarianized.

Of course there are non-political explanations for this relatively elite position of Italians in immigrant society; Italian immigration benefited from large established groups of compatriots and relatives already in France, while the Poles lacked this advantage. Italy also had a larger pool of skilled workers to export than did Poland,

Table 9   Occupational and Class of Distribution of Italian and
Polish Workers, 1931

Occupation/ economic status	Italians No.	%	Polish No.	%	French %
Agriculture	70,272	14.7	50,337	17.5	35.6
Mining	25,518	5.4	96,405	33.6	2
Industry	283,283	59.7	110,078	38.4	31.6
Transport	24,009	5.1	5,708	2.0	4.9
Commerce	44,279	9.3	12,639	4.4	12.6
Free professions	5,886	1.2	2,482	.9	3
Domestic service	19,682	4.2	8,753	3.0	4.2
Public service	1,759	.4	592	.2	6.1
Total	474,688	100	286,402	100	100
Employer	55,015	11.6	8,635	3	28.9
White-collar	22,472	4.6	6,705	2.3	14
Blue-collar	325,297	68.5	252,035	87.8	42.3
Self-employed	54,388	11	12,489	4.4	12.7
Unemployed	17,834	3.9	7,138	2.5	2.1
Total	475,006	100	287,002	100	100

Source: France, *Résultats statistiques du recensement général de la population*, 1, no. 5 (1931), 76–78 and 1, no. 3 (1931), 96.

especially in the important construction and metal goods industries. Yet the superior position of Italians in France was also a result of the Italian state's intervention in the distribution of emigrant labor. It blocked the kind of organized immigration under the control of employers, which had channeled the Poles into primary industries and had limited their mobility.

Furthermore, French employers were keenly aware of the counter-vailing power of the Italian state and its ability to frustrate their manpower plans. Edouard de Warren and other parliamentary representatives of French business had sponsored a national immigration office in 1921 in part to give French business a state-level counterpart to the Italian CGE (see p. 53). R. Blanchard, representing the Alpine hydrochemical and metallurgical industries, complained in 1924 that the Italian government had, since 1920, created "obstacles and restrictions blocking the peaceful invasion of its nationals. . . . and it is to overcome these difficulties . . . that the industrialists have used all their powers to induce contingents of other nationalities to come [to France] despite their inadequate numbers and quality in comparison to the Italian immigration."[32] Employers were often obliged to tolerate Italian "interference" when they had no alternative sources of labor.

The promotion of Italian national identity under conservative sponsorship, however, had mixed results. As in the case of the Poles, employers sometimes appreciated the conservative goals of these nationalist welfare agencies in France. For example, the Opera Bonomelli was generally "well liked in industrial circles," for it provided non-communist workers through its job placement services.[33] The French trade-union and communist press agreed that the Opera Bonomelli served the interests of French employers: its mutual-aid societies were alternatives to unions, and the Opera recruited "backward elements" into regions and occupations, especially near Paris, weakening trade unions.[34]

Yet the nationalism of these agencies contradicted the interests of French employers. For example, Robert Pinot, the president of the Comité des forges in the early 1920s, probably had the greatest experience among French entrepreneurs with Italian immigration. Writing to the Conférence permanente de la main-d'oeuvre étrangère in December of 1920, he complained that the Italian clergy's nationalistic preaching undermined his attempts to "stabilize Italian labor" in France; it served the foreign-policy goals of the Italian government. Pinot claimed that this policy included encouraging emigrants to change jobs frequently to prevent their attachment to a single job or location. "Italy knows," he said, "that if its emigrants permanently settle in France, they will not send back . . . their earnings." He feared that they might "unite and fortify themselves around an Italian clergy established in France under the patronage of the Pope."[35] Unlike the Polish church, which moved into and divided an already organized mining community in the north, Italian missionaries served as a trade union substitute where often none existed. Both Italy and Poland attempted to create colonies in France led by patriotic, conservative, and often clerical elites. Obviously, when this policy divided immigrant and French workers or maintained the docilitiy, credulity, and fertility of imported workers, French employers supported it. Clearly, when and where it united or articulated immigrant interests, even if an attempt to prevent assimilation, employers opposed it. For Pinot, a "yellow union" run by priests was almost as bad as a "red" one.

The foregoing analysis suggests that Italian policy probably helped to improve the economic status of emigrants in France and certainly frustrated French employers. Yet did it realize the ultimate goal of the Italian government—the substantial inflow of foreign exchange in repatriated wages or the return of newly skilled Italians? Despite governmental efforts, savings returned to Italy from the continental emigrants was significantly lower than repatriated savings from transoceanic emigrants. In 1923, a year of high continental savings, only 168 million lire were returned to Italy from European emigrants compared to 510 million from the transcontinental savers. For the period 1903–23, the deposits per emigrant saver in France was only 223 lire compared to 899 for the Italian who emigrated to the United States.[36]

Moreover, the expected bonanza of repatriated labor failed as well. Although seasonal laborers returned regularly to Italy, especially during the winter months, they contributed little to Italy during their annual leaves. The emigrants who obtained skills and capital when in France often did not return to Italy. Rather, they naturalized or settled permanently in France. This is indicated by the repatriation figures which declined significantly after reaching a peak of 109,529 in 1925. Returning emigrants dropped to 85,123 in 1926 and slid to 46,296 in 1927 and 31,845 in 1928.[37] The number of individual contracts may also reveal a trend toward permanent migration: many Italians hired under individual contracts were relatives of Italians already settled in France. Thus a large number of individual contracts indicated a pattern of Italian families bringing kin to France for permanent settlement. In the early twenties, the number of these individual contracts increased from 8,228 in 1922 to 31,824 in 1923. The number of collective contracts rose only from 30,756 in 1922 to 33,907 in 1923.[38]

The impact of the CGE's policy, then, was ambiguous: it benefited Italian emigrants in France, yet was unable to provide a significant return on the social investment of Italy in her expatriated labor force.

This failure became increasingly evident to the fascist leadership in Italy as the 1920s wore on, leading by 1927 to an important modification of the CGE's program.

Fascist Modifications of Emigration Policy

Despite Mussolini's seizure of power in 1922, the fascist regime was slow to penetrate the state apparatus involved in emigration. As late as 1925, Mussolini expressed his full confidence in the CGE and the policies of its director, de Michelis. Indeed the goals of this holdover from the liberal state were basically consistent with those of the fascists. Yet the stamp of fascism was gradually placed on emigration policy. In an effort to eliminate the CGE's autonomy and make emigration a part of fascist foreign policy, Mussolini, in January 1923, subordinated the CGE to the Ministry of Foreign Affairs.[39] Two years later the CGE was abolished and replaced by the Directorate of Italians Abroad, a name signifying the fascist belief that emigrants remained a part of the nation and participants in fascist plans of expansion.[40]

Moreover the fascists rejected the implicit assumption which guided CGE policy—that Italy was overpopulated and required emigration to disgorge her unemployable masses. Rather, fascist leaders decreed that Italy's high fertility was a mark of vitality. Indeed in 1926 Mussolini declared that his regime would promote more births in order to raise Italy's population to sixty million by mid-century.[41] Emigration, as a French consul noted in 1927, was a word which grated in the ears of fascists,[42] a symbol of the backwardness which the fascists pledged to abolish.

Beyond this visceral ideological rejection of emigration, the fascists and their allies objected that the economic benefits of emigration were meager, helping only the receiving nations. Francesco Coletti, writing in *Corriere della sera* (July 1926) complained that the French "receive especially young or adult men. They choose the immigrants who are the most useful to them. As a result, the entire population [of France] is improved both from the biological and productive points of view." Without immigration, Coletti noted, French capital would have to be invested abroad.[43]

Dino Grandi, Undersecretary of Foreign Affairs, summed up the fascist approach to emigration in a speech in March 1927, shortly before the abolition of the CGE:

> The General Commissariat of Emigration is today in obvious contradiction with the principles and aims of Fascism. . . . Italian colonies abroad should each be reproductions of the home country on a small scale. . . . Since emigration has now changed into a political phenomenon, the General Commissariat must become a political organ and must form an undivided whole with . . . the Ministry of Foreign Affairs. . . . We as Fascists must have the courage to declare that emigration is an "evil" when, as at the present, it is directed towards countries under foreign sovereignty. Emigration is necessary, but towards Italian countries and possessions.
>
> . . . Henceforth [Italy] will send only members of her governing classes beyond the frontiers of her sovereignty, not as a remedy for her poverty but to fulfill her need for expansion. . . . Why should our race form a kind of human reservoir for the replenishment of the small or declining populations of other nations? Why should our mothers continue to bring into the world children who will grow up into soldiers for other nations?
>
> Fascism will cease to encourage emigration, which saps the vital forces of race and State.[44]

Instead of massive expatriation, the fascists promoted a program of internal colonization and agricultural colonies in Northern Africa, especially Somaliland and Eritrea. These projects were not successful and led the Italians into the disasterous military adventures of the late 1930s.[45] The fascist decision to de-emphasize emigration was an expression of nationalist pride and a recognition that emigration was not the best utilization of Italian manpower resources. Yet behind this anti-emigration rhetoric was the unspeakable fact that Italy could no longer place her unemployed in the economies of other nations. Both the catastrophic restrictions of movement into the United States and the uncertain and fluctuating demand for Italian labor in France was evident by 1925. Mussolini had attempted through the international conferences on emigration and immigration held in

1921 and 1924 to improve the conditions for economic emigration and to weaken the impact of American quotas. Yet these efforts had indifferent results.[46] The decline of opportunity for Italians in France after the completion of the reconstruction in 1924 was more bad news (see Figure 1). Finally, French revision of its naturalization law in 1927 capped the failure of the CGE's emigration policy. This law significantly eased the process of naturalization in France, in effect frustrating Italian government hopes of retaining the national identity of emigrants in France.[47] In the light of these developments, the boisterous rejection of emigration as a social policy was a smokescreen for the inability of Italy to carry out a successful emigration program.

Yet Italy could hardly rid herself of the need for emigration or abandon the long-held policy of making emigrants an instrument of national economic growth. The fascists would simply try harder, first to improve the economic position of those who were allowed to emigrate, and secondly to redouble efforts to encourage emigrants to remain Italian nationals and to contribute to Italy's economic development. Toward these ends, Mussolini placed even greater restrictions on emigration than had the CGE and promoted a strong nationalist movement among the emigrants.

Following the suppression of the CGE in April of 1927, Mussolini issued a series of decrees which more strictly regulated emigration. A circular of June 3 to the prefects declared that henceforth permanent emigration was to be discouraged and that passports should be granted would-be emigrants only after careful scrutiny. Edicts required Italian consuls to approve of work contracts and limited the rights of emigrants to petition visas for their relatives in Italy. At the same time, Mussolini instructed the consuls to encourage repatriation.[48] Because the fascists considered individual migration as likely to lead to permanent settlement abroad, they placed numerous restrictions on it. For example, in 1928 importers of Italian labor such as Alpine metals and chemical industries, who hired specific workers, were denied their requests.[49]

Beginning in April of 1928 the Italian state allowed employers to hire only twenty emigrants by name; others had to be recruited by the Italian government under collective contracts.[50] Finally, in January of 1929, control over migration at the frontiers was taken from the emigration services and placed under the general security police. This change meant greater surveillance of the frontier to prevent clandestine emigration that naturally increased as additional emigration restrictions were imposed.[51]

While the shift in policy in 1927 was directed against massive emigration and especially permanent resettlement, the fascist regime continued to uphold the objectives of the CGE by attempting to encourage temporary migrations of skilled and highly paid workers. Emigration, according to a fascist deputy in 1927, was to be "reserved for those elements best armed for the economic struggle."[52] Thus engineers, skilled building and metal workers, as well as managerial personnel were freely granted passports.[53] Not only were these Italians more likely to return with savings and experience than less skilled workers, but they would enhance Italian prestige abroad. On the other hand, the fascist-dominated Directorate of Italians Abroad was even more severe than the CGE in restricting migration of unskilled Italians: for example, in July of 1928, French employers were denied requests for domestic labor and farm workers, a policy which greatly aggravated the French in the departments of the Bouches-du-Rhône and Isère.[54]

Partially as a result of these policy changes, emigration to France declined significantly from 1927 to 1929. If, for 1927 this decrease could as well be explained by the recession of that year as by Italian restrictions, in 1928 and 1929, years of economic growth in France, the Italian controls obliged employers to shift their foreign labor needs to Eastern Europe.[55] However, rhetoric and formal decrees aside, the number of Italians entering France in 1930 increased sharply (by 87 percent). The onset of the economic crisis of the 1930s stimulated Italian ingenuity at sidestepping government controls. Economic realities limited the political objectives of the fascist regime.

The style more than the substance of Italian emigration policy changed with the fascist suppression of the CGE. This was as true for the semi-private cultural and assistance programs as for the policy of the state. Indeed, just as the fascists abolished the CGE only to continue its broad objectives, so it eliminated private, often religious emigration services only to carry out similar programs under the aegis of fascism. The fascists attempted, with indifferent results, to impose a nationalist-conservative leadership on the Italian community in France and to assure its continued loyalty to Italy.

In 1925 Mussolini cut off the state subsidy to the Opera Bonomelli, forcing a number of its offices to shut down. By September 1926 he had purged the nonfascists on the Opera Bonomelli's board and replaced them with his appointees. Finally in July 1928 Mussolini induced the pope to disband the organization altogether. Most of the established missions were turned over to the fascists.[56]

Beginning in 1923, fascist trade unions gradually gained control over most collective recruitment,[57] gradually eliminating the recruitment services of the Opera Bonomelli. Fascists often infiltrated emigrant work groups in France in order to spy on those who were tempted to join French unions. They also attempted to organize fascist mutual-aid societies as alternatives to these unions, which, like the Polish ZRP, intervened in workers' compensation cases and even demanded that employers contribute to their emergency-aid funds.[58] Fascist unions were sufficiently active to annoy French employers and to force Mussolini at the Congress of Fascist Unions in 1926 to order them not to intervene in disputes and controversies in France.[59] Mussolini was, of course, not about to allow the formation of class attitudes among emigrants any more than at home, nor would he needlessly antagonize French entrepreneurs.

Fascist infiltration of the Italian community in France was, however, allowed to divide French unions. A delegate to a conference of independent construction workers complained that a fascist-led influx of Italians into many construction trades had seriously undermined the eight-hour day because Italian work-teams labored ten-hour days.[60] The French unions complained that employers kept fascist supporters on the job after others were laid off.[61] Even if one generously allows for exaggeration, fascist influence must have had a considerably divisive effect in those sectors where Italians were important.

Mussolini, however, found the fascist trade unions to be too unreliable. They were purged in 1928. The fascists also found the consuls to be too bureaucratic and, of course, the Opera Bonomelli too religious to serve his nationalist goals. As a partial replacement for these agencies, Mussolini created foreign-based *fasci,* modeled after the local Italian fascist organizations. As early as November 1922 the first *fascio* was set up in Paris. In 1923 it had 200 members and published a monthly newspaper, *L'Italie nouvelle.*[62] It became the funnel for many of the cultural and welfare projects of the fascist state.

For example, the Comitato d'assistenza per li lavoratori italiani in Paris was controlled and financed by the *fascio* of Paris. By 1926 there were fasci in most Italian centers.[63] The consular staffs often led these *fasci*, while local Italian businessmen, clerks, and artisans composed most of the membership. For example, police reported only eighty members of the fascio of Lyons. The secretary was an employee of the Banque de Rome; other officers included a tailor and a butcher.[64] One of their principal functions was to distribute *Il Lavoratore d'Italia* to Italian workers in the industrial towns of the Loire valley. In Nantes and doubtless elsewhere the Italian consul established a mutual-aid society, which was administered by the local *fascio*.[65]

Teamwork between the consuls and *fasci* extended into every nook and cranny of Italian life in France. This was particularly true as Mussolini purged career diplomats from consular posts. In February 1927, for example, the most important consulate in France at Marseilles went to a fascist deputy E. Barduzzi. He took over the local *fascio* as well as various veteran, patriotic, and mutual-aid organizations. He seized the Opera Bonomelli's facility and also took over the local Italian-language newspaper, *Eco d'Italia*. Barduzzi's vice-consul, an agent from the Italian General Security, spied on so-called Italian communists and anarchists and demanded their expulsion. While Barduzzi bullied the established Italian business class (apparently sufficiently to induce some of them to subsidize anti-fascist groups), he also catered to apolitical workers. He organized festivals for Italian fishermen and sponsored summer camps in Italy for the children of Italian workers. His excesses greatly annoyed both the Italian elite of Marseilles and the French prefect; their dissatisfaction probably contributed to his early departure at the end of 1927.[66] In any case, other Italian consuls worked in a similar direction.[67]

Several innovative programs paralleled this expansion of fascist influence within the emigrant "colonies."[68] In December 1925 Mussolini instructed the consuls to develop programs for the moral and patriotic training of Italian emigrants.[69] They were to organize groups called *dopolavoro*.[70] In some places the *dopolavoro* concentrated simply on Italian language classes for French-speaking Italian children.[71] Others sponsored sporting events, political indoctrination, and propaganda to encourage savings and temperance.[72] The *dopolavoro* served the goals of nurturing national identity (and with it, the desire to work hard, avoid alcohol, and save) as well as of stifling class consciousness. The fascists discouraged Italian citizens from becoming naturalized citizens of France. Italy often refused to send to French authorities civil documents required for naturalization. Beginning in 1928, the *fasci* subsidized trips to Italy for expectant mothers in order to assure the birth of Italian citizens.[73] From 1928 until the Second World War the consuls and fascists organized a series of summer camps in Italy for Italian children in France in the hope of encouraging nationalism. About 800 children from the Paris region went yearly.[74]

Despite these efforts, the fascists seemed to make little headway. It is, of course, difficult to determine the number of Italians even minimally affected by this nationalism. But because Italian immigrants, unlike the Poles, never constituted a large, stable, and homogeneous colony, they could hardly maintain a nationalist culture. Only immigration into the southwest and the Lorraine provided any parallel to Polish immigration into the northern coal field. Yet in January 1927 the *commissaire spécial* of Toulouse claimed that only 5 percent of the Italians in the French southwest were fascist. Sixty percent of these immigrants were Christian Democrats and the rest, Nitti socialists.[75] Although 78,945 Italians had concentrated in the French Lorraine by 1926, there were only eight Italian organizations with a total of 600 members in 1924 in this region and no regional Italian press or schools.[76] The fact that the fascists chose to supplant rather than use the church for its nationalist propaganda may explain its failure when compared to the Poles. For many Italians in France, especially those in the skilled trades or old established emigrants, the fascists were the enemies of democracy and the working class. By contrast, the more conservative Poles rallied around the church as the carrier of the nationalist tradition.

Italian nationalism was a failure especially among workers. No workers' names appear on lists of the leaders of fascist-led organizations in France. In contrast, Polish workers participated in many nationalist organizations. In a word, Italians had no substitute for the Polish ZRP. Fascist strength in France was concentrated in older centers of Italian penetration where middle-class emigration was more deeply rooted.[77]

The Italian state, however, more successfully regulated labor emigration. Unlike the Polish state, Italy controlled its labor supply, thus affecting where and, to a degree, at what price it would enter the French labor market. Although this policy was subordinated to the fascists' nationalist goals in 1927, and had limited economic impact, it remained the logical means by which a labor-supplying country might gain from the export of its citizens. Thus Italy became the model for others such as Poland and Spain in the late 1920s.

Other Labor-Exporters Adopt the Italian Model, 1928–30

The great advantage which France had over labor-supplying nations in the early twenties rapidly dissipated by 1928. Not only had France a growing need for labor, but Poland, Spain and other labor exporters had begun to learn from the Italians and demand a quid pro quo from the French. As the French economy heated up, coal operators, sugar beet planters, building contractors, textile manufacturers, and steel industrialists all claimed labor shortages by 1928.[78] Moreover, these industries faced a period of sharp diminutions of young native labor as the impact of the low fertility rates of the First World War reached the labor market. Alphone Pichon, president of the Union of Metal and Mining Industries, predicted in 1929 a yearly shortage of 310,000 workers which would last until 1939. He feared that this would lead to "increased instability of labor, more contract breaking, and a rise of wages and inflation."[79] One of the few acceptable solutions to this problem was still greater immigration.

Yet, at the same time, Poland and other labor exporters were becoming less dependent upon France. While Poland's unemployment rate declined in the late 1920s she found new outlets for emigration: her farm workers again were in demand for Germany and new agricultural settlements in South America called many Poles who otherwise might have had no choice but France.[80]

Given the apparent effectiveness of Italy's policy, it was adopted by Poland. In 1928, Poland began to restrict immigration to France in order to force improvements in the wages and the working and living conditions of Polish emigrants. In that year the Polish government reduced the number of the highly prized female farm workers who were allowed to go to France despite the objections of French farm associations.[81] In 1929, the Polish government suspended farm labor emigration altogether, pending improvements in the housing, wages, and "moral protection" given to these peasant women.[82] In 1929, despite the French request for 96,000 Poles for all industries, the Polish government allowed only 61,000 to go to work in France.[83] The Polish government had begun to doubt the wisdom of exporting potentially useful labor, especially skilled miners.[84] Moreover, by 1929, Polish business began to insist on a share of the emigration trade, then monopolized by the French SGI. They demanded that the Polish government aid them in displacing the SGI.[85]

Even the relatively backward Spanish government established an emigration council in early 1926.[86] In August of that year, Spain belatedly signed a migration treaty with France which provided Spanish emigrants with legal access to French social welfare benefits. The Spanish also set up an office in Paris to review work contracts and to aid Spanish emigrants with legal problems. Again, reminiscent of the Italians, the Spanish minister of labor in 1928 reduced emigration under pressure from Spanish farm employers. The authoritative newspaper *ABC* cited frequent repatriation of destitute emigrants and the inability of many Spaniards to compete with other nationalities as additional reasons for the policy of restriction.[87]

French response to this imitation of the Italian policy was first to make compromises: for example, the French Ministry of Agriculture in 1929 sponsored Committees for the Protection of Polish Farm Women in an attempt to satisfy Polish complaints that their young women in France received inadequate moral protection (see chapter VIII).[88] However, when a policy of accommodation was not so easy, the French state attempted to weaken the bargaining position of Poland, Italy, and Spain by tapping new sources of labor. In 1929 and 1930 France signed migration treaties with Yugoslavia, Rumania, and Austria which gave official backing to new missions controlled by the SGI.[89] As a result, immigration became increasingly Balkanized. Although the core nationalities (Italians, Poles, Spaniards, and Belgians) constituted 88 percent of the immigrant in 1926, by 1929 they formed only 76 percent and by 1930 only 72 percent.[90] The balance was composed of increasingly large groups of Yugoslavs,

Rumanians, and other nationalities. If the depression had not intervened, even greater ethnic diversity would have resulted. The French would have recruited workers from increasingly less developed nations, ever further from its frontiers, even Arabs and blacks. The culmination of this trend, however, had to wait until the Fourth Republic and the contemporary period.

The 1920s closed an era in which laissez-faire principles guided international migrations. Economic factors increasingly were supplanted by politics in determining population movements. Not only were the interests of employers (and labor) in the receiving countries articulated through the state, but the labor-supplying nations became involved with the fate of their expatriated citizens. French employers utilized their government to facilitate immigration on favorable terms in order to meet their demand for labor and to counteract the pressures of advanced nations like Italy. This trend was evident in 1919, when the French government signed a migration treaty with Poland.

Yet it would be barely a decade before Poland would adopt the methods of Italy. Inevitably, as migrations became politicized, the French had to bargain at the state level with supplier nations. No longer could the employer, backed by his nation state, exercise full hegemony over the immigrant worker. The labor-exporting states became the defenders of their citizens abroad, even if they were less interested in the emigrants' personal fates than in using them to enhance their nation's prestige and economic advantage. Ironically, often authoritarian and nationalist regimes, more then the labor movement, represented the international working class in France. Yet the effectiveness of this effort was limited. Labor suppliers lacked the receiving nations' advantage: there were many nations seeking buyers of their surplus labor and few markets for them. If the French were frustrated by the interference of Italian and Polish nationalists, they had the advantage of moving to other sources.

Finally, how does one assess the affect of this complex politicized climate on the individual migrant? If he was increasingly "protected" by his home government, this support often contradicted his economic and even political interests. The migrant seeking economic and political freedom was less able to find it in this new worlf of international migrations.

VI   Foreign Labor in a Period of

Growth

WHAT distinguished immigration after World War I in France was the role of the state and business organization: beyond the push and pull of the labor market and population, the individual immigrant was manipulated by the agencies of the French state, corporate business, and his or her home government. Each migration was affected by a different mix of these three agencies which competed for control. This pattern seems particularly applicable to the Poles and Italians. Yet, by the end of the post-war period of growth (1931), of all the immigrants in the French labor force only 30 percent came from Italy and 18 percent from Poland. In fact the foreign work force was Balkanized with thirteen nationalities which each comprised at least one percent of that labor force.[1]

Some of these nationalities lacked the influence of their home governments, for example, French subjects from North Africa or stateless refugees from Russia or Armenians from Turkey. Despite France's negative reaction to colonial and refugee labor during the war, the shortages of labor in the 1920s made it impossible for French employers to dispense with them entirely. As important, workers from several of the bordering nations entered France with little organized encouragement and minimal regulation. Much as before the war, they were attracted to jobs in the economies of the frontier regions or were drawn to the diverse labor market of the capital. Moreover, while some employers, especially the coal mine operators, tried to organize and stabilize the foreign population, others had neither the resources nor the incentives to undertake this effort. Instead they relied on a loose and mobile labor market and on a plentiful supply of immigrants for their immediate and diverse manpower needs. The result was a highly complex foreign labor system, only part of which was organized, and which served the disparate needs of French employers.

Colonial and Refugee Labor

The political and economic chaos in postwar Europe and in the Mediterranean basin produced a stream of immigrants from French North Africa and refugees fleeing to France from Russia and Turkey. While colonials and refugees never constituted more than 10 percent of the foreign work force, they played an important role in the manpower program of French industry during the 1920s. After the war, controls were not liberalized for orientals as they were for the European immigrant. Employers had alternative sources of unskilled labor and they generally believed that orientals were inferior laborers; for these reasons French industry employed North Africans and Armenian refugees for the least attractive jobs. Demand for their labor also was more sensitive than that of European immigrants to economic change.

World War I brought the first sizable introduction of North Africans to France. While this category included Tunisians and Moroccans who were nationals of French protectorates, many of the available statistics included only Algerians, who were true colonial subjects. The Colonial Ministry imported 132,421 North Africans between 1916 and 1918. After the armistice, however, the state feared that French veterans would protest the competition of colonial labor; as a result the police summarily deported North Africans after raids on their neighborhoods in Paris and Marseilles.[2] Probably only about 6,000 remained by the end of 1920.[3] The government continued to isolate North Africans in special camps until at least April 1920; Algerians in Marseilles complained of arbitrary arrest and expulsion as late as January 1921.[4]

North African immigration was allowed, however, during the

expansion between 1922 and 1924. The Labor Ministry established a special colonial labor service in Marseilles in 1919, which throughout the interwar period segregated North Africans from European immigrants.[5] Algerians, especially, were pulled by the prospect of wages which were 75 percent higher in France than in Algeria. They were also pushed into the French labor market by the takeover of land by French settlers (colons) which increased 300 percent between 1901 and 1926.[6] As a result, in the 1920s, 471,330 Algerians entered France to work (see Table 10).[7]

Table 10   Algerian Migration to France, 1922–1931

| Year | Controlled entries | Controlled exits | Ration exits/entries | |
			Algerian	*Foreign*
1922	61,349			
1923	69,625	51,933	.74	.31
1924	71,426	57,467	.80	.24
1925	24,753	36,328	1.47	.31
1926	48,677	35,102	.72	.30
1927	21,472	36,073	1.68	1.40
1928	39,726	25,008	.63	.55
1929	42,948	42,227	.98	.22
1930	40,250	44,882	1.12	.20
1931	20,847	32,950	1.58	.91

Source: Michel Huber, *La population de la France pendant la guerre* (Paris: presses universitaires de France, 1931) p. 793.

Unlike the European immigrants, however, they were much more likely to repatriate as is shown by the ratios of repatriations to entries. In part, this may indicate a continued reluctance of French employers to hire Algerians for anything but temporary jobs or to retain them during a reduction in the labor force. When the Labor Ministry tried to funnel Algerians into farm jobs, the agricultural societies resisted, strongly preferring Spanish or Polish workers.[8] In several surveys of employer opinion on the value of immigrant workers, North Africans were rated lowest. Employers thought that they were physically inferior and less stable than other immigrants.[9] In fact, Algerians frequently failed the medical examinations for military conscription because their physical size and strength was often below European standards.[10]

This high rate of repatriation may also indicate another characteristic of Algerian migration: as is common with peasant populations in pre-industrial regions, Algerians often sent members of families to France for a short stint of work merely to be replaced after a few months by another family member.[11] Clearly these North Africans had little expectation of settling permanently in France. Only 3 percent of the North African immigrants in 1931 were women, a fact which suggests that male workers left their families at home and intended to return. Thus, despite the fact that nearly one half million Algerians entered France in the 1920s, only 98,153 remained by 1931.[12]

Most of the Algerians were hired by the military or by large enterprises where they were assigned the worst jobs.[13] Continuing a pattern set during the First World War, 42 percent of the North Africans were employed in military construction, while 17 percent worked in metal plants (especially auto factories); gas works, chemical plants and mines were other major employers of North Africans.[14]

Only in growth periods, when French or European immigrants could not be found for the worst jobs, were the North Africans hired. Again, Table 10 indicates the sensitivity of Algerian migration to shifts in the economy. Note the downturns in 1925, 1927, and 1930. The drop in the demand for North Africans in 1925 was paralleled by government restrictions on its supply. A decree from the Interior Ministry (September 1924) allowed North Africans to embark for France only if they possessed a validated work contract and a certificate of health. Complaints from French colons that farm labor was being drained to France for industrial work probably prompted these restrictions. Soon the colons demanded even more severe controls while the French government anticipated a new recession; thus, in August 1926, the Interior Ministry required Algerian immigrants to deposit 150 francs before embarking for France to pay for their later repatriation.[15] The sum was prohibitive for many Algerians. Immigrants from the French protectorates of Tunisia and Morocco were even more restricted.[16] North Africans circumvented the rules by passing false work contracts and visas as well as undertaking illegal landings on the French coast near Marseilles; professional labor smugglers also brought North Africans to France.[17]

French employers also found a limited supply of labor among penniless refugees: the communist victory in Russia as well as the Turkish persecution of Armenians brought a wave of refugees to Western Europe. As they had during the war, French employers seized the opportunity to hire many of these stateless people. Following the pattern of her treatment of the Greeks from 1916–1918, the French state simply issued visas in Sofia and Istanbul to these displaced persons, shipped them to Marseilles, herded them into tightly supervised camps, and, as rapidly as possible, disseminated them throughout France. Russians were employed primarily in auto and metal plants in Paris, Lyons, Le Creuset, and Lille. Although Armenians were also hired in these industries, about 18,000 remained in the south to work in the textile industry. By 1926, France had roughly 67,000 Russians and somewhat less than 45,000 Armenians. As displaced persons, they did not necessarily belong to the working class. As a result, they often quickly abandoned their unskilled jobs in order to engage in petty commerce.[18]

Unlike the Poles or Italians, employers did not aggressively recruit colonial and refugee immigrants. They served primarily to supplement the immigrant work force. They were small but significant streams which flowed into the labor reservoir required by the turbines of French capitalism. They were not permitted to move freely into and within the labor market as were the immigrants from border nations. Unlike Western European immigrants, colonials and refugees brought few skills; had no established patterns of immigration; and in most cases lacked cultural affinities to the French. Most importantly, because refugees and colonial immigrants were stateless, discrimination was inevitable. No organized power defended their dignity, freedom, and working conditions, as the Belgian, Italian, Polish, and Spanish states at least occasionally did for their citizens. In addition, French racism, especially directed against the North Africans, hampered their mobility. In a word, these "undesirables," as the French frequently called them, were used only when the well of other labor sources ran dry, but were not allowed the mobility of other immigrants.

The Persistence of Traditional Patterns of Migration

While the new organized immigration dominated France's attention during the 1920s, older streams of migrants continued as before the war to flow into the French economy. These migrations were relatively unrestricted movements of neighboring nationalities into areas adjacent to their homelands and into the Paris region. As members of well-established migrations these individuals were often aided by family ties that already existed in France. With no concerted effort to channel their labor into a few industries, they moved rather freely within regional labor markets. Many became self-employed. Yet these traditional migrations declined during the 1920s, particularly in the rapidly growing industrial regions of the north, east, and the Paris suburbs. Here an organized influx of Poles gradually supplanted traditional sources of Belgian and Italian labor.

In contrast to colonial and refugee workers, immigrants from the border regions were relatively unrestricted. Unlike Eastern Europeans, the Swiss, Luxembourgeois, and Belgians did not even need passports, while Spanish and Italian immigrants needed passports only, but not visas. Only in 1928 were any restrictions placed on the 60,000 Belgian *frontaliers*. In addition, with the significant exception of Italy, these border states did not control immigration. Only the push of low wages and unemployment at home and the pull of job opportunities in France regulated their migration.[19]

Belgians continued as they had before the war, albeit in decreasing numbers, to migrate seasonally to northern French brickworks, sugar refineries, and fruit and grain harvests. Likewise, Spanish vineyard laborers continued their yearly journey into the Hérault. Unskilled farm migrants often shifted into temporary and seasonal jobs in industry, especially in construction. As a floating population often hired for short-term jobs, the frontier nationalities tended to gravitate toward Paris or provincial urban centers like Lille, Marseilles, and Lyons.[20] At the same time these older migrations continued to flow into a vast number of skilled occupations, such as forestry, leather crafts, masonry, and quality furniture and clothing trades, which had become lost arts to the French.[21]

Despite the continuing importance of migrations from border regions, they declined proportionately to more distant migrations in the 1920s (see Table 11).[22] The share of neighbor nationalities in the alien workforce in France dropped by over 30 percent between 1911 and 1931. This was due to the large influx of Eastern Europeans, especially Poles, and to the improved economic climate in Western Europe, which gave these peoples alternatives to migration. This was particularly true of the Belgians (60 percent decline) and the Germans (78 percent decline). On the other hand, the less developed economy of Spain resulted in a slightly increased proportion of Spanish workers in France by the end of the 1920s.

If the prewar pattern of spontaneous migration was on the wane, this trend was hardly universal. Traditional patterns of immigration remained important in Paris and in many southern departments. Even in an age when French employers were increasingly committed to corporate and state-controlled labor migrations, many businesses still required an unregulated pool of immigrant workers. Petty

Table 11 The Declining Impact of Border Nations on Alien Manpower in France, 1911–1931

Nationality	1911		1921		1931	
	No.	%	*No.*	%	*No.*	%
Border migration						
Belgian	169,480	24.9	203,140	22.2	156,870	9.8
German	63,575	9.3	35,795	3.9	38,840	2.4
Italian	258,027	37.9	279,351	30.5	475,006	29.7
Spanish	61,136	9.0	146,296	16.0	194,200	12.1
Swiss	46,938	6.9	55,383	6.0	60,846	3.8
Total	599,156	88.1	719,965	78.6	925,762	57.8
Non-Border migration						
Polish			28,438	3.1	287,002	17.9
Other	81,094	11.9	168,311	18.4	386,460	24.2
Total alien labor	680,250		910,714		1,599,224	

Source: France, *Résultats statistiques du recensement général de la population* 1, no. 5 (1931), 68, or (1936), 66.

capitalists, especially in the still large artisan sector, could not afford to recruit labor over long distances and instead required a ready supply of cheap immigrants whom they could hire through personal connections or off the street without burdensome restrictions. This pool of labor formed spontaneously, as it had before the war in Paris and along the frontiers where immigrants were attracted to the diverse employment and economic mobility that these regions offered.

The capital had long attracted foreign workers because of its diverse cultural environment as well as its relatively high wages and varied opportunities for employment.[23] As Table 12 indicates,[24] in the city of

Table 12 Foreigners in the Economy of the Seine, by Occupation, 1926

| Occupation | Paris | | Suburbs | |
	Self-employed & employers	*Workers*	*Self-employed & employers*	*Workers*
Food processing	298	4,539	151	2,468
Clothing	6,043	14,508	1,281	1,517
Leather	2,325	7,320	516	956
Wood	1,325	7,948	429	4,104
Chemicals	103	2,393	135	8,000
Printing	402	5,383	88	496
Metal work	1,753	20,164	844	30,623
Construction	1,371	23,506	1,071	8,084
Goods handling	110	1,039	1,457	656
Transport	318	2,674	298	2,171
Food commerce	2,760	3,032	918	1,037
Restaurant/hotel	1,674	8,678	766	614
Entertainment	1,166	413	418	97
Commerce	7,530	14,700	968	1,585
Finance	794	4,837	41	60
Free professions	10,256	4,434	971	1,031
Domestic service	435	17,623	168	3,041
Public service		2,830		825
Other	2,477	4,448	1,580	5,121
Total	41,140	150,469	12,100	72,486

Source: Georges Mauco, *Les étrangers en France* (Paris: A. Colin, 1932), p. 308.

Paris, immigrants competed successfully in a number of occupations; in no industry did more than 12 percent of the foreign labor force concentrate. Moreover, a strikingly large percentage of these immigrants were self-employed or employers (23 percent in 1926, which was high for the city, for almost half of the foreign employers in France were farmers).[25] Many participated in the traditional artisan sector, which was still significant in Paris: they were skilled craftsmen making quality watches, shoes, clothing, and fine woodwork. Others were entertainers, hotel personnel, taxi drivers, and petty merchants. Paris attracted not only immigrants from the bordering nations but also eastern Europeans. Of the 22,800 foreign craftsmen in Paris, 4,100 were Russian, 2,600 were Polish, and 7,600 were natives of Balkan nations, many of the Jewish religion. Immigrants sent for members of their families and villages to work in these foreign-owned enterprises in Paris.[26] Clearly Paris continued to be a center of traditional spontaneous immigration, largely because Paris remained a city of small businesses and artisans.

By contrast, the suburbs of Paris attracted a different type of immigrant. The suburban immigrants were concentrated in only a few industries, especially metal goods which comprised 35 per cent of the immigrant workforce. Only 14 percent of these foreigners were self-employed or employers. The vast majority were unskilled laborers drawn to jobs in the thriving heavy industry of the suburbs of Billancourt, St. Denis, Aubervilliers, and Puteaux.[27] This reflects an economy very different from the city of Paris—the predominance of modern large scale industries. Clearly, it was the newer pattern of the suburbs which was gaining ground in the 1920s over the older immigration of Paris: while the proportion of alien workers in the suburbs grew 146 percent between 1921 and 1931, it increased only 46 percent in Paris.[28]

These labor pools which formed in the Seine quite naturally suited employers who were thus able both to select their personnel with greater choice and to weaken the bargaining position of labor. Yet, as will be discussed in the next chapter, this also created tensions with the French work force who had to face the immigrant competition. This concentration of often intermittently employed immigrants also led to the kind of social problems familiar to contemporary American cities with their black and hispanic populations. While a large influx of foreign labor into a complex and burgeoning Parisian job market had obvious economic advantages, it posed also the threat of labor unrest and the necessity of policing and pacifying an unstable foreign population.

Employers in the frontier regions had, like businesses in the Seine, an easy access to immigrants. By 1931, southeastern departments had exceptionally high percentages of immigrants (e.g., Alpes-Maritimes with 28 percent and Bouches-du-Rhône with nearly 23 percent). The same was true of departments facing the Pyrénées (e.g. Pyrénées-Orientales with almost 16 percent). France's northeastern industrial frontier also drew on a large pool of workers from Italy, Germany, and Belgium. This was particularly true of Moselle (19 percent immigrant), Meurthe-et-Moselle (17 percent) and the Nord (11 percent).[29]

Like the capital, these frontier regions had long been magnets for a relatively spontaneous migration; and, as a result, aliens had penetrated deeply into the class and occupational structure of these regions. This pattern was evident especially in the south where short-distance migration of Italians and Spaniards still dominated. For example, in the Bouches-du-Rhône, generations of Italians had migrated into the port of Marseilles: as a result, 32 percent of the foreign work force had penetrated the employer and self-employed classes by 1931 (see Table 13).[30]

Another effect of spontaneous immigration was the rather wide occupational distribution of foreigners in the Bouches-du-Rhône. Reflecting the impact of the port of Marseilles, 16 percent of the foreign labor force or 13,320 was employed in the shipping industry, primarily on the docks. Other important concentrations were in construction (9 percent), agriculture (10.6 percent), chemicals (8.7 percent), and metal goods (6.3 percent). Another striking feature of immigrants in the Bouches-du-Rhône was that 12.3 percent worked in commerce, often as petty tradesmen or cafe owners, 38 percent above the national average for foreigners. While the Italian work force predominated (52 percent of the immigrants), substantial numbers of Spaniards (13 percent), North Africans (7.3 percent) and other nationalities floated into this cosmopolitan region.[31]

A rather different southern border department was the Pyrénées-Orientales. By 1931 this land-locked and underdeveloped region on the Iberian frontier attracted mostly Spanish manpower (89 percent) and a near majority (48 percent) worked in agriculture. Here too, effects of an older migration is evident: 41 percent were self-employed or employers of labor; this also indicates a degree of economic mobility for individual immigrants.[32]

For both southern departments we see signs of the economic integration of the foreign work force. While, as Table 13 indicates, the foreigners were much more concentrated in the working class than was the labor force of the entire department, immigrants more closely approximated the class distribution of these two departments than did the alien work force in the French economy as a whole (compare ratios, especially in the employer and self-employed categories). This suggests that in these frontier regions, immigrants from neighboring nationalities would experience the earliest and most thorough assimilation (see chapter VIII).

Yet the older pattern of short-distance individual immigration into border regions declined in the 1920s relative to long-distance and organized immigration. In a pattern which parallels that of migrations to the United States a generation earlier, the older migratory streams to France from neighboring countries dried up. As immigrant families acquired property and economic knowledge in France, they moved out of the wage-earning classes, or, at least, low status laboring jobs. While this had not yet become a problem for employers in the south, largely because economic development lagged in this region, in the rapidly growing regions of the northeast, traditional sources of foreign labor were clearly insufficient. As we have already detailed, an organized immigration of Poles supplemented these workers. This contributed to a foreign population more concentrated in a few industries and less mobile than in the southern departments. An analysis of two departments will illustrate this phenomenon.

In the Nord, despite a long history of migration from nearby Belgium, nearly a third of the immigrant work force was Polish by 1931. This reflected ten years of organized immigration into mining and agriculture. Still 18 percent of foreign manpower worked in textiles; this industry was mostly supplied by Flemish workers who had been attracted to jobs in Lille, Roubaix, and Tourcoing since the mid-nineteenth century. Nevertheless, even more immigrants worked in mining (18 percent) and a substantial number in the metal goods

Table 13 A Comparison of Economic Status Profiles, by Department, 1931

Economic Status	Foreign %	French & foreign	Ratio
Bouches-du-Rhône			
Employer	9	15	0.60
Self-employed	23	19	1.21
White-collar	10	21	.48
Blue-collar	54	42	1.29
Unemployed	4	3	1.33
Pyrénées-Orientales			
Employer	23	39	.59
Self-employed	18	16	1.13
White-collar	9	13	.69
Blue-collar	49	32	1.53
Unemployed	0.1	0.1	1.00
Nord			
Employer	7	13	.54
Self-employed	6	10	.60
White-collar	5	13	.38
Blue-collar	79	62	1.27
Unemployed	3	2	1.50
Moselle			
Employer	3	16	.19
Self-employed	3	7	.43
White-collar	11	19	.58
Blue-collar	81	56	1.45
Unemployed	2	2	1.00
France			
Employer	10	29	.34
Self-employed	10	13	.77
White-collar	9	14	.64
Blue-collar	68	42	1.62
Unemployed	4	2	2.00

Source: France, *Résultats statistiques du recensement général de la population,* 1, no. 5 (1931), 206, 207, 59, and 1, no. 3 (1931), 174–177.

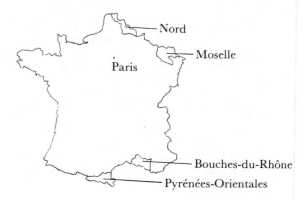

Nord

Moselle

Paris

Bouches-du-Rhône

Pyrénées-Orientales

industry (10 percent), both of which were growth industries in the 1920s and drew the eastern European workers.[33] In contrast to the pattern of the Bouches-du-Rhône (see Table 13), few immigrants were able to rise out of the working class.

In the eastern department of the Moselle, we see an even greater deviation from the traditional pattern of border region migration: despite its proximity to Italy and Germany, it was the Poles with 30 percent that dominated the foreign work force in 1931. Italians trailed with 26 percent and the Germans constituted only 21 percent. Even a smaller proportion than in the Nord had left the ranks of the working classes (19 percent) and a majority worked in the related industries of mining (30 percent) and metallurgy (22.4 percent).[34] Finally, as the ratios in Table 13 show, the immigrant work force deviated sharply from the class distribution of Moselle as a whole. This suggests a minimum of social integration in French society. Clearly, traditional immigration from the frontier nations into the border departments was declining in significance. Employers replaced Belgians and Italians with Poles. Along with this new foreign worker went a pattern of economic segregation.

The Imperative of Informal Migration

Despite a trend toward a more rationalized foreign work force, especially in the modernizing sectors, definite limits to change remained. First, many industries, especially those employing seasonal labor, had neither the resources nor the incentive to organize an immigration. Yet these industries, often far from traditional streams of migrants,[35] had critical needs for foreign labor. Second, many companies with large resources, such as those in the steel industry, had no incentive to complete the rationalization process by stabilizing their foreign manpower. In both cases, employers relied on informal substitutes for a rationalized manpower program: labor contractors, pirating immigrants from other employers, and ultimately the relatively free flow of foreign workers into France.

Labor subcontractors, both foreign and French, recruited and managed work teams of Italians and Spaniards, who formed an essential supplement of seasonal labor for large construction projects; these labor gangs did hard physical work extending railways, building canals, digging subways in Paris, and laying tramways in other cities. They also were essential for France's extensive program of military fortifications (for example, the Maginot Line).[36] Other industries, such as cement, plaster, and stone quarrying also used temporary teams of immigrants. Few French could be found for this hazardous and often only temporary employment. Because they were usually distant from urban labor markets, these industries were dependent upon the subcontractor for skilled labor. In many stone quarries Italians and Spaniards formed the bulk of the skilled cutters and shapers. In a survey of 220 brick factories cromprising about 8,550 workers, only 33 percent were immigrant in the off-season, but during peak periods that proportion rose to 65 percent.[37]

The *unstables,* as the French called them, migrated frequently between France and their home villages. Typically, they worked in the warm months for a subcontractor and migrated south in the winter. Seasonal but regular migration was institutionalized when in 1922 the French government granted immigrants annual leaves of absence, during the "dead season" in winter. This eliminated any red tape when the employer recalled them.[38]

French trade unions in Paris, Armentières, and Lyons complained when employers brought these teams of foreign workers into construction sites. Because these gangs moved from job to job as a group under the control of a subcontractor, they were isolated from the labor organizer. Usually they worked ten or twelve hour shifts and thus ignored the eight-hour-day law. Pay rates (obscured by the piece-rate system) were well below local standards. Subcontractors sometimes profited from the immigrants' ignorance of local wages and took a share of the team's earnings. These workers were often housed in flimsy temporary barracks near the work site and fed in company canteens.[39] Under this system alien workers could be relatively easily maintained and dismissed. When their work was complete, they could be laid off, transferred to other jobs as a part of a work team, or simply forced to disperse. For example, in March 1925 at Amiens, although 2,000 foreign laborers had just been discharged from a public works project the prefect reported no noticeable unemployment in the area.[40] Having no roots or permanent residences in the district, the unemployed foreign workers quickly moved on.

The subcontract system not only created a flexible and cheaply maintained labor force, but guaranteed its segregation from the French. Foreign *unstables* were effectively isolated from the regular French workers by both working conditions and outlook. This was at least suggested by one disgruntled French unionist, who complained that

> foreign workers accept almost anything. They have no ambition, no desire to elevate themselves. We French want to be as well dressed as our employers; we want an easy life; we try to be well housed. The foreign workers accept being housed in barracks and fed in canteens.[41]

Not only were they different in culture and language from their French fellow workers, but they had the outlook of a migrant: a willingness to forego the "civilized" living standards of the French for the opportunity to work and save for their return home.

In Paris also the subcontract system was employed. It sometimes took the form of "yellow unions." In 1927 the Confédération national du travail and La Liberté du travail recruited foreign and colonial workers as strike-breakers, according to the Paris Prefect of Police. He reported that these organizations masqueraded as mutual-aid societies but in fact were illegal placement services, directly subsidized by big construction companies.[42]

Other industries also took advantage of pools of available foreign labor to avoid recruiting immigrants abroad. Even before the war the glass industry had become notorious for employing immigrant children as apprentices, often under illegal conditions.[43] *Le Peuple* reported in 1930 that Portuguese youths, who entered France under contract as woodsmen, were immediately diverted to glass factories in Bordeaux.[44] In 1929 recruiters promised Polish miners a bounty of seventy francs per month to apprentice their children to glass works in the Somme, although they received only forty francs.[45] Some petty manufacturers, especially in the textile and clothing industries of Marseilles and Paris, hired laborers from the mass of illegal and thus powerless immigrants, who worked under hazardous and illegal conditions.[46]

Some companies hired the immigrants recruited by others. Textile firms, often within commuting distance from stable immigrant centers in the northern mine fields, pilfered the daughters of Polish miners for so-called apprenticeships, much to the annoyance of the mine operators. As a result, they avoided both the cost of recruiting and housing their manpower.[47] Many employers lured foreign workers from companies which had recruited and transported them to France. Only about 20 percent of the unmarried immigrants who had entered France under a contract in 1926 completed a year of service to the company which had recruited them. Most of them broke their contracts for other jobs. The chief of the departmental placement office for Isère estimated that in 1923 only 60 percent of the immigrants entering Isère under work contract ever picked up their identity cards.[48]

Being able to obtain a cheap, tractable work force simply through the looseness of the foreign labor market, many employers had no interest in a rigidly controlled foreign labor system. Despite the trend toward a more rationalized manpower program in France, a free, informal, and indeed often illegal market for alien labor flourished. It fed upon the half-hearted efforts of government to regulate the foreign influx and lived off the labor recruited by organized business, especially the SGI. The massive influx of alien workers in the 1920s engendered opposition from those seeking social stability in France; yet those who relied on this unrestrained influx of labor helped to retard pressure for greater regulation (see chapter VIII).

Even employers who used the organized sector of the foreign labor system, those who were the clients of the SGI or patronized the government's job placement service, did not always complete the rationalization process: they did not attempt to stabilize their immigrant manpower. By their failure to reduce turnover, they contributed to the loose market of alien workers. Good examples are the iron mining and basic steel industries of the Lorraine and the hydroelectric industries of the Alpine region.[49] The ferrous metal industries relied heavily on alien laborers, especially in the Briey and Longwy districts of Moselle and Meurthe-et-Moselle. Unlike construction or farming, they had the resources to undertake a program of stabilization. Yet, with a few exceptions, these industries did not follow the path of the coal operators and build houses, encourage the immigration of families, or launch a cultural program to root the immigrant to the mill or mining pit.[50] Instead single male immigrants were recruited and housed in overcrowded company barracks. Far from encouraging stability, these living quarters helped to create a transitory labor force. The Commission of Hygiene in Meurthe-et-Moselle reported in 1928 that barracks lacked windows and the beds of Moroccan workers had no sheets or blankets. Labor inspectors (Labor Ministry) noted in 1926 that twenty miners in Longwy were lodged in company barracks adequate for only two. A government study of miners' housing in the Meurthe-et-Moselle in 1928 revealed only 10,904 of 37,904 immigrants were sheltered in family apartments; 10,073 were housed in dormitories, while the rest found shelter with other families or in attics, barns and other usually unsuitable private lodgings.

Not only poor housing but inferior pay and working conditions stimulated turnover: a CGT organizer from Moselle reported in 1928 that Polish iron miners were promised twenty-eight frances per day in their contracts but earned barely seventeen francs because they were placed on a piece rate. This was much below prevailing wage standards in French industry for unskilled labor (about twenty-seven francs). Immigrants at the iron mine of Sainte Marie complained that they received only 351 francs of the 460 earned per month after the company deducted numerous dues and insurance premiums. Some found themselves endebted to the company store as a result of high prices. Furthermore, immigrants faced an extraordinarily harsh management which since the turn of the century had adopted a sink-or-swim policy for new workers: companies provided little training in the difficult work of mining and refining iron and steel. In fact few workers could endure the drudgery of deep mining which characterized the region. Finally, immigrants had many alternative job opportunities if conditions in the mines or mills of French Lorraine were too difficult: they could flee the short distance across the frontier to heavy industry in Germany or Luxembourg; they might find work in the construction of French military fortifications; or they could dash off to Paris or other large job markets and compete with the French for work.[51]

As a result of these conditions, the Lorraine bled immigrants over the body of France. For example, at a large iron complex in Moselle, immigrant terminations reached 2,020 for an average of 2,690 employed in 1928. This is a turnover rate of 75 percent (in contrast to a rate of 12 percent for the French). In a metallurgical plant in the Calvados, 3,287 of the 4,000 aliens hired in 1928 terminated before the end of a year.[52]

Not only the iron and steel industry but chemical, aluminium, and other heavy industries had similar problems with retaining foreign labor. For example, in the hydroelectric-based chemical, paper, and metals industries of the Alpine regions, immigrants continually came and went. Since the turn of the century, industries thrived in the valleys and moutains slopes in Isère, Alpes-Maritimes, and Hautes-Alpes. Because of the sparse native population and large requirements of labor, immigrants were essential. Of the 110,000 factory workers in the Alpine departments in 1928, 35,000 were foreign (31,000 of whom were Italian).

Labor recruitment was a major and constant management chore. Companies not only sought workers from Italy, but recruited North Africans and refugees from Marseilles. By 1925, the hydro-electric companies were even hiring Poles from the SGI. Yet like the iron and steel industry they had no serious program designed to stabilize this manpower. Although these industries maintained fixed plants and regularly operated them, because of their reliance on water power, they reached optimal output only in the warm months. During the winter many of the immigrants were laid off, creating an unstable work force. Partly because of the seasonal nature of the industry, housing was rudimentary (e.g., old army barracks continued to be used a decade after the war); few immigrants brought their families; and thus turnover was substantial.[53]

The onerous nature of the work and seasonal employment may explain part of the instability of foreign labor in these industries. Yet employers had little incentive to reduce turnover. The revolving factory door kept wages low, for few workers remained long enough to earn raises. High turnover rates also discouraged unionization which had practically no success in the Lorraine or Alpine region.[54]

Furthermore, these industries had an alternative to a stabilization policy for creating docile and productive workers: a program of mixing nationalities. It had already been advocated in 1917 by the War Ministry's Colonial Labor Service as a way to "diminish the cause of strikes and to facilitate an exact assessment of the value of each worker."[55] Following this advice in 1926, an auto company employing 13,537 workers used 4,366 immigrants or 32 percent of the total. This company relied heavily on Arabs and refugees; their numbers varied with the plant. From 2.1 percent to 3.4 percent of all workers were Armenian, 6.9 percent to 9.1 percent were Arab, and 5 percent to 13 percent were Russian, while only 2.1 percent to 5 percent were Italian. In 1925 the iron mines of the Lorraine were almost equally divided between Italians (12,179) and Poles (11,574). Indeed, even in the coal mines, the Poles in 1925 constituted only 61.5 percent (72,969) of the foreign miners. The others included 11,945 Germans, 10,245 Italians, 5,481 Spaniards, 6,449 Belgians, 5,785 Czechoslovaks, 3,079 Moroccans, and 1,696 Hungarians.[56] In 1924 R. Blanchard, in *Les Alpes économiques*, gave a colorful description of the impact of mixing nationalities in the Alpine industries:

> When one rises in the morning, one encounters an odd assortment of swarthy men: some wear a turban or a fez; some are blinking Chinese; others, Spaniards with blue chins or Russians still wearing the uniform of the Czar, all mixed in with French and Italian peasants.[57]

He observed that this multi-national work force helped to prevent strikes because "peoples with such marked differences cannot communicate." Another inexpensive means of assuring managerial authority was for employers associations (such as the Association française des industries alpines and Comité des forges) to agree to blacklist foreigners who broke contracts.[58] In the potash industry an immigrant could secure a new job only by presenting a satisfactory reference from his first employer.[59] This provided a cheap substitute for a policy of family housing to stabilize immigrants. Finally, for all their complaints about labor instability, many employers were apparently willing to tolerate high turnover rates if new labor was readily available. For this reason employers pressed the government to expand the foreign sources of labor.

Parallel to the organized market of immigrant labor, there functioned a free market: seasonal, backward, and marginal industries relied on spontaneous migrations of foreigners from border nations to meet their demands. Others made use of labor contractors or immigrants recruited by their competitors. This unorganized and sometimes illegal alien labor market was vital to the success of a highly diverse French capitalism. The availability of this labor discouraged employers from making the investments necessary to satisfy and thus retain this foreign manpower.

The past three chapters have analyzed the foreign labor system which emerged in the 1920s. They have stressed the innovative factors, especially the mix of agencies which impinged upon the new immigration: the French state, organized business, and foreign governments. Yet this chapter showed an even more complex picture: the use of stateless refugee and colonial labor as well as the survival of a relatively unregulated migration. All of this suggests an immigration which served a highly diverse market and accommodated different managerial strategies. The foreign labor system was not always satisfactory to employers; for many, foreign governments had too much influence over their citizens in France; for others, immigrants were too free to seek their economic advantage. Yet the system gave employers most of what they wanted in a complex blend of organization, regulation, and laissez-faire. This was the final result of the failure of an integrated or corporatist immigration policy in the 1920s.

But this system was far less pleasing to other elements of French society. Labor, the principle losers in the struggle over immigration policy in the early twenties, naturally feared the influx of foreign labor which the government encouraged and business, to a degree, organized. Trade unions had hardly abandoned their hope for a role in policy making. They continued to seek guarantees against the competition of cheap foreign labor. Other critics saw in the flood of new immigrants the makings of serious social problems: they feared the formation of alien cultural enclaves in France, the emergence of a criminal society from the uprooted immigrants, and the threat of communist influence within this exploited laboring class. Instead of a narrow manpower approach to immigration, these critics advocated a program of assimilation and social control in order to reduce these social problems. For both labor and the advocates of assimilation, the state was the instrument of reform. The bureaucracy attempted throughout the 1920s to accommodate these groups, in a kind of informal corporatism, without, at the same time, threatening business interests. It was a formidable task.

VII   Acceptance without Integration: Regulating Immigrants in the 1920s

A LARGE and rapid flood of foreign workers into a community often leads to conflicts with native labor. French workers reflected this hostility in the industrial regions of the East in the thirty years before World War One when an essentially unregulated influx of alien labor competed with Frenchmen. Yet, despite the doubling of the percentage of foreigners in the decade after the war, native opposition to the immigrant was muted, sporadic, and strictly localized. How can we understand this anomaly?

Two broad and interrelated changes in the labor relations system after the war may explain much of the greater toleration of foreign labor: 1) the trade unionists, both more numerous and more disciplined after the war, rejected confrontation. Instead, the dominant reformist wing, which controlled the CGT, supported massive immigration while lobbying the government to limit and channel it. The CGTU, the communist-influenced minority wing of the labor movement, denounced regulation but also discouraged confrontation. Instead they favored organizing foreign workers into unions and opposed discrimination. 2) The state attempted to minimize direct competition for jobs between French and foreign workers. Although its regulations usually served the interests of employers and were not allowed to impede economic growth, the state in fact controlled immigration in order to minimize potential French labor unrest.

French Unions and Foreign Labor

The war brought an end to the ambiguous attitude of French labor: until 1914, unions expressed a formal solidarity with international workers and with it a commitment to organizing their foreign-born comrades; yet they often evidenced a real hostility to immigrant workers when they invaded local job markets. During the Union Sacrée of the war, the CGT leadership briefly tasted the fruits of collaboration with business and government. They had adopted a "politics of presence" rejecting the old program of class confrontation for a nationalist policy of cooperation. They defended massive immigration and discouraged local union opposition to alien labor in the name of French economic growth. In exchange the CGT demanded a share of power with government and business in regulating the size and distribution of foreign labor.

Léon Jouhaux and other reformist leaders of the CGT fought the internal opposition to their cooperative strategy, especially the communists, whom they expelled from the CGT in 1921. While weakening the unity of the labor movement, the schism allowed the CGT leadership to pursue their new policy of collaboration with French business and government.

The CGT, however, did not entirely abandon the effort to organize foreign workers and to defend their interests. In the early 1920s the Construction Federation tried to recruit formerly unionized Belgian workers employed in the repair of the North. Against nationalist opinion the CGT supported German workers' entering the old war zones to take jobs in the reconstruction. Since 1919 the CGT advocated equal pay for foreigners holding the same jobs as the French; opposed the expulsion of aliens for union activity; and supported their right to become elected union officials.[1]

Nevertheless, the CGT's organizing drive was made with little sustained effort and meager success. Not until September of 1924 did the CGT establish a national office for organizing immigrants.[2] By 1929 only about 7,500 of the over 90,000 Polish miners had joined the CGT's miners union. Perhaps as few as 15,000 Italians were enrolled in all CGT unions in 1926 from a pool of 428,221 Italian workers in France.[3]

The failure of the CGT's organizing efforts flowed from its

weakness in the industrial sector. The schism of 1921 reduced CGT membership from a conservative estimate of 1,011,913 in 1920 to about 554,896 by 1929. Further, its strength was not in industries where immigrants were concentrated but rather in the tertiary sector: government (95,028 members), teachers (66,022), and railways (70,507) in 1929. By contrast, only 11,566 construction laborers and only 16,315 metal workers belonged to the CGT. The CGT was impotent in agriculture where it had merely 1,433 members in 1929. In summary, only 29 percent of her members in this year held jobs in agriculture, mining, and industry where 71 percent (1931) of the immigrants worked.[4]

Organizing immigrants was difficult under any circumstances. French law barred foreigners from voting for or being elected to leadership positions in the unions. Language and cultural differences were an insuperable obstacle for union organizers. In some Parisian metal factories, for example, as many as twelve languages were spoken, making communication impossible.[5]

Greatly contributing to the difficulty were the attitudinal differences between immigrants and French workers. Immigrants were difficult to organize because most lacked union experience in their home countries, coming directly from peasant backgrounds. In a 1950 survey of 96 Italian construction workers (77 percent arriving before 1940), 67 percent came from rural backgrounds. In a similar study of Polish miners, only 26 percent had been miners before emigrating.[6] Mussolini's fascists destroyed independent trade unionism between 1920 and 1925, thus depriving emigrants of roots in the trade union movement.[7] Polish miners were also diverted from the CGT by the aggressive competition of the conservative Polish mutual aid society, the ZRP (see chapter IV). Furthermore, skilled Belgian and Swiss workers often belonged to strong unions back home and thus were reluctant to join French unions which provided few benefits or strike funds.[8]

Perhaps most important in explaining the difficulty of organizing alien workers was that they, like the immigrants of today, had very different views of working and living conditions in France than did union militants. Upon arrival in France Polish miners and farm workers were impressed with the high living standards in comparison to conditions in Poland. One Polish miner was amazed to see fresh fruit available, the use of coal to heat houses, and the wonder of white bread. Others were impressed with the more democratic and free social relations—the absence of police and the closer relations between worker and boss. Polish immigrants escaped the low pay and degrading working conditions of Polish agriculture for the opportunity for higher pay and greater personal freedom in the mines of France. Italian construction workers (Seine) expressed similar impressions of work in France: it was a step up from the hard life back home. A Polish miner, upon arriving in France, explained to his wife: "We are in paradise."[9] Many immigrants expected to remain in France only as long as necessary to accumulate sufficient savings to return home to buy or extend a family farm or business. As a result many were willing to work twelve or even fourteen hours daily, live in barracks, and move quickly from job to job in search of quick earnings and low living costs. This was hardly the social material of trade unionism. Given these obstacles to organizing immigrants it is not surprising that the CGT made only a token effort to recruit them.

Certainly rank-and-file French hostility to foreign workers had hardly disappeared after the war. As we have already observed (see p. 136), French unionists saw those immigrants who worked beyond the eight-hour day and accepted poor living conditions as a threat to the French labor standard. Surely not unusual was the remark of a French miner to a recent Polish immigrant: "Go back to Poland. You came here to eat our bread." Surely the French worker was hardly immune to cultural chauvinism. Italians were often called "Macaronis" and the Poles, "Boches" (because some spoke German). Polish miners reported "indifference if not hostility" from French miners when they arrived at the pits. After twenty-five years, a surprisingly low level of interaction between Poles and French miners was reported in a government study of 1950–1952. Ninety percent of ninety-four surveyed had married Poles. Few had close French friends. This lack of communication between French and alien workers doubtless contributed to rank-and-file opposition to foreign workers.[10]

The 1921 recession produced scattered protests against foreign competition, especially in the war-devastated departments.[11] Since immigration outside the old war zone was unimportant until the reconstruction was completed, widespread anti-immigrant feeling did not appear until 1924. Late that year, however, construction unions in Paris demanded a stop to immigration in the reconstruction regions because they feared that immigrants already in the old war zones would soon descend upon Paris in search of work. Other CGT unions, especially the food service and hotel workers, persistently opposed immigration and advocated strict ceilings on foreign employment.[12]

Yet these concerns did not govern leadership policy. It never deviated from Jouhaux's position, which emerged in 1917, despite the many local manifestations of anti-immigrant feeling. In fact, the CGT centralized power in the 1920s, denying autonomy to the formerly often activist locals.[13] In effect the CGT hid under a blanket the hostility of unions to immigrants. No evidence of riots or other violent confrontations between immigrants and French workers was found in a review of the press in this period.

Instead of encouraging either internationalism or confrontation, the CGT pursued its politics of presence: it lobbied for a national manpower office, through which the CGT along with business and government would make policy. The CGT was willing to trade off their support for large-scale immigration in exchange for negotiated levels of immigration into sensitive labor markets. Despite their moderation, however, the right wing political shift after 1919 and the return of economic liberalism doomed these efforts (see chapter III). Yet the CGT did not abandon its corporatist strategy.

The communist-led CGTU, created after the schism, sharply opposed this program. For several years, CGTU leaders issued confusing policy statements, e.g., in 1924 demanding controls on the immigration of unskilled workers because they were used to lower wages. By 1926, the CGTU settled into a policy of opposing all restrictions on immigrants.[14] During the ultra-left "Third Period" phase of the communist party (1927–1934), leaders proposed "open frontiers" and free individual migration rather than any government manipulation of the flow of immigrants.[15] As a result of this rejection of collaboration with the bourgeois state, the CGTU had only "class solidarity" as their line of defense against employers using the immigrant in an attack on labor standards. J. Racamond, in his report as general secretary of the CGTU in 1925, observed:

If you do not support the foreign workers they will be formed in the hands of the capitalists as a mass of labor which can be used to beat you in all the demands which you make.[16]

To this message of solidarity it was necessary to add practical measures for their defense. The CGTU miners union in 1926 advised "strong protests in cases of the repression of any foreign workers," equality in trade union rights, and the abolition of the identity card for foreigners.[17]

These efforts to win over the foreign worker, however, did not meet with success. Despite much effort, the CGTU miners' union could claim in 1925 only 2,200 Polish members or about eight percent of Polish miners. During the 1920s the communist unions declared a membership of between 10,000 to 25,000 Italian workers,[18] while 438,221 Italians were employed in France in 1926. By 1926, only forty of the 300 local unions of the CGTU had organized immigrant sections into which all foreigners were to be organized.[19]

Obviously the CGTU failed to integrate the foreign worker into the French working class. The CGTU was even weaker than the CGT (merely 370,260 members in 1928) with only a slightly better implantation than the CGT into industry and agriculture, sectors comprising 36 percent of CGTU membership in 1928.[20] Other reasons for its failure include the conservatism of many foreign workers, the indifference of the CGTU rank and file to organizing immigrants,[21] and the government's sustained repression of aliens who joined the CGTU (see chapter VIII). Instead of CGTU's ideal of international class solidarity, the CGT's nationalist policy dominated French labor from the 1920s. In fact, after 1935, when the CGTU merged with the CGT, the communists dropped their independent position.

The State Accommodates Moderate Labor

Despite the failure of corporatist politics in parliament, the French bureaucracy continued to mediate between the interests of businesses and labor. Without any legislative sanction the state used decree powers to carry out a complex immigration program. Its regulations were strongly biased in favor of business and never violated the essential needs of powerful employer groups like mining and agriculture. Yet both from fear of potential social unrest and because the demands of the CGT were largely consistent with business, the state gave labor a voice in regulating immigration in the 1920s.

An accommodation with French labor was relatively simple. In general the market and organized business tended to assure that alien workers were concentrated in the jobs which most French avoided. Regulation was required when and where this dual labor market broke down—during periods of high unemployment and in urban markets, especially Paris, where job competition was severe. Government also channeled foreign manpower into jobs disfavored by the French; this served not only the interests of domestic labor but powerful employer groups. Regulation then was a rather politically painless expedient.

In 1918 the French government made an unprecedented decision— to assume the responsibility of regulating the foreign labor market and in so doing to reduce job competition and potential social conflict. No longer was the employment market "free" and labor unrest, borne of its fluctuations, treated simply as a police matter. Central to this new function was government control over the entry of aliens into France and thus their access to her job market. The state opened and closed the frontier to labor immigration as if it were a faucet. Anticipating serious unemployment of French veterans, the Ministry of Labor's Foreign Labor Service closed the frontier to further immigration immediately after the armistice.[22] Yet because of labor shortages, it opened the faucet in January of 1920 to fill the hiring lists of construction, mining, and other employers of manual labor.[23]

This pattern of opening and closing the frontier in accordance with the labor market occurred again and again during the 1920s. In December of 1920, the Foreign Labor Service shut off most new labor immigration in anticipation of the recession of 1921. The minister of the interior used his police power to deport immigrants who lacked work papers, while the prefects appealed to large enterprises to lay off foreign workers before placing the French on furlough.[24] Again in March of 1922, in response to encouraging economic signs and the massive needs for labor for the reconstruction of the war zones, all restrictions were lifted. However, as reconstruction funds dried up and economic growth sagged in late 1924 and 1925, a surplus of unskilled laborers and construction workers developed. As a result the Foreign Labor Service again curtailed immigration. The most expendable labor, that of North Africa, was also limited in late 1924. The same pattern of restriction took place in December of 1926, shortly before the 1927 recession, to be followed by a return to open immigration between 1928 and 1930. Figure 1 indicates the close correlation between growth and the magnitude of immigration.[25]

Figure 1 Production Index* Compared with Controlled Immigration, 1920–1937

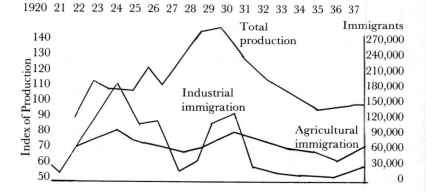

*1913=100

Source: *Bulletin du Ministère du travail* (January–March 1936), p. 25, (July–September 1936), p. 290, and (January–March 1938) p. 17.

Of course, this relationship could be explained by the market. Demand for foreign labor would decrease during recessions, hence the decline in immigration. Yet government restriction of immigration during general recessions may also have blocked unemployed foreigners from seeking jobs in France or prevented employers from importing desperate immigrants willing to work at substandard wages. Government restrictions mollified labor competition during recessions when it was most visible.

A second method of limiting competition was to direct foreign workers into the least desirable jobs. The Foreign Labor Service had several means of channeling foreign workers: first, it was empowered to reject the entry of immigrants hired by private recruiters. The Foreign Labor Service (at the Ministry of Labor) reviewed all work contracts in order to exclude immigrants from entering France to take jobs for which French applicants were readily available. Second, the Foreign Labor Service maintained a string of job offices along the frontier to provide jobs for immigrants seeking legal jobs in France. Similar offices, located in all major cities in France where unemployed aliens gathered, also found jobs for foreign workers. These offices provided jobs which often could not be filled at departmental placement offices or which officials knew attracted few French workers (e.g., unskilled jobs in mining, construction, and building materials). Foreign workers applied for these jobs because the job offices automatically granted them work permits necessary to live in France legally.[26] Between 1921 and 1930 the Foreign Labor Service channeled some 1,345,093 aliens into jobs (see Table 14).[27] The occupational distribution is highly revealing. Some 20 percent of this total were sent to iron or coal mines while another 23 percent went into construction. Note, however, that less than 2 percent of labor in France (1926) were miners and 3.5 percent, construction workers. Many immigrants avoided regulation by entering France as tourists and obtaining permits after finding jobs.[28] Yet most immigrants were relegated to a secondary work force.

Table 14 Alien Manpower Regulated by the Foreign Labor Service, by Occupation, 1921–1930

Occupation	No. of immigrants	% of total
Iron mining	112,928	8.4
Coal mining	167,242	12.4
Metal work	126,746	9.4
Construction	319,230	23.7
General labor	224,112	16.7
Agriculture	115,138	8.6
Other	279,697	20.8
Total	1,345,093	100.0

Source: *Bulletin du Ministère du travail* (1921–1931).

The leadership of the CGT completely agreed with this policy. Although the CGT did not participate in the decision-making process of the Foreign Labor Service, this agency made regulations with their approval and even under their pressure. A good example is the government's response to the recession of 1927. As a result of the revaluation of the franc in August 1926, which raised prices for French exports, the government expected a recession. Indeed, the index of production dropped from 126 in 1926 (1913=100) to 100 in 1927. The government anticipated the need to shut off the flow of immigrants before the full impact of the recession translated into a sharp increase in French unemployment. By mid-December the Foreign Labor Service was already rejecting foreign work contracts.[29] Only in early January 1927, did the CGT mobilize its forces sufficiently to send a delegation to the minister of labor, Pierre Laval, demanding that he restrict new immigration. Laval could claim that just such a policy had been already introduced since mid-December. Furthermore, Laval promised the anxious trade union leaders that unemployed foreigners in France were to be sent to jobs and regions in which there was no unemployment; if this was not possible, the minister of labor told the CGT delegation, "action was to be taken to encourage their repatriation."[30] The Labor Ministry also won the support of CGT construction workers in Paris when it promised them that it would encourage immigrants in this field to accept jobs in the provinces or to repatriate.[31] This policy was systematically applied by the Foreign Labor Service's placement office in Paris. In 1927, 85 percent of the 9,486 immigrants who applied for jobs at this office were sent at least one hundred kilometers from Paris. The Prefecture of Police of Paris encouraged employers to follow this same policy. Reportedly shoe, furniture, metallurgical, and other industries sent immigrant employees not needed in their Paris plants to provincial factories or "had them returned home."[32] The government made serious and well-publicized efforts to reduce the competition of foreign labor, especially in the sensitive urban market of the Seine during this major recession.

The government's goal was in part to placate the CGT. However, its regulations were also consistent with the needs of employers: the Foreign Labor Service's actions reduced the costs of unemployment benefits to be paid to foreigners. Indeed the Ministry of Labor insisted that even qualified recipients of unemployment compensation be sent whenever possible to jobs which had no French applicants instead of being granted aid.[33] While the government attempted to save French workers from foreign competition, it was also sparing French taxpayers the burden of social expenditures for indigent immigrants. Furthermore, these same policies also meant the return of many immigrants laid off in the cities to their original employers in the mines and farms of provincial France.[34] The recession was an opportunity for the government to redistribute immigrants to suit French employers' economic needs. Finally, where this restrictive policy did not fit business desires, it was revoked. In March of 1927 sugar-beet lobbyists and representatives of the National Confederation of Agricultural Associations pursuaded the government to allow skilled farm workers to enter France. The sole condition imposed on the farm groups was that they report any movement of foreign labor out of rural areas as a guarantee that new immigrants would not further flood the urban labor market.[35]

Although the regulatory machinery was by no means directed solely toward the interests of labor, it was nevertheless an acceptable substitute for the CGT's corporatist immigration policy. Especially in the cities, the CGT embraced these controls as a way of preventing low-wage foreign labor from battering down the living standards of the urban and skilled workers whom they represented.[36] This will become clearer when we consider another regulatory mechanism—the departmental placement office—in which the unions participated directly.

Since 1915 the departmental placement offices had been the key to local control over the labor market. After the war this was the one institution which retained the principle of parity or tripartite control. Throughout the 1920s the CGT hoped to make these offices the vehicles for protecting the rights of settlement of indigenous labor—preventing employers from hiring outsiders, especially foreigners, in preference to locally unemployed French.

From October of 1920, the government gave the placement offices the power to control the hiring of immigrants. They were authorized to review the job contracts of all aliens seeking work in their departments and to issue work permits, which were required before the immigrant could obtain an identity card or residence permit. This requirement especially affected the false tourist, who entered France to seek work. In theory, the placement offices gave this authorization only if no French worker were available for the foreigner's job. The permit was to be granted only if the pay and working conditions offered to the immigrant met local standards.[37] Although aliens frequently switched jobs after obtaining an identity card (valid up to three years), and thus avoided government control, the work permit did slow down their mobility.

While the work permit seems to be still another way of guaranteeing French priority on the job market, the regulation was effective only in urban departments. First, neither immigrant farm workers nor miners needed this authorization. Further, the work permit rule was merely a formality in those departments where the placement office was run by a career official. In theory, all placement offices were to be regulated by parity commissions—representing local labor and employer groups. Yet only in those departments where labor organizations, primarily the CGT, were strong enough to insist on an active parity commission was the potential of the work authorization to control or limit foreign job seekers actually realized.[38] There is evidence that placement office directors, even without the prodding of labor on parity commissions, actively used this power to prevent immigrants from being hired at substandard conditions,[39] or when French workers were available.[40] The officials sometimes recognized that they had a responsibility not only to provide labor to French enterprise but to reduce French unemployment and to prevent a decline in the local labor standard. Yet, in those departments where labor was the strongest, especially in Paris (Seine) and Marseilles (located in the Bouches-du-Rhône), the work permit powers were clearly used to restrict access of foreigners to jobs.

In these urban departments the parity commissions were divided into subcommissions for each sensitive trade which allowed the commissions to specialize in detailed review of applications for permits. Labor and employer associations nominated commission members and often chose them from their representatives on the conseils de prud'hommes (Labor Courts). The commissions usually reflected the rather narrow interests of the skilled trades and local family enterprises.[41] The CGT, but generally not the CGTU participated on them. By the 1920s these subcommissions existed in the

Bouches-du-Rhône for the chemical and furniture industries as well as for barbers and dock workers.[42]

In the Seine the parity system developed into a major influence over the labor market of Paris. In 1929, a year of economic growth, we find that 68 percent (23,587) of the applications for work permits were approved by the commissions of the Seine placement office. Yet there were wide variations between trades. For example (see Table 15)[43], the commissions in charge of construction approved of only 39 percent of the applicants. This was a trade which showed signs of competition between the French and immigrants in the mid-1920s. Immigrants were particularly a threat to French construction workers during the "dead season" of winter.[44] Following a similar pattern were the commissions dealing with furniture workers (only 23 percent approved) and restaurant workers (22 percent), both with histories of union opposition to foreigners. On the other hand, the vast

Table 15 Immigrant Work Authorizations in the Seine, by Occupation, 1929

Commission	Work contracts authorized	% of requests authorized
Restaurant/hotel/bar	231	22
Furniture	233	23
Construction	1,473	39
Leather	199	54
Clothing	1,091	58
Bread baking	26	61
General male labor	766	66
Barbering	222	69
Electrical work	164	74
General female labor	1,942	77
Paper	314	81
Domestic service	2,813	82
Manual laborers	2,177	83
Butchers	108	85
Metal work	3,204	88
Total	14,963	68

Source: Office départemental de placement de la Seine, *Rapport au conseil général* (1930), p. 59.

majority of foreign metal workers and general laborers received permits. These obviously were not skilled trades which the French sought to protect for themselves.

The effectiveness of the commissions in restricting foreigners can be seen by noting that in 1929 a full 88 percent of the applications were approved in the departments immediately surrounding Paris and 93 percent were approved in the department of Isère (Grenoble) where, despite large numbers of foreign workers, the parity commissions were weak.[45]

The public placement offices, then, gave French unions, especially those in large cities, some veto power over foreign access to choice job markets. This bargaining structure within the job placement system gave labor unions an alternative to the local riots which pitted French against foreign workers. It also gave them an alternative to the negative demand often heard before the war for across-the-board restrictions of immigration.[46] To a limited degree the organized portion of the French working classes had gained a direct and indirect voice in the decision-making process.

A major drawback of the parity commission was, of course, that it had only local powers and was impotent in regions of significant immigration such as the Lorraine or Picardy. Since the war, the CGT favored an extension of the commissions to the national level. As described in chapter III, the parliamentary right blocked these appeals for class cooperation and no consensus on immigration policy was achieved. Yet in 1925 the Cartel des Gauches government finally gave the CGT its opportunity to practice corporatist politics by promulgating the National Manpower Council (Conseil national de la main-d'oeuvre). Its membership comprised the CGT, employer groups including the SGI, as well as job placement and immigration officials.[47] Although the council had only advisory powers dealing with national manpower problems, for the CGT it was the beginning of the longed-for national labor office. Premier Painlevé's speech opening its deliberations anticipated a significant role for the council in finding a corporatist solution to France's manpower problems. It was to:

protect workers in the fields and factories against the risk of unemployment that threatens them always in the present capricious fluctuations of the exchange rate; to give employers the security of having workers necessary for their enterprises; and to preserve and increase our population reserves especially with reference to the importance of foreign manpower.[48]

Painlevé expected that the revaluation of the artificially low franc (which was delayed until August 1926) would lead to higher unemployment and increased pressure on French business to lower costs in order to compete on the international market. In this situation the council had the contradictory duty both to protect French labor from immigrants while jobs were scarce as well as encourage employers to import more workers in order to dampen wage pressure, improve productivity, and thus enhance their competitiveness. Clearly consensus was an illusory goal.

Despite the inherent limitations of the Council, the CGT offered it a number of concrete suggestions for improving France's manpower management and protecting French labor from foreign competition.[49] The CGT targeted the problem of ineffective controls over immigration into the farming and mining sectors. This hole in the regulatory net weakened unions and probably slowed wage increases in these industries. Immigrants also fled the farms to seek jobs in urban industry and services, a trend which threatened the more unionized sectors of the economy, which the CGT represented.

In order to slow down immigration into the primary sector, the CGT proposed that the Farm Labor Service and labor exchanges (then administered by the Ministry of Agriculture) be placed under the Ministry of Labor, where the unions' interests would receive a more favorable hearing. The CGT also proposed that the immigrant miner and farm worker be required to obtain work permits.[50] In order to discourage immigrants already working in farms and mines from fleeing to the urban job markets, the CGT made two additional proposals: first, that the government provide credit for farmers to build adequate lodgings for farm workers and second, that the iron mines and steel mills of the Lorraine improve working and living standards. Both of these measures would have reduced turnover and thus spared the urban French worker the competition of the immigrant. Not surprisingly, the employers' representatives had no interest in any of these proposals which would have raised their costs and limited their freedom to employ foreign labor. To the first two proposals, the CGT met with "irreducible opposition"; to the second set, the response was merely a resolution requesting departments to set up rural housing credit offices and encouraging industrialists to "continue" to improve conditions in the Lorraine.[51]

Consensus between management and labor was possible, however, over one issue: the problem of immigrants' breaking their work contracts. Since the reconstruction period both farm and industrial employers had called for governmental controls over contract breakers.[52] Frustrated in their efforts to reduce the flow of immigrants by other means, the CGT gave its approval to a plan to compel foreigners to remain under contract.[53] This proposal, presented by the Labor Ministry to the National Manpower Council in 1925, required that immigrants work one year in the occupation for which they were first admitted to France and prohibited employers from hiring any worker before that year had expired. This measure became law in August of 1926 under the title, "Law for the Protection of National Labor," the only legislation concerning immigrants during the 1920s.[54]

Although the enforcement of this law was sporadic, its intent was to serve the concerns of almost all interested parties.[55] Agriculture, mining, and other basic industries were to be assured of a more stable foreign work force without having to pay the price of higher wages or improved working conditions. Reformist labor, already weak in the primary sector, gained at least an abatement of the spread of substandard wages and conditions to industries where it had a foothold. The limit of the term of indenture to one year was necessary because a longer period would have provoked diplomatic protests from the labor-exporting states and would have antagonized employers who sought access to the foreign labor supply in France.[56] The losers by this law were French workers in immigrant-dominated industries who had to compete with this foreign labor force; the immigrants themselves saw a further deterioration of their rights of occupational mobility and with it a loss of bargaining power against their French employers. This sacrifice of the freedom of foreign labor probably mollified class tensions within the French community. It served the purposes of groups that had otherwise few interests in common.

The CGT's support of this law as well as the web of regulation was a confirmation of a trend evident since World War I: the majority wing of organized French labor viewed immigrants not as workers to be granted rights equal to the French. Rather, immigrants were seen as tools for economic expansion, but not to be allowed equality of opportunity. While the CGT eschewed xenophobia, it also rejected the integration of foreigners into the French working class.

Social Legacy of Organized Immigration

The 1920s saw the decline of liberal immigration, a pattern which before the war produced a mobile immigrant work force but also engendered social tensions. In its place emerged a massive immigration, partially under the collective control of employers and regulated by the French state. It is now appropriate to ask: what was the social impact of this organized immigration? Clearly it led to an important shift of the alien work force toward the lower rungs of the occupational and class ladder in France. This trend helps explain reduced social tensions in France during the 1920s for it placated French labor while, at the same time, it served the interests of many employers. This decline of the economic standing of immigrants becomes clear when we compare the economics status of immigrants in 1906 (in the last suitable prewar census) with the pattern revealed in the 1931 census.

Table 16 Percentage of Foreigners in Major Social Classes, 1906 and 1931

| Economic status | % of foreigners | | % change |
	1906	1931	
Employer	1.2	2.4	100
White-collar	2.3	4.9	113
Blue-collar	4.4	11.9	170
Self-employed	3.2	5.7	78
Unemployed	5.5	12.9	40
Mean	3.0	7.4	147

Source: France, *Résultats statistiques du recensement général de la population* 1, no. 5 (1936), 58.

One basic measure of the trend toward a more proletarian foreign population is the change in the proportion of immigrants in major social classes (see Table 16).[57] While Table 16 shows that immigrants increased proportionately in all classes, the rate of growth was substantially greater in the working class. During these twenty-five years there was also a dramatic increase in the percentage of foreigners in a number of key industries, especially mining, agriculture, construction, and industrial goods (see Table 17).[58] The increasingly working-

Table 17 Percentage of Foreigners in the Labor Force, by Occupation, 1906 and 1931

Occupation	% of foreigners		% change
	1906	*1931*	*% change*
Mining	6.2	40.1	548
Metallurgy	17.8	34.8	96
Quarrying	8.7	26.1	200
Construction	10.2	24.1	132
Glass, ceramics	8.1	21.9	170
Goods handling	8.4	19.7	135
Stone/pavement work	10.2	17	66
Entertainment	11.2	16.2	45
Rubber, paper	3.6	10.7	197
Chemicals	10	14.7	47
Metal work	4.5	10.5	133
Leather	5.6	9.4	68
Personal service	4.8	8.5	77
Textiles	5.2	7.5	44
Domestic service	7.0	7.6	9
Fine metal work	4.8	7.3	52
Foods	3.8	7	84
Wood	3.3	6.8	106
Commerce	4.2	5.8	38
Clothing	5.1	5.4	5
Agriculture	.9	3.3	266
Transport	2.7	3.2	19
Banking, insurance	3.1	3	−4

Source: France, *Résultats statistiques du recensement général de la population*, 1, no. 5 (1936), 51.

Table 18 Class Distribution of Immigrant and French Workers, 1906 and 1931

Economic status	% of immigrants			% of French		
	1906	*1931*	*% change*	*1906*	*1931*	*% change*
Employer	11.7	9.6	−18	31.0	30.5	−2
White-collar	7.7	9.4	25	10.3	14.4	40
Blue-collar	56.6	67.4	19	37.5	40.2	7
Self-employed	21.9	9.8	−55	20.1	12.9	−36
Unemployed	2.1	3.6	71	1.1	2.0	82
Total	100	100		100	100	

Source: France, *Résultats statistiques du recensement général de la population*, 1, no. 5 (1931), 59.

class complexion of the foreign population in France can also be measured by comparing the change in its class distribution between 1906 and 1931 with that of the French (see Table 18).[59] The foreign population experienced a disproportionate loss of employers and the self-employed. On the other hand, there was a sharper rise in the percentage of foreign workers as compared to the French. When making the same comparison while using an occupational distribution, one observes a trend toward the concentration of immigrants in the onerous jobs of primary production (see Table 19).[60]

Table 19 Occupational Distribution of Immigrant and French Workers, 1906 and 1931

Occupation	% of immigrants			% of French		
	1906	*1931*	*% change*	*1906*	*1931*	*% change*
Agriculture	12.7	16.6	28	43.3	36.9	—15
Mining, quarrying	3.1	10.4	235	1.3	1.3	0
Industry	47.1	48.8	4	27.5	30.3	10
Transport	7.5	4.7	− 37	4.1	4.9	20
Commerce	14.3	9.7	—71	9.5	12.6	33
Free professions	3.6	2.6	—31	2.2	3.1	41
Domestic service	.4	3.4	—15	6	6.3	5

Source: France, *Résultats statistiques du recensement général de la population*, 1, no. 5 (1931), 52.

While the proportion of French employed in primary production declined or was static, the proportion of immigrants in these occupations increased sharply. The opposite happened in the tertiary sector. In the postwar period immigrants became increasingly concentrated in the working class and in basic production.

These trends were the net effect of the change in immigration patterns after World War I. Before the war, the French state and the *patronat* made little effort to organize or regulate immigration. As a result, it was relatively small, with a sizable number of skilled alien workers and self-employed entering the French economy. After the war, however, the organized efforts of business and the state channeled a much increased migration into lower working-class occupations such as farming, mining, and heavy industry. Without this organized immigration, a very different French occupational structure and economy would have resulted: the tertiary sector (or the peasant population) would have had to be smaller. Labor shortages in the mining and industrial sectors would have led to less economic growth. Furthermore, after the war, the state (and business) actively discriminated against alien labor, denying it full occupational mobility. French workers therefore were allowed to move up the class and occupational ladders, whereas aliens were held back in the race.

In effect, this organized and regulated immigration made it possible for the French to abandon many essential but objectionable jobs and enter more secure, higher paying, and less arduous occupations. One way to indicate this trend is to calculate the impact of the growth of immigration on employment in the twenty-one major occupational groups. For this purpose we found the difference between the actual numbers of French active in each industry in 1931 and the number we would have expected if the ratio of French to total employed (including aliens) in 1906 had been maintained. This number measures the degree to which immigrants (or French) had displaced their counterparts in 1931 relative to the base year of 1906. By translating this number into a percentage of the work force in each industry, one has a useful indicator of the degree to which each industry was becoming more (or less) dominated by foreigners. One might suppose that much of this displacement of the French was due to the decline of the French population (due to war and demographic stagnation) which was available to join the work force. In order to

Table 20 Occupational Displacement, 1906 and 1931

Group A (abandoned by French)	%
Mining	30
Construction	27
Metallurgy	19
Stone work	16
Entertainment	15
Quarrying	13
Glass/ceramics	9
Goods handling	7
Rubber, paper	3
Metal goods	2
Chemicals	1
Group B (favored by French)	%
Fishing	6
Free professions	5
Banking, insurance	5
Transport	4
Domestic service	4
Public industries	4
Wood	3
Printing	3
Straw-feather goods	3
Commerce	3
Textiles	2
Clothing	2
Foods	1
Agriculture	1
Personal service	1
Fine metals	1
Leather	1
Government	1

Source: Data derived from France, *Résultats Statisques du recensement général de la population*, 1, no. 5 (1931), 107, and *Annuaire statistique de la France* (1909), pp. 126–129, and (1935), pp. 188–190.

discount this factor and to isolate the impact of occupational migration, we subtracted from the displacement percentage of each occupational group, 4.4 percent, which represents the decline of the French work force relative to alien manpower over the 1906–1931 period. These percentages arranged in a two part scale show the degree to which the French abandoned or moved into these occupational groups. This measure of occupational migration graphically reveals French economic mobility and its relationship to the channeling of foreigners into the lower occupational groups (see Table 20).[61]

Group A shows the degree to which the French abandoned the dirty and onerous jobs, while Group B shows that they in effect received an excessive share of the more attractive jobs in the craft trades and tertiary industries. With the exception of entertainment, all of the top eight classifications under Group A were characterized by large numbers of unskilled, dirty, dangerous, and often isolated jobs. The bottom three categories were characterized by relatively modern, expanding plants. The position of these industries may indicate that the French were more prone to abandon the unpleasant traditional jobs than to avoid the new mass-production industries.

It is somewhat more difficult to interpret Group B. The second and third occupations were relatively prestigious and thus naturally targets of French penetration. Yet why the transportation and domestic categories became French preserves is less obvious. The lower half of the chart is characterized by artisan-dominated or stagnant industries which relied primarily on French women (for example, textiles and clothing). Finally, the greatest anomaly is agriculture's position on the scale: despite an increase in the proportion of immigrants employed in agriculture in the 1920s and their increased role in the farm population, they still did not migrate into agriculture at a rate sufficient to displace the French. There was a sizable influx of foreigners into farming, but once we controlled for the war loss, this number was absorbed into the still large French peasant population.

These tables show a general trend toward an occupational concentration of immigrants and a degree of French upward mobility. Obviously, the French did not all become managers or skilled workers. They did, however, tend to abandon or avoid the least attractive industries. This led to a segmentation of the labor force in France divided between the French citizen and the marginalized alien. This trend is reflected in a profound shift in working-class ideology and practice. It greatly undermined consciousness of class and further weakened the old ideal of international class solidarity. Instead, native labor increasingly identified with its nationality and the power of the French state to improve its life chances. Also this trend toward segmentation helps explain the decline of antagonisms between the French worker and the alien, for the immigrant became less a competitor in the real world of the job market than he had been before the war.

French labor during the 1920s abandoned confrontation and came to accept immigrants on the worksite, but they refused to allow their full participation in the French working class. Immigrants were viewed primarily as extra hands—vital during periods of expansion but expendable during contractions—and, because of their status as non-citizens, to be denied equality of opportunity in the job market. The government encouraged this outlook by providing a legal structure which guaranteed that immigrants would be a necessary but strictly secondary workforce, concentrated in the lower rungs of the occupational ladder. This allowed native labor to avoid significant conflict with the immigrant but also discouraged integration.

The government implemented a portion of the CGT's immigration program. In doing so it mollified social tensions which an unregulated immigration, dominated by business groups, would have intensified. Yet this web of regulation hardly quelled all objections to the massive immigration of the 1920s. A policy concerned only with the labor market ignored a series of social problems which inevitably resulted from so large a migration: these included the appearance of the ethnic ghetto, economic exploitation which stimulated foreign radicalism, and social disruption which produced crime and other forms of social malaise within immigrant communities. By the mid-1920s these social effects of immigration gave rise to appeals for a more explicit social policy—one which would modify the manpower bias of the immigration program and which would be modeled after the American policy of assimilation.

VIII Limits of Assimilation

THE coming of nearly two million immigrants in the 1920s was an important factor in the steady growth of French capitalism: it not only helped to assure prosperity but also social stability. Through a complex pattern of private initiative and public control, immigrants filled job orders without seriously competing with French job-seekers. This foreign labor system would become the norm for other western European nations a generation later. Yet despite its success this immigration program posed a series of conflicting policy questions: (1) the choice between manpower or social criteria for admitting foreigners into France, (2) the conflict between a policy of encouraging temporary migration to meet short-term demand for labor or permanent immigration in order to facilitate social integration and population growth, and (3) the option of creating a subclass of foreign workers through tight regulation or tolerating their free access to and mobility within the labor market. These issues which France faced in the 1920s are similar to policy dilemmas more recently encountered by other industrialized nations, including the United States.

In the face of the broad choice between a manpower and social policy, the French in the 1920s heavily stressed economical goals. Since 1919, the French government's immigration policy was directed almost exclusively toward expanding the supply of manpower and, to a lesser extent, to regulating aliens' access to jobs in order to prevent French unemployment. Neither employers of immigrants nor many

French workers had an interest in assimilation. Yet the social question could not be entirely ignored.

Parliamentary efforts from 1921–1924 to establish a national immigration office signified an interest in broadening policy to include non-economic issues. As we have seen, political conflicts and the refusal of the dominant right-center government to accept an expanded government role foiled these efforts.[1] Still, politicians, especially from the left-center Radical Party as well as health, police, and other government officials continued to demand a more balanced policy. By 1925, when it became obvious that immigration was not a temporary phenomenon of the postwar period but was to become a permanent feature of French society, the demand for a social policy on immigrants was again heard. Critics identified three broad problems of national policy: (1) the existing policy allowed the formation of alien colonies in the cities and industrial regions (e.g., coal basins). This threatened French cultural and political hegemony in these key industrial districts. (2) The demand for temporary or seasonal immigrant labor created a class of floating alien workers. These immigrants were often illegal residents and escaped governmental controls. Their rapid mobility, lack of community ties, and clandestine behavior made them a source of social disorder. (3) Finally, a policy which served only economic interests concentrated immigrants into the lower job levels and isolated them from French society. This made foreign workers susceptible to political radicalism and thus a threat to the French status quo.

In response to these social problems posed by the new immigration, critics raised solutions which were patterned on the experience of American immigration in the early 20th century: they advocated that immigrants be preselected to reduce the number of socially desirable foreigners in France. They also proposed that socially and economically acceptable immigrants be assimilated in order to increase France's stagnant population.

Despite widespread and diverse support for these reforms, policy changed little in the 1920s. The reforms were inconsistent with the policy already in place: government restriction of foreigners to a secondary labor market and its discouragement of immigrants' participation in the social and political life of French labor. As a partial alternative to the "Americanization" model, the government stressed administrative and police controls over immigration. These measures reinforced rather than contradicted the policy of channeling immigrants into a secondary workforce. This chapter will analyze the social problems which immigration engendered, the debate over reform, and the failure of the French to seriously modify the manpower bias of their policy.

Foreign Enclaves, the Dangerous Class, and Communism

Foreigners and the social problems which they engendered were not new to France in the 1920s. Yet the rapid pace of immigration and the arrival of new nationalities made ethnic differences far more visible than ever before. Before World War I, the foreign population increased slowly, rising from .38 to 1.16 million between 1851 and 1911. The only sharp increases were during the periods 1881–1886 (12 percent) and 1906–1911 (11 percent). After the war, the number of immigrants rose dramatically, reaching 2.7 million by 1931. Between 1921 and 1926 alone, the foreign population increased 57 percent.[2] Furthermore, immigrants after 1918 were no longer recruited primarily from neighboring nations, usually with close cultural affinities to the French. Rather, as Table 21 indicates,[3] eastern and southern Europeans as well as Arabs and other ethnically distinct groups entered France. These nationalities concentrated in highly visible enclaves in the cities and the mining regions of the northeast. French xenophobia was the inevitable result.

Concentrations of foreigners on French soil excited anti-foreign sentiments for several reasons: first, police and the press feared that slum-dwelling Arabs would cause an epidemic of exotic diseases and crime in French cities. In the Nord, for example, the popular newspaper *Reveil du Nord* complained in 1924 that the "Sidis," as the Arabs were frequently called, lived in overcrowded lodgings. According to this investigation, 563 Arabs lived in only 181 rooms.[4] In 1924, René Martial, a professor at the Paris Institut d'hygiène and a specialist on immigration, observed that North Africans in Paris were "lured by unscrupulous landlords who exploit them by placing four, six, and even more in a single room which normally held two; they have no way of sleeping properly or keeping clean."[5] Georges Dequidt, an influential public health official, warned in 1926 that France not admit the "degenerate, the sick, and the vagabonds of the Mediterranean" and prophesied that if France did nothing she would become like the "U.S. where the most prolific population was foreign, with a propensity to crime, disease, and indolence." To substantiate

Table 21   Foreigners Residing in France, by Nationality, 1911–1931

Nationality	1911	1921	1931
Western European			
Austrian	14,681	2,090	9,780
Belgian	287,126	348,986	253,694
British	40,378	47,356	49,143
German	102,271	75,625	71,729
Luxemburger	19,193	29,269	21,286
Swiss	73,442	90,149	98,475
Southern European			
Greek	2,902	12,771	19,123
Italian	419,234	450,960	808,038
Portuguese	1,262	10,788	48,963
Spanish	105,760	254,980	351,864
Eastern European			
Czechoslovak		5,580	47,401
Hungarian	3,170	630	18,824
Polish		45,766	507,811
Rumanian	8,080	15,852	15,387
Russian	35,016	32,347	71,928
Yugoslav			31,873
Non-European			
African (French colonies or protect.)	3,120	36,277	101,939
Armenian			29,227
East Asian			12,337
Other	44,200	72,593	145,875
Total	1,159,835	1,532,024	2,714,697

Source: France, *Résultats statistiques du recensement général de la population*, 1, no. 2 (1931), 57 and 81.

his claim, Dequidt later calculated that immigrants filled 14 percent of the beds in public hospitals and that they comprised in 1924 18 percent of the sentenced criminals even though they were less than 6 percent of the population.[6]

For different reasons the European immigrant enclaves were also perceived as a threat. As we have seen, they were often tightly knit communities with well-organized nationalist cultural and even political organizations. Police, for example, claimed that Polish communities in the coal districts of the northeast could not be controlled: they harbored illegal aliens and criminals as well as practiced their customs and laws in defiance of the French authorities.[7] The police and press also feared that Italian nationalism in the southeast was a threat to national security. The Interior Ministry monitored the activities of Italian nationalists in Nice and Marseilles for signs of irredentism: Italian agitation to return territory annexed by France to Italy.[8] In the southwest, Italian agricultural colonies became frequent targets of the press which wrote darkly of an Italian takeover of French soil. Even the CGT condemned this concentration of Italian peasants as a "state within a state."[9] In 1924, the French ambassador to the United States, drawing on the American experience, warned the French government that "compact masses of people of many races made complete assimilation difficult. They could influence political elections when they became naturalized."[10] The new concentrations of foreigners therefore posed the threat of crime, disease, cultural separatism, and political dissent.

The French were also suspicious of the highly mobile foreign individual. As an uprooted person who floated from one temporary job to another, this immigrant could not be trusted. Thus the individual immigrant was automatically in a suspect class, a *classe dangereuse*, similar to that class of French men, described by Louis Chevalier, which had migrated to bourgeois Paris in the first half of the nineteenth century.[11] Especially singled out were the immigrants without families in France. They lived in boarding houses near factories and, according to the prefect of the Nord (1925), they "often constituted an undesirable element. Drunkards, violent and immoral, unfortunately they appear all too often in the chronicles of crime and scandal."[12] One might expect this hostility toward these immigrants from the rightist press (*L'Action française, L'Ami du peuple* and *La*

Victoire, for example), but it also appeared in *L'Homme libre,* the organ of the liberal Society for the Rights of Man and Citizen. This newspaper, in June of 1926, advocated that the government eliminate those "undesirables" who were concentrated in the cities.[13] This identification of the single immigrant with criminality was nearly universal among the French.

There was a third factor that made the new immigration a social problem: the assumption that the immigrants were sympathetic to communism. French authorities believed that their lowly economic and social status made them likely candidates for communist organizing efforts. In France, communists could poll from 8 to 12 percent of the vote in national elections in the 1920s and could command the support of significant working-class districts. Thus, it seemed plausible that communists could recruit immigrants. The following statement published in the highly influential *Revue politique et parlementaire* in 1924 summed up much of public opinion:

Among the foreigners, who are normally passive, the attitude of revolt is more slow to appear than among the French; but once it has taken root it does not dissipate so easily in words and gestures. These elements need direction and discipline. If they do not receive them, they become confused and sometimes even troublemakers.[14]

Even a leader of the CGT miners' union, which was then anti-communist, claimed that if the Polish miners were not quickly organized into the CGT, they would "move toward the Moscovite demagoguery."[15] Another veteran leader of the mine workers claimed that the Poles had a natural disposition towards "autocracy," which from his anti-communist perspective, had both red and black varieties.[16]

As if to confirm these anti-communist suspicions, the French communist party undertook a serious effort to organize immigrants into their party and the communist-controlled unions (CGTU). The communists devoted about 16 percent of the CGTU's budget in 1926, for example, to propaganda directed at immigrants, a significant amount when only 56 percent of this sum was provided by immigrant workers. Most of these funds were used to publish foreign language weekly newspapers. Although all were short-lived and were often simply translations or reprints of standard communist material, they represented an effort to reach all nationalities working in France.[17]

Yet the communists had no success organizing immigrants which justified the fear of their influence. The earliest records on immigrants in the CGTU indicate that only about 3,000 foreigners belonged in 1923 and half of these were Italian. Most of these members were probably refugees, formerly enlisted into the Italian communist party, and were not recruited out of an immigrant milieu.[18] Years later, the communists had little better success: despite the fact that the CGTU had established in Paris a special office in 1928 to recruit North Africans, only a few hundred of the nearly 30,000 Arabs in the area belonged to the CGTU by May 1930.[19] This failure extended throughout the immigrant community: the CGTU could organize no more than 8 percent of the Polish miners (1925) and 5 percent of the Italians (1926).[20]

Yet upholders of the status quo in France continued to agonize over the communist threat. This was probably because the communist doctrine on immigrant labor was both potentially appealing to foreign workers as well as subversive. In contrast, the CGT's policy was neither attractive to immigrants nor threatening to the status quo. The CGT perceived the French worker to be a citizen entitled by his birth to protection against cheap foreign labor. CGT leaders were willing to collaborate with the state and employer groups to assure this protection. The communists, on the other hand, saw less distance between French and foreign workers. They observed that a working class divided between nationalities was incapable of successfully bargaining with employers, much less of overthrowing the capitalist system.[21] As discussed in chapter 7, the communists advocated a "class solidarity" which included the foreign workers as the only solution. By 1927, they favored the elimination of the entire legal machinery which discriminated against the foreigner (identity card, work permits, and exclusion of immigrants from union offices). Communist leaders, if not always the rank and file, supported equal treatment for immigrants within the labor movement and society. To the French authorities it was intolerable for immigrants to adhere to such an ideology. This subversive influence would have to be nipped in the bud wherever it appeared.

The French perceived the problem of immigrants in terms of the

American experience: that France might become another "nation of national minorities." Likewise the French looked for a solution to this threat in the United States.[22] The American solution was to exclude foreigners who were potential social problems and to assimilate and naturalize those immigrants who were socially acceptable. French efforts to follow the American path, however, were to prove largely unsuccessful.

France Tries the "American Model": Preselection and Assimilation

After five years of nearly unrestricted immigration, a wave of proposals for tightening admittance standards appeared in 1926. Critics demanded that diseased immigrants and political activists be excluded.[23] Charles Lambert, a prominent Radical deputy from Lyons, advocated setting quotas on each immigrant nationality. Inspired by the American immigration law of 1924, Lambert hoped that these quotas would prevent ethnic enclaves of Poles and other nationalities from forming.[24] In 1926, Lambert became president of the short-lived High Commission for Immigration and Naturalization which a cabinet of his party had sponsored. He hoped to make it into a permanent governmental agency similar to the American Bureau of Immigration and Naturalization. It would administer all aspects of immigration, independent of special economic interests, and thus assure that the "national interest could be served."[25]

The objective of national control over the selection of immigrants, however, had scanty success: in February 1928, the Interior Ministry required new immigrants to present a medical certificate before they could enter France.[26] In the same year, Armenians and other Middle Eastern immigrants, considered to be a health hazard, were barred from landing at Marseilles.[27] Advocates of reform, however, hoped to go much further in order to stem the flow of "undesirables" and prevent ethnic enclaves. Still, preselection was considerably more difficult in France with its relatively open and poorly patrolled frontiers with five countries than in the United States with its Ellis Island and Atlantic Ocean. Apart from the formidable geographical problem, there simply was no support from the business interests who imported labor. Particularly important was the General Immigration Society (SGI). This agency, which imported virtually all the Eastern European labor which entered France in the 1920s, had no interest in accepting governmental controls. With its powerful contacts with the parliamentary right, it was able to prevent any infringement upon its activity. The failure of the new right-center government in 1926 to continue Lambert's High Commission capped the failure of this approach.[28]

If preselection was difficult to implement, assimilation was even more problematic. Most French agreed that the foreign resident should be integrated or assimilated into French society, at least in theory.[29] Generally, assimilation and eventually naturalization were also to increase the French citizenry and the pool of men for military conscription.

The favorite method of assimilation followed the well-worn American path—through the education of immigrant children. William Oualid, a prominent former official in the Ministry of Labor, advocated a vigorous effort to enlist foreign children in French schools in order to counteract the cultural influence of foreign nationalists over their compatriots in France.[30] Since the 1880s, the public school had become a vehicle for reducing the cultural distance between classes and regions in France.[31] The idea of winning the children of immigrants to "French civilization" was but a minor adaptation of this well-established principle.

Integration was more difficult for the adult immigrant, however. Besides the obvious problems of adult education, particularly language training, French authorities were often ambiguous about assimilating the immigrant worker. Social integration could make the immigrant less serviceable to the French economy: it could reduce the social distance between foreign and French workers, make possible labor unity, and thus could put pressure on wage levels. In the northern coal mining region, for example, employers encouraged Polish separatism rather than assimilation by placing Poles in segregated housing and subsidizing Polish Catholic activities. The result was division between the French and Polish miners.[32] A final problem was into which "French Civilization" were the immigrants to be assimilated—the secular-liberal tradition of the Radicals, the Catholic-conservative position of agrarian and bourgeois groups or even the revolutionary-egalitarian movement of the socialists and communists. We will consider briefly two efforts at assimilating adult immigrants which will illustrate some of the dimensions of these problems.

The first organization, Le Foyer français, was formed in Lyons and Paris in February of 1924, largely to counteract the ultranationalist influence of Italian fascists over their compatriots in France. Sponsored by a committee of lawyers and Radical politicians, the Foyer was closely identified with the liberal tradition in France. The Foyer attempted to encourage assimilation by organizing a variety of programs including French language classes for adults and legal aid for foreigners seeking naturalization. The Foyer illustrated an attempt to assimilate immigrants into the mainstream of French liberalism. Its influence was restricted to the well-established communities of middle-class Italians in Lyons and Paris. There is no evidence that it penetrated the enclaves of immigrants in the coal and steel regions of the northeast.[33]

A second and more conservative effort to assimilate immigrants was organized by the Comités d'aide et de protection des femmes polonaises—CAPFP. Like the Foyer, they organized a program of French language instruction and sponsored French cultural events. Yet, unlike the Foyer, the CAPFP were organized by the employers of these immigrants—the farm associations of the northeast—who imported these young Polish women to work on their farms. Not surprisingly, the committees' commitment to assimilation was colored by their desire for a stable immigrant workforce. For example, the committees monitored attempts of industrial employers to hire Polish farm workers. A principle function of the CAPFP was to reduce discontent and thus turnover.

One means of encouraging immigrant stability was to support the traditional Catholicism of the Polish women workers. According to official minutes, the CAPFP were to offer "paternal advice to acclimatize [the women immigrants] to France . . . and to protect them from the dangers which threaten solitary girls. Wholesome and engaging distractions are needed so that their religious beliefs may suffer no attack."[34] Toward this end the CAPFP worked with Polish nationalist organizations to provide Polish religious festivals and clerical visitations. Far from counteracting the nationalist influence over the Poles, the committees attempted to use Polish influence to maintain a docile workforce.[35] Assimilation for the CAPFP had a very different meaning than for the Foyer français: it was not to make French citizens; rather it was to link the Catholic conservative background of the Polish worker with a similar culture in France, thus isolating the Poles from other significant cultural and economic options in France. Given these sharp differences over strategies of assimilation, private efforts to integrate foreigners met with little tangible success.

Despite these differences, both liberals and conservatives agreed that assimilation required occupational and familial stability.[36] Reflecting this sentiment, the French government encouraged married foreigners to send for their families. In 1928, for example, a Franco-Polish Protocol required that employers pay 60 percent of the costs of bringing immigrant families to France.[37] Family immigration would help to reduce the turnover rates of foreigners as well as increase the young population—important for the army as well as the economy.

Yet many foreign workers lacked the stabilizing influence of spouse and children. A rough indication of this is found in the relative shortage of foreign women and children. For every foreign woman in 1931 there were 2.03 foreign men, while for every French woman there was .88 men. Furthermore, despite the very low French birth rate, still a larger proportion of the French population was under fifteen (23 percent) than was the foreign (20 percent).[38] Another means of stabilizing the immigrants was to encourage them to become sharecroppers in the depopulated regions of the southwest. This idea was widely aired in the 1920s but with little practical success. The old belief that in order to be a true Frenchman one had to have his roots in the peasantry and French soil was nostalgically expressed in this unrealistic proposal.[39] To many French in the 1920s, the assimilated foreigner was to mirror their idealized image of the French worker of the 19th century—the sturdy independent artisan, the docile farmhand, or the stolid peasant. How unrealistic this was becomes clear when we consider France's naturalization policy during the 1920s.

The Narrow Road of Naturalization

Naturalization laws are surely a good indicator of a nation's commitment to assimilating a foreign population. Up to 1927 French procedures, unchanged since 1893, were hardly an encouragement for assimilation. Not only were immigrants required to reside in France ten years before they could apply for citizenship but even then they could be granted only the status of permanent resident for three years pending a decision on their naturalization petitions.[40]

A number of groups sought the revision of this law, including the Catholic church, trade unions and political parties.[41] The Congrès de la Natalité, an influential proponent of population growth, sought to liberalize naturalization procedures in the hope of increasing the French population in the child bearing years and thus reversing France's demographic decline.[42] Others sought increased naturalization as an antidote to the cultural influence of nationalist groups, especially from Italy.[43] As the French Minister of Justice observed in 1927, "naturalization can, in many cases, free citizens of foreign nations from the tutelage of the representatives and agents of their governments . . . [and] help absorb them into the French nation."[44] Naturalization was also advocated as a means of integrating the middle-class immigrant into French society: "we must not offend the foreigners who have reached a certain position in our country . . . it is necessary that they not be discouraged."[45]

The revision of the naturalization law in 1927 was addressed to these concerns.[46] The new law reduced the residence requirement to three years for those seeking naturalization and abolished the three year waiting period. As a result, the number of naturalizations rose sharply: while 38,589 were granted between 1920 and 1926 before the revision of the law, the number of naturalizations rose to 119,276 between 1927 and 1932. Furthermore, the age of naturalized French dropped after the law was adopted, a fact pleasing to the pronatalists, who wanted more French fertility: the mean age of naturalization dropped from forty-three years for both men and women in 1927 to thirty-two years for men and thirty-eight years for women ten years later.[47] The revised law seemed to be serving its purpose of integrating more foreigners into French life and of increasing the French population.

Yet, if we break down the data by nationality and occupation, we see that naturalization remained a narrow option. The law primarily benefited the older migrations. For example, the Italian share of naturalizations increased from 30 percent of the total in the period 1923–1926 to 50 percent in 1927–1930. In contrast, a newer migration of Poles, almost entirely dating from after World War I, remained a small proportion of naturalizations: only 6 percent of the total between 1927 and 1930 were Poles, rising only to 9.5 percent from 1931 to 1935, despite the fact that the Poles in 1931 comprised 19 percent of the foreign population.[48] This tendency for naturalization reform to serve disproportionately the most established and oldest migrations is indicated also by a comparison of status profiles (see Table 22).[49]

Table 22   A Comparison of Naturalized, French, and Foreigners, by Class, 1931

Economic status	Naturalized		French		Foreign	
	No.	%	*No.*	%	*No.*	%
Employer	42,093	22.5	6,040,390	30.5	143,108	9.6
White-collar	22,195	11.9	2,852,523	14.4	119,809	9.4
Blue-collar	86,216	46.2	7,977,336	40.2	955,134	67.6
Self-employed	29,892	15.9	2,567,698	12.9	138,396	9.8
Unemployed	6,567	3.5	387,764	2.0	21,642	3.6

Source: Pierre Depoid, *Les naturalisations en France* (Paris: Presses universitaires de France), p. 51, and France, *Résultats statistiques du recensement général de la population*, 1, no. 5 (1931), 59.

Except for the unemployed, the naturalized more closely fit the status profile of the French than they did of the foreign population (compare the worker category). The fact that a higher proportion of the naturalized were self-employed than were the French indicates that the artisan and petty merchant classes were routes of integration into French society. To a degree, naturalization was a reward for moving up from the working class. Finally, naturalization would play a far smaller role in France than in the United States, even after the revision of the naturalization law. Only 11 percent of the foreign population in France was naturalized in 1931 compared to 55 percent in the United States in 1930.[50]

Why did not more immigrants naturalize, especially more foreign workers? Intermittent or temporary residence in France may have precluded many workers from seeking naturalization.[51] Close proximity to native countries may have helped to preserve immigrants' identity with their homeland. In a government survey of Italian and Polish immigrant assimilation conducted in 1950–1951, a number of immigrants retained a strong loyalty to their nationality. As one Italian put it, "my nation is where I remember being a child and a youth." Yet economic reasons were probably as important for low naturalization rates. Application fees of up to one or two thousand francs (two or more months' pay for most workers) clearly was a discouragement for many of the respondents to the 1950–1951 survey. Furthermore, no campaigns to promote naturalization were sponsored by government or business groups. Indeed, as previously noted, some employers, especially in mining, were hostile to naturalization. A study of successful applications for naturalization in the Rhone (Lyons region) between 1927 and 1946 found that they were often arbitrarily administered, taking up to four years to process; during the depression years between 1931 and 1936, applicants were especially scrutinized. After 1936, officials appear to have favored the naturalization of those susceptible to the draft or with male children. In a postwar survey, Poles noted that their applications for naturalization were delayed or rejected in the 1930s because they were too old to be conscripted or had only female children.[52] Obviously the French made little effort to assimilate aliens through naturalization.

Despite the powerful social and demographic motives for increasing naturalization, the French had compelling economic reasons for not encouraging immigrants to acquire citizenship. First, foreign status allowed the government to deny immigrants the right to political representation. Their diplomatic counsels served as substitute lobbyists but with minimal impact. By contrast, the French employers, through access to political power, were able to shape the immigration in their interests. Lack of citizenship also meant denial of the right of settlement in France. Especially during economic contractions, the immigrant could be repatriated. This reduced the expense of welfare and other social services for the French taxpayer. The social costs of the business cycle—the need to maintain the labor pool during periods of contraction—could be shifted to the immigrants' native countries. Furthermore, the non-citizen worker was deprived of the right of occupational mobility. Legal residence in France depended upon obtaining a work permit, which was granted only for occupations in which there was a labor shortage. This discriminatory regulation assured that immigrants would remain in a secondary labor market of low-paying, arduous, and socially undesirable jobs (see pp. 145–158). This would protect French labor from foreign competition as well as assure French employers a labor supply. To have encouraged naturalization would have contradicted all of these economic advantages for the French. Besides the economic drawbacks of assimilation and naturalization, the government had alternatives to assimilation which minimized the social costs of immigration but did not violate French economic interests: these were administrative and police control of the immigrants.

Administrative Controls of Immigrants

In addition to the controls over the occupational movements of foreign labor, the French state imposed, by decree, extraordinary restrictions on the civil and political freedoms of foreigners. Since 1916, foreigners were obliged to obtain and carry an identity card. This device served two crucial purposes. First, it allowed the government to monitor and control the movements of immigrants. The identity card designated the geographical limits within which immigrants could travel (until 1920 and after 1935) and identified their occupation. Upon each change of residence, the immigrant had to register his identity card with local police. In addition, the Interior Ministry maintained and constantly updated these records of immigrants. In effect the identity card was an internal passport, similar to the livret which French workers were obliged to carry in the nineteenth century. It minimized the possibility that "undesirables" could move anonymously within France or hide from detection within the immigrant ghetto. Second, the identity card also served as a residence permit which the police could withdraw at any time. Loss of the identity card removed the foreigners' right to reside in France (*refoulement*) and, when authorized by the Interior Ministry, could lead to formal expulsion. Thus the identity card placed the immigrant on permanent probation in France.[53]

While the identity card was a tool for social control, it did not impede the flow of immigrant labor in the French economy. In fact, the government selectively enforced identity card regulations to complement economic activity. Regulations were liberalized during the period 1922–1924 in order to facilitate the movement of foreigners into the work of reconstructing the war zones and expanding the coal production of the north.[54] No bureaucratic controls were to impede the flow of immigrant labor when it was in demand.

Yet the threat of *refoulement*, expulsion, and other controls was necessary to minimize the threat of a dangerous class of immigrants. The process of refoulement and expulsion was entirely administrative: it involved none of the juridical guarantees provided for citizens. Grounds for expulsion were not codified, nor were there any of the normal provisions for due process of law. *Refoulement* was warranted if, in police opinion, the immigrant failed to "provide suitable guarantees."[55] Apologists justified administrative control as an act of the sovereignty of the state "to prevent foreigners from attacking the vital interests of the nation."[56] Immigrants were to "respect public order" and "abstain from all action which might trouble the tranquility of the population," according to a circular from the Interior Ministry of A. Sarraut (1926).[57] The correct relationship between the state and the foreigner was one of host and guest.

This doctrine assumed that the immigrant population was transitory, while in fact it had become an integral part of French society. The state's power to expel was a retention of the legality of old regime absolutism in an era of liberal civil and political rights. This power could be imposed on the portion of the working classes who, because of their birth, lacked citizenship. This status of non-citizen reinforced the immigrant's economic position as a secondary worker. It also augmented their economic and social separation from French workers, for immigrants were not only channeled into the lowest occupational levels but subject to a separate and illiberal legal status.

How was this power of expulsion used by the French state? Out of an immigrant population of 2.7 million in 1931 some 93,130 foreigners were expelled between 1920 and 1932. The reasons for expulsion were extremely arbitrary: the vast majority were expelled after a prison sentence.[58] Yet only a small proportion of foreigners convicted of crimes were expelled and many "undesirables" were *refoulée*, i.e., denied their identity card but not expelled.[59] This served as a kind of probation. The power of expulsion was clearly used selectively.

These police controls, however, were not purely arbitrary or limited to malefactors. They were consistently applied against political radicals, especially communists and militant trade unionists. The power of expulsion was used to deny the foreigner the full right to political participation (something which could not be denied to the French radicals). Although data do not reveal the extent of political expulsions (many were hidden in criminal expulsions) documentary evidence suggests a persistent pattern of deportation for participation in communist organizations and militant strike activity. Police often attended meetings or demonstrations singling out those immigrants who "spoke out" for discrete expulsion or *refoulement*. Interior minister C. Chautemps in September 1924 directed the police to warn any foreign activists that they "exposed themselves to severe sanctions unless they followed /police/ advice" that they quit communist groups. Indeed, those who frequently attended CGTU meetings were expelled.[60]

Given the practice of open union organizing among the foreigners, the police had little difficulty identifying and expelling agitators. For example, in early 1925, Czech, Russian, and Italian leaders of the CGTU were expelled.[61] As a result, the communist unions shifted from mass open meetings for foreigners to small workers' circles to avoid expulsions.[62] Furthermore, active involvement in any communist-led strike was sufficient grounds for expulsion. In the northern coal fields, participants in a strike in February of 1923 were expelled, a practice repeatedly followed thereafter.[63]

Finally, through a nineteenth century decree law, the Interior Ministry could adminstratively outlaw any "subversive" foreign language publication and seize subscription lists. Between 1923 and 1932, the government suppressed twenty Polish-language publications.[64] Police also rooted out communist newspapers printed in Italian, Spanish, Russian, and Hungarian.[65] Names on the subscription lists were investigated for participation in communist activities and often signaled for expulsion.[66]

Besides the obvious effect of weakening the communist unions, administrative expulsion had a sobering effect on would-be militants. One policeman in a coal district boasted that his checking identity cards of immigrants at the entrance to a communist meeting "instilled fear in the workers and drove them away from the communist organizations."[67] The threat of expulsion could easily have dissuaded immigrants from participating in unions as well as the communist party. "The fear of expulsion," said another police report from Longwy, "is the beginning of wisdom. . . . [It] makes them submit more easily to the bosses."[68]

It may have also reduced the loyalty of long-term resident foreigners to France. As one Pole surveyed in 1950–1952 declared: "how can one love a country where one feels undesired and hated?" A number cited the experience of family members being repatriated during the economic crisis of the 1930s. Not only did they resent this treatment but they never felt secure enough in France to feel "at home."[69] The point is that the thrust of French policy was not to make loyal citizens of immigrants (even though the government certainly hoped that they would be loyal and probably naturalized those whose "loyalty" could be translated into military service). Their goal was instead to create "subjects" in the old regime sense of the term—subjects whose outward demeanour and behavior was "correct."

By the mid-1920s a large influx of foreign workers in France stimulated a demand for a social program to balance the manpower bias of immigration policy. France's similarities with the United States—a permanent need for foreign labor and the threat of numerous unacculturated aliens—made appealing the American immigration policy of preselection and assimilation. Yet the French retained an essentially economic approach. Differences in geography partially explain the failure of the American model in France: France could less easily select than it could repatriate the immigrant as a means of social control. Further, a socio-political factor was central to the differences in policy: France was less a homogeneous political culture and the employers had less influence over the political ideology of its laborers than was true in the United States. Thus, while in the United States assimilation meant integration of foreign workers into a society where business values dominated, in France such integration would have been into a French laboring class strongly influenced by socialist and communist ideas.

The key to the difference in policy, however, is economic. France was not an undeveloped frontier economy like the United States was until the early twentieth century; employers required fewer immigrants and needed many for only temporary and seasonal jobs; thus, business had less incentive for encouraging assimilation. The privileges of citizenship which gave native workers an advantage on the job market also gave French labor little practical need to sponsor massive assimilation or naturalization. Despite French unions' frequent support of immigrant trade union and civil rights, they seldom undertook campaigns to gain naturalization status for their immigrant members. The goals of assimilation, then, had few consistent advocates.

The alternative to the American model of selection and assimilation was a policy of administrative controls. The threat of the ethnic ghetto, the *classe dangereuse,* and radicalism could be met negatively through police efforts to identify and purge potentially distruptive immigrants. This approach had the added advantage of reinforcing the manpower goals of French immigration policy. The identity card system and its implied threat of expulsion placed the immigrant in a legal world apart from the French citizen. He was forever merely a "guest" in France—welcome only to serve specific economic purposes.

The French labor system which emerged during the 1920s did far more than bring nearly two million immigrants and their families into France. It created a highly flexible subservient laboring class, not through racial segregation or forced labor, as had been practiced by less liberal societies, but through a policy suitable for a relatively small and dispersed class of non-citizen workers. The French denied immigrants full occupational mobility. This served not only the interests of employers but also of French labor, whose moderate leadership participated as much as it was allowed to in the regulatory process. The French also avoided some of the social costs of immigration by excluding the immigrant from the right to permanent residence in France. When immigrant workers became "undesirables," France had no responsibility for them. In a democratic age of rising economic and social rights, denying non-citizens these rights meant public savings and economic flexibility. It also compromised French liberal and democratic values.

This foreign labor system, which had contributed so much to French prosperity and social stability in the 1920s, would be greatly transformed in the next decade. When the depression finally descended on France in mid-1931, anti-immigrant sentiment, which had been so muted in the 1920s, again dominated policy debate. Pressure to make immigrants the scapegoats of the crisis was inevitable. Yet, despite a new regimen of restrictions, the French could not rid themselves of their need for foreign labor.

IX Regulating the Immigrant Worker during the Depression

SOCIETY bears the cost of economic crisis unequally. Those with economic and political power often displace the burden of economic hardship on those lacking such power. In modern times this has meant mostly the layoff of wage-labor.[1] Yet after World War I, in France and other capitalist democracies, the state rather than merely the "market" has allocated hardship by denying rights and entitlements to the less powerful. The burden of economic crisis began to fall upon a new but significant sector of the population—the non-citizen immigrant worker.

Universal male suffrage and the consequent threat of socialism forced the state to accommodate those interests of the native working classes which did not threaten the vital needs of the economically dominant classes. The result was that the costs of economic crisis were less easily deposited in the laps of French wage earners. To a limited degree the political rights of French workers counterbalanced their economic dependence. This was not true, however, for those workers who lacked voting rights: the non-citizen immigrant.

There were powerful incentives for shifting the social costs of and responsibility for the depression onto the immigrants. Not only did they not share in the national community, being—like the Jews in Germany—perceived as cultural outsiders, but also they had no political and few civil rights. Thus the state denied to the immigrant services and protection to which the French citizen was entitled. The government not only intensified its well-established policy of excluding new immigrants from the labor market, as it had done during the recessions of the 1920s, but it went further; it attempted to flush immigrants out of the national economy no matter how long they had been working in France. Discrimination against the non-citizen worker provided a relatively inexpensive and popular alternative to other forms of social crisis management. Public works, increased unemployment compensation, nationalization or price supports were positive means of stimulating the economy, but they were also divisive. In contrast, most Frenchmen could rally to the nationalist appeal of blaming the foreigner for the depression and expelling him as a solution to the crisis. Placing the burden of the depression on the immigrant served a conservative purpose: it placated French workers, who might otherwise seek structural reforms. It shifted the responsibility of unemployment onto the immigrant (for taking Frenchmen's jobs) and away from the economic decision-makers or the economic system itself. These strong motives for blaming the immigrant and making him pay the price of the crisis were acted on in a variety of government decisions in the 1930s.

Yet equally powerful forces restrained this scapegoat policy. Immigrants had become an integral part of the workforce. They were critical in the secondary sector of a dual labor market in which the French dominated the primary sector. As a result, both French workers and employers resisted a policy of purging aliens from these jobs and shifting these professions to the French. As miners, ditch diggers, steel workers, and fruit pickers, immigrants were irreplaceable. Few Frenchmen would accept these jobs. A wholesale attack on the limited rights of immigrants was also inconsistent with the desire of many French to assimilate a *portion* of the foreign population. In the face of French demographic stagnation and thus an inadequate manpower pool for the military, young foreigners were a national asset.

The result of these contradictions was an immigration policy in the 1930s which was torn between extremes: on the one hand, French governments periodically blamed immigrants for French unemployment and offered to purge them from the workforce. These campaigns coincided with particularly sharp dips in the economy and the rise of a demogogic right. On the other hand, all governments of the 1930s recognized the necessity of immigrants in the French economy and society. They used the opportunity of the depression to further restrict the immigrant to the secondary labor market. At the same time they granted a small degree of mobility to classes of immigrants which the government hoped to assimilate. In any case the government forced the immigrants to bear a disproportionate share of the costs of the depression, placed them in an even more regulated environment, and caused them to suffer profound insecurity owing to the constant shift of policy.

The Xenophobic Response to the Depression

With the first signs of economic crisis in late 1930 came agitation to remove the immigrant worker. Beginning with organized labor, it soon became a cause for the nationalist right. Initially, the depression stimulated a spontaneous and often illegal immigration which intensified competition between French and foreign workers. France's delayed entry into the depression and thus her relatively favorable employment situation led jobless Italians to scramble across the Alps in search of work. Some 70,000 foreigners found jobs after irregular entry in 1930, as compared to only 43,928 in 1929 and 21,505 in 1928.[2] As early as June 1930, trade unions in southeastern France, especially Corsica, complained that Italian workers with no work permits were being hired in preference to the French.[3] Placement office officials and police reported a flood of irregular Italian workers entering the Marseilles and Grenoble regions and noted the potential for labor unrest.[4] Despite relatively smooth relations between *frontaliers* and French unions, the prospect of depression excited bitter opposition to these commuters from Belgium and Germany.[5]

The construction and other vulnerable trades throughout France's urban centers were also threatened by immigrants. The construction industry was hit by early and particularly severe unemployment; further, the French worker was often at a disadvantage against the cheaper and more skilled Italians. In September 1930, the CGT construction unions claimed that Paris was "flooded with foreigners" who threatened to take the few jobs available during the winter's "dead season."[6] French employed in seasonal or unstable occupations such as the garment trade, hotel and restaurant services, or entertainment also feared foreign competition, for immigrants could easily be hired illegally, often through private placement services.[7]

Protest took a variety of forms. CGT hotel and restaurant unions in February 1930 requested the Labor Ministry to outlaw the private recruitment of foreigners.[8] Entertainment unions demanded that the Paris prefect encourage employers to give priority to the French.[9] The garment unions even joined with management in November to demand government controls over immigrant-owned sweat shops, which employed many illegal immigrants. Because of the low pay offered these foreigners, the immigrant shops were a threat, the delegates declared, "as harmful to the employers as to French workers."[10]

At the request of the construction and garment unions, the CGT sent a delegation to the Labor Ministry in late October 1930. It demanded that immigration be controlled and that foreign work permits be shortened. Minister Pierre Laval agreed to limit new immigration to temporary construction projects and to sharply curtail new work permits.[11] As early as November placement offices rejected most applications for work permits from irregular immigrants and limited the validity of the permits for temporary workers to the period of employment (three to six months).[12] Police also stepped up their enforcement of identity card rules and increased five-fold its prosecution of violators of the law of 1926, which prohibited immigrants from changing occupations for one year after being admitted to France.[13] These measures, similar to those taken during the recessions of the 1920s, were designed to limit new immigration, restrict the mobility of immigrants already in France, and thus prevent their competing with Frenchmen in sensitive urban job markets.

Such efforts could hardly placate labor for long. They affected mostly immigrant job seekers rather than the 1.4 million immigrants already employed. However, with increased layoffs in 1931, some unions began to demand that employers discharge the immigrant first.[14] The CGT leadership, long committed to a policy of regulating foreign labor through the work permit system, was slow to favor a policy of discriminatory layoffs. Repeatedly in 1931 the CGT's executive council reminded French workers that immigrants with work permits had a legal right to their jobs and condemned xenophobia.[15]

Yet, as the depression deepened, both labor and nationalist groups began to demand that immigrants be purged from the workforce and replaced with unemployed French.

Conservative deputies reported to the Chamber that French citizens were discharged rather than immigrants in the textile, chemical, metals, and construction industries.[16] Veterans' groups defended the French against immigrant taxi drivers and sponsored a boycott of restaurants that used foreign orchestras.[17] In January of 1931 a small but active nationalist group, the Confédération des syndicats unionistes, began agitating against foreign workers in the Paris region. This group had been organized by G. Hervé, the former anarcho-syndicalist, turned ultranationalist. The unionistes plastered working-class districts with posters which called for "jobs first for the French, who never hesitated to do their duty in war."[18] Hervé's newspaper, *La Victoire*, proposed a law to limit foreign workers to a percentage of each occupational group.[19] Communist organizers of the unemployed in the Paris suburbs feared the impact of this nationalist campaign on French workers. At a conference of committees of the unemployed held in December of 1931, a communist organizer admitted that "the majority of the French workers will accept only with difficulty being treated equally with foreign comrades."[20] In order to counteract the propaganda of the unionistes, a special edition of *L'Humanité* was distributed in the industrial suburbs of Boulogne and Billancourt.[21]

In the fall of 1931, as unemployment rose sharply, the conservative and ultra-right press also exploited the anti-immigrant theme. Included in this group were *L'Action française, L'Ami du peuple,* and *L'Intransigeant.* They emphasized the need for French solidarity against the "invasion" of foreigners. A common theme was that every job taken by an immigrant was a job stolen from an unemployed French wage earner. If the foreigners were only dismissed, the French could all have jobs.[22]

In the face of this tide of xenophobia, a law to reduce the immigrants in the workforce seemed inevitable. However, countervailing forces from the right as well as the left checked this trend. Many business groups who shared the conservatism of the xenophobes on the right, did not, however, wish to lose their access to immigrant labor. For example, a delegation from the Confédération nationale des Associations agricoles and de Warren of the Societé générale d'immigration (SGI) lobbied the government to continue the flow of farm labor. They claimed that any attempt to substitute the unemployed French for immigrants would fail, for Frenchmen would not take farm jobs. Construction employers and textile interests made similar appeals against restrictions which impeded the flow of immigrant labor.[23] In November 1931, the influential daily newspaper of heavy industry, *La Journée industrielle*, denounced rash measures, arguing that "for the sake of the future, immigrants must be allowed into the trades in which the French will never work." The same message came from *Le Temps, Bulletin quotidien, Le Nord industrielle,* and *L'Usine.*[24]

This dependence of the French economy on foreign labor was obvious: in March 1931 still 42 percent of the miners, 30 percent of the construction workers and 38 percent of the metallurgical laborers were immigrants. Any policy of sharply reducing foreign employment and shifting unemployed French into immigrant jobs would have been difficult at best. Yet if the business press was correct in proclaiming the economic folly of the anti-immigrant proposals of the nationalist press, their stance was hardly disinterested. After all, immigrants were generally cheaper and more docile than the French.

Despite their rhetoric, the xenophobic right did not seriously threaten the heavy users of immigrants for the right defended primarily the privileged or popular occupations from foreign intrusion. Likewise, union opponents of immigrants sought protection from the encroachment of cheap foreigners in their specific trades rather than the wholesale purge of immigrants from the French economy.

Moreover, the labor leadership as well as the socialists and communists stalled the stampede toward xenophobia. While the CGT leadership and the socialists were committed to defending French workers from foreign competition, they supported immigrants who were threatened with involuntary repatriation. In 1932, the CGT Miners' Federation organized the Fédération des émigrés polonais en France which lobbied for extended pension and union rights for Polish miners. In the depths of the depression, *Le Tribune des mineurs* (CGT) argued that the repatriation of Poles would lead only to a speed up of French workers and decreased production.[25] In 1933, the CGT leadership declared: "in spite of bad appearances . . . . /immigrants/are an element of stability, of activity and prosperity which the nation can scarcely spare, without leading to grave harm."[26]

The communists in the early 1930s were even more bold in their defense of immigrants. At their 1933 congress, the CGTU pledged support for unemployment benefits for aliens and denounced expulsions. Their communist-dominated trade union reaffirmed its support for "free borders" for "colonial" as well as European workers and the elimination of government regulation of foreign labor. This alone would "safeguard the rights and work of all the proletariat." In Paris the communists organized foreign labor sections of their unemployment committees and in the northern coal mining region they organized protests of Polish miners who had been expelled. This defense of foreign workers doubtlessly isolated the communists from many French workers (they admitted as much at their 1933 Congress) and contributed to the success of a nationalist workers' movement in the 1930s (led by Jacque Doriot and Marcel Deat); yet it may have also diffused the xenophobic pressure within the working classes.[27]

This ambiguous political climate jelled in November 1931 during a debate in the Chamber of Deputies over growing unemployment. Quickly the debate turned into an attack on immigrants and to a series of proposals presumably to protect French labor from foreign competition. The far right led the way. Throughout the 1920s, ultra-conservatives called for a labor tariff, a tax on businesses that hired foreign wage earners. This was based on a moral appeal to French solidarity rather than any careful analysis of economic realities.[28] However, in 1931, their position changed somewhat by their efforts to link the tariff to French unemployment. For example, Paul Ledoux submitted a bill which obliged employers to deposit five francs per day for each foreign worker into a fund for work relief. Amedieu du Clos, in addition, proposed that the rate of taxation be linked to the level of unemployment. Claiming that France had become the "milch cow of Europe," he advocated increased funding for the expulsion of indigent illegal aliens rather than putting them on relief. The right linked French unemployment to the presence of immigrants. Employers who hired foreigners were to pay the cost of relief which was the consequence of foreigners taking jobs which rightfully belonged to the French.[29]

The socialists, of course, opposed these illiberal appeals for massive expulsions.[30] In *Le Populaire* Paul Ramadier stressed that a socialist bill would attempt to protect the immigrant from the nationalist onslaught.[31] The socialist proposal promised unemployment relief for laid-off immigrants and equal status with the French for immigrants with French spouses or children and for the *frontaliers*. Yet the socialist proposal also sought to prevent "so-called immigrant farm workers" from taking French jobs in industry and to prevent "unscrupulous subcontractors" from using hapless aliens as a battering ram against French labor standards. Thus the socialists advocated that the border be closed to new immigration and that a limit of 10 percent be placed on all new hiring.[32] A similarly restrictive bill was proposed by the left-center Radical Socialist Party.[33]

Neither the proposals of the far right or those of the left gained the support of the Labor Commission of the Chamber. These bills were too inflexible to appeal to the right-center majority. In deference to the concerns of business, the relatively mild bill of Leon de Tastes and Pierre Taittinger was adopted by the government. Instead of a flat 10 percent maximum on hiring immigrants, the government's proposal authorized merely the possibility of quotas. These would be determined by a complex procedure: only after a petition from a labor or employer association would the National Labor Council initiate an investigation to determine a specific quota.[34] This procedure guaranteed that only those industries which were organized by strong unions with serious grievances against foreign competition would be affected. Industries where unions were weak but that also had large numbers of immigrants (e.g., auto, steel, and chemical) would be unlikely candidates for quotas. This bill also encouraged conservative local unions to collaborate with employer associations (e.g., the garment industry) against immigrant workers and employers. Furthermore, despite socialist efforts to include agriculture, farm interests in the Chamber excluded agriculture from the bill.[35]

The result was a second "Law for the Protection of National Labor," promulgated in August of 1932.[36] It would hardly fulfill the promise of its title. Indeed, it was probably the most moderate measure possible in response to the economic crisis of the winter of 1931 which finally brought the Great Depression to France. Pressure for additional legislation quickly faded in 1932, especially with the election of a center-left parliament.[37] Anti-immigrant reaction, so strong in 1930 and 1931, gave way in 1932 to the relatively moderate and prosaic administrative manipulation of the foreign workers by government and employers.

The Government Retakes the Initiative: 1932–1934

Despite the success of anti-immigrant opinion in imposing the quota law on the nation, the Ministry of Labor had little enthusiasm for it. Indeed, the state bureaucracy felt threatened by this law for it competed with the regulatory machinery already in place, and, from the standpoint of the functionary, it gave unreasonable power to local special interest groups.[38] Yet even these groups were slow to participate. While the CGT encouraged its unions to request quotas, few did so. Not surprisingly, only two employer associations took the initiative (from the hat and public works industries). As late as October 1934 (when records cease), only unions from the construction, leather, clothing, hat, barber, hotel, food service, and entertainment industries had petitioned for quotas. A number of local unions, both from the CGT and independent, also filed requests to limit foreign employment. The law was used only by the more conservative unions (no communist locals filed petitions) and these primarily represented craft trades. No national union in heavy industry, where most of the immigrants were concentrated, requested a ceiling on foreign employment.[39] The quota law, which was initiated with such demagogic fever in 1931–1932, was scarcely more than a public relations measure. It surely served the conservative idea of linking unemployment to immigration and it may have mollified small groups of skilled workers from especially aggrieved trades. Yet, with the exception of the construction industry, it did not touch industries in which immigrants were concentrated. Neither employers, the state, nor even the unions seriously pressed for its implementation. Furthermore, it was clearly impractical. To be effective the quotas had to force employers to lay off the number of immigrants above a legal ceiling allowed for that industry. Then presumably French workers would replace these foreigners. In effect, French occupational migration was to solve the unemployment problem. However, this was easier said than done. As Stephane Wlocewski observed in 1935, 42 percent of the immigrants worked in towns of less than 3,000 inhabitants. These workers, in small and often isolated labor markets, could not easily be replaced by natives without great cost and probably greater resistance. Even in Paris, the presumably expendable foreigners were concentrated in trades which could not easily find French applicants (for example, brick, glass, chemical, and excavation industries).[40] The Coal Committee was probably right when it declared that the Poles were irreplaceable, especially in underground mining.[41] Furthermore, even if French replacements were available, it was likely that they would be older, less skilled, and thus less productive than immigrants. Finally, the fact that no national union in heavy industry applied for quotas may indicate that not enough French wanted immigrant jobs in these industries to prompt a movement for quotas.

If the Law for the Protection of National Labor of 1932 was a failure, there were still other ways of controlling immigrant employment. The state already had a large tool chest of regulations which were more consistent with economic realities than the quotas. First, in order to reduce the immigrant labor pool the state drastically restricted

Table 23 Controlled Introduction of Foreign Labor, 1930–1939

Year	No. of foreigners			
	Industry	Agriculture	Seasonal agriculture	Total
1930	128,791	92,828	47,534	221,619
1931	25,804	76,462	40,034	102,266
1932	12,817	56,675	34,379	69,492
1933	12,200	62,375	37,471	74,635
1934	11,188	60,350	41,217	71,538
1935	9,989	46,517	40,134	56,506
1936	10,062	52,645		62,707
1937	13,997	77,212		91,199
1938	12,521	45,904		58,425
1939	6,684	20,200		26,884

Source: Henri Bunle, Institut national des études économiques, *Mouvements migratoires entre la France et l'étranger, Études et documents*, 4 (Paris: Presses universitaires de France, 1943), p. 96.

new immigration after 1930 (see Table 23).[42] Not only was there a precipitous decline of immigration but much of the post-1930 influx was in agriculture, especially the seasonal sector. Also, about 60 percent of the industrial immigrants were hired for temporary sugar and distillery jobs.[43] These seasonal workers were automatically repatriated at the conclusion of their contracts and thus prevented from entering the permanent job market.[44]

The state also used its administrative powers to encourage repatriation. Beginning in March 1932, the Labor Ministry provided funds for local officials to transport unemployed immigrants to the French frontier. If the offer of a free ride was not sufficient, the prefects were to "persuade" them to accept it.[45] The placement offices sharply reduced the proportion of work authorizations granted, thus denying the immigrant the obligatory identity card. For example, only 32 percent were granted in the Seine in 1932.[46] Immigrants who were unable to obtain authorized work or who attempted to change jobs were encouraged to repatriate.[47]

In addition to limiting the size of the labor pool, the state continued its already long-established policy of restricting immigrants' job mobility. The placement offices routinely denied work authorizations for jobs favored by the French and channeled immigrants back into agriculture and mining.[48] The Foreign Labor Service continued to send foreigners out of large urban areas: in 1931, for example, 74 percent of its job placements were outside urban regions.[49] Finally, to supplement these economic restrictions, the police increased expulsions.[50]

Business much preferred this plethora of administrative restriction to the quotas for they did not enhance trade union power, nor did they interfere as directly with employers' rights to make personnel decisions.[51] Yet some industries did carry out their own policy of massive dismissals of immigrants. In the iron mines, for example, 23 percent of the foreign workers were laid off in 1932 in contrast to only five percent of the French.[52] The Coal Committee reported that only 17 percent of the French were dismissed between 1931 and 1935, while 33 percent of the immigrants lost their jobs.[53] To a degree, government controls were unnecessary for industry carried out a parallel policy. Between 1932 and 1934 administrative controls and private business initiatives dominated immigration policy.

A Period of Constriction: November 1934 to the Popular Front

This fairly moderate immigration policy of 1932–1934 could not withstand the tide of popular discontent over unemployment and the rightist exploitation of the immigrant issue. By the end of 1934, the political climate was again ripe for anti-immigrant demagoguery: unemployment had been rising sharply in the fall of 1934[54] and a rightist movement had been growing rapidly ever since the violent anti-republican demonstrations in February. The right was ready to lead the call for "France First for Frenchmen."

Opposition to foreign labor mounted from many quarters in the fall of 1934. Unemployment prompted construction and food service unions to complain that the government was lethargic in implementing their requests for quotas.[55] A series of reports on unemployment from local governments, submitted to the Labor Ministry between October 1934 and August 1935, reveal deep hostility to immigrant workers. All but four of the thirty-four reports called for greater restrictions on foreign labor as a solution to unemployment.[56] A concise summary of the stronger resolutions came from the Meuse in eastern France:

> Shall we finally decide to get rid of those who desert our farms, who come from who knows where to take bread from the mouths of our unemployed, empty the treasury, exhaust the funds of the welfare offices, and who too often join the criminal class?[57]

The departments of Isère, Gard, Moselle, Loir-et-Cher, Loiret, Cher, and Creuse also proposed tough new barriers on immigrants shifting from agriculture to industry. A number of communal councils resented spending local funds on unemployment benefits for immigrants. Some requested the Paris government to repatriate all foreigners on the dole.[58]

By the end of 1933, the right again proposed draconian restrictions on immigrants as a solution to the ever deepening depression. A clause added to the finance bill of 1934 would have required a tax of five francs a day for each immigrant worker over 5 percent of the labor force in any workplace. On March 8, 1934, Paul Deudon proposed an immediate ceiling of 10 percent on foreigners employed in any trade because in his opinion the 1932 quota law was too low, and Paul Raynaldy went to the extreme by offering a bill in November which demanded that all foreign workers be fired by a fixed date.[59]

Xenophobia in the mass-circulation press also reappeared. In November 1933 *L'Ami du peuple* and *L'Action française* echoed the slogan "Le travail aux français d'abord." Even the radical-inspired newspaper *L'Homme libre* demanded that more illegal aliens be expelled. It justified this proposal by quoting E. Herriot, who said, "we intend to love all nations, but we love ours first." *Le Jour* was more direct on November 3: "In Paris there are sixteen unemployed French for every twenty-three foreign workers; in the provinces there are thirty-nine for one-hundred."[60] In spite of this upsurge in anti-immigrant sentiment, none of these bills got beyond parliamentary committees. They did, however, produce a hostile reaction from the major employers of immigrant workers, including agricultural, construction, textile, and coal interests as well as the Confédération générale du production française, the major national employers' organization who again defended their right to immigrant workers.[61]

Despite the opposition of employers, pressure for more decisive action led the government to accommodate the protectionist sentiments of the right with whom it was increasingly identified. In March 1934, the center-left government gave way to a right-leaning one, the National Union of Gaston Doumergue, and later cabinets led by Flandin and Pierre Laval. Soon after becoming premier, Flandin promised "priority to French workers in the job market" so as "to show the workers that the union of Republican parties can only be a benefit to them."[62]

The government demonstrated its solidarity with the French wage earner in a series of extraordinary measures which claimed to do the impossible: eliminate French dependence on foreign labor to the benefit of national workers. Besides placating public opinion, these measures further tightened the net of regulation and control around the immigrant. In response to the xenophobic campaign, in November of 1934 the government formed the Comité interministeriel pour la protection de la main-d'oeuvre française (Cabinet Committee for the

Protection of French Labor). Under the leadership of Edouard Herriot, the sometimes Radical premier, the committee had the responsibility of drafting new immigration legislation. Herriot committed himself to "remedy a situation revealed by a comparison of two figures: 350,000 unemployed French workers on relief and 800,000 foreign workers with jobs.[63] After the manner of the ultra-right, Herriot directly linked unemployment to immigrant workers.

Yet, despite a public call for a purge of immigrants from the workforce, the Committee for the Protection of French Labor in fact preserved most of the traditional policy of using foreign labor as a tool of manpower management and repopulation. The Labor Ministry continued to insist that immigrants be used to fill gaps in the workforce and to restrict immigrants to those occupations and regions. Immigrants also continued to be seen as part of the solution to French demographic stagnation, especially in anticipation of sharply reduced supplies of young workers and draftees in the late 1930s owing to low birth rates during the war. Because the French desired a permanent increase in their population, assimilation was necessary. This posed a dilemma. As an investigator for the Labor Ministry, A. Loroque, observed, "a national policy of assimilation presupposes that the foreigners not be treated . . . in a manner too different from French workers. . . . This is the only way to assure their ultimate stability."[64] The fact that immigrants were denied citizenship rights made them useful tools in the shaping of the workforce. Yet, because this involved obvious discriminatory treatment, immigrants had little reason to develop loyalties to France. This, in turn, posed a social threat which grew more grave as the war approached and compromised French repopulation plans. Immigrant loyalty and assimilation required equality of opportunity, a goal which contradicted the main thrust of French policy.

In response to these complex problems Herriot's committee proposed a policy of both increased constraint and greater liberality toward immigrant workers. First, it recommended a number of measures designed to encourage foreigners to repatriate. Secondly, it fashioned rules which made aliens serve French manpower needs. Third, it granted privileges, which were to encourage some immigrants to assimilate.[65]

In an effort to expand the quota system, the committee decreed that all industries which employed more than 10 percent immigrants were to submit a proposal for a quota. Within six months there were 170 new quotas, one hundred more than in the two years since the passage of the law.[66] The government also began in May of 1935 a program to encourage repatriation. The Interior Ministry hired a transportation company (perhaps not surprisingly dominated by the SGI) to ship eastern European immigrants to the frontiers of their home countries. Although this program lasted barely a year, it was an improvement over the previous policy of dumping penniless immigrants on the eastern French frontier; for Swiss and Belgian authorities had simply sent them back across the border.[67]

As a further encouragement of repatriation, the Labor Ministry asked local governments to carefully screen immigrants for relief payments and to repatriate indigents. The Interior Ministry also demanded that the prefects exercise more rigor in expelling undesirable foreigners, reminding them in a circular of January 1935 that they could expel any immigrant, even those who had not violated a law.[68]

The Labor Ministry also significantly modified the rules governing work authorizations, increasing the requirement for continuous residence in France from five to ten years before an immigrant could be granted an automatic renewal of his work permit.[69] This threatened the jobs of many foreigners who had made short visits to their homelands despite an otherwise long stay in France. The placement offices were to find Frenchmen to take these immigrants' jobs.[70]

Finally, in an effort to increase the efficiency of the controls, in December of 1934 the Labor Ministry gained authority over the agricultural foreign labor service, much to the irritation of farm interests.[71] Also, in April 1935, the Labor Ministry's inspectors were given police powers over immigrants which had formerly been in the ineffective hands of the local gendarmes.[72]

Business also did its part: for example, in 1934 coal mining companies organized and financed special trains to repatriate unwanted Polish families to their homeland, resulting in the exodus of 7,687 miners (18,922 Poles, including family members) between 1933 and 1934.[73] As a result of these policies, there was a 60 percent increase in recorded repatriations in 1935 (67,215).[74]

At the same time as the government sought to purge France of unwanted foreign workers, the Committee for the Protection of French Workers affirmed established manpower policy by restricting the mobility of alien workers. In February of 1935, the government prohibited immigrants from leaving the department where they had obtained their identity card without the approval of the prefect. Even more stringent was a rule which required immigrants to obtain work permits for each change of occupation. Formerly this was necessary only when renewing the identity card (valid for up to three years). These measures put a lid on the movement of foreigners into competitive job markets.[75]

Most of these immigrants accepted silently their repatriation to an uncertain future but police in the coal regions of the north reported in 1934 that Polish miners waved red flags and shouted "down with France" as their trains left the station bound for Poland. Others complained through their unions that their employers forced them into taking "long vacations" in Poland. This was a particular hardship for not only was there little work in Poland but Poles of Westphalian origin and the young had no roots in their "homeland."[76] The ZRP (Polish Workers' Society) of Lille complained in a letter to Premier Flandin (August 1935) that the new regulations had created an "uncertain situation" even for those Poles able to avoid repatriation: one unemployed Polish miner could not move from the Nord to the Loire, where his family lived, because of the new travel restrictions despite the fact that he had lived twenty-five years in France. Polish families, the letter continued, faced these dilemmas: men over fifty-five years old were retired on a pension of thirty francs per month, too low to cover the one hundred franc cost of a non-laborer's identity card. Others were denied unemployment benefits or the renewal of work permits. Desperate Polish families who tried to find work for their teenage children found that the placement offices rejected their requests for work permits. One thirteen-year-old Pole from Lens (Pas-de-Calais) was repatriated in October of 1935 to Poland although he had no relatives there and found himself "without a home and in the greatest misery." Nevertheless, despite pledges that relatives in Lens would support him until he found a job, the Foreign Labor Service rejected his request for reentry because of the "state of the job market." This experience of the period 1933–1936 left Poles interviewed in 1950–1952 still bitter toward France.[77] In these and many other ways the new regulations hemmed in the immigrants.

Yet, having just taken away significant civil and economic rights, the Committee for the Protection of French Workers, within three months, tempered the blow for favored groups. For purposes of encouraging assimilation, the government suspended the rule requiring a ten-year residence for an automatic renewal of the identity card for immigrants with French spouses or children born in France. This same rule was abrogated for favored nationalities—the Swiss and Belgians—whom the committee believed to have strong affinities with the French nation. Within a year, however, this privilege became meaningless as other nationalities won the same right after their home governments pressured the French into conceding equal status for their nationals.[78]

What was the impact of the government's relatively stringent immigration policy of 1934–1935? While the Committee for the Protection of French Labor hoped that their policy of encouraging repatriation and occupational immobility would help French workers obtain jobs, there is no evidence that they were successful. While unemployment decreased in 1935, a temporary expansion of the economy was more responsible than were the new anti-immigrant regulations.[79] Furthermore, placement offices noted that unemployed French workers refused to take many jobs vacated by immigrants, for they required an unacceptable move or loss of status.[80] The committee's assimilation policy was hardly more effective. It is true that in 1935 more immigrant children born in France opted for French citizenship (a 245 percent increase over 1934, or 28,026). This increase, however, probably is less an indication of assimilation than the desire of immigrant families to win protection from expulsion. Furthermore, while the government claimed to favor assimilation, the number of naturalizations granted declined sharply from 27,052 in 1933 to only 16,043 in 1935. Professional and commercial groups opposed increased naturalization for it gave citizen rights to the foreign-born worker and competitor. Despite the compelling demographic arguments for assimilation, it remained, as it had in the 1920s, subordinate to the economic advantages of denying the immigrant citizen status.[81]

The Impact of Government Policy, 1936

For five years the public policy of France had been to make room for the native worker in a shrinking economy by encouraging the removal of the foreign wage-earner. We have already suggested the limits of this policy. But what precisely was the impact of French discrimination on the immigrants? This subject is best approached by comparing the censuses of 1931 and 1936. Despite their limitations (e.g., undercounting immigrants), they provide our best picture of what happened to the foreign laborer.

First, immigrants suffered a vastly disproportionate share of the economic hardship of the depression. The impact of discriminatory government policy and layoffs is shown in the decline of the immigrant wage-earning population (see Table 24).[82] Between 1931 and 1936, the number of foreign laborers dropped from 1,079,993 to only 689,898; while the foreign working class decreased by 36 percent, French wage earners declined only 12.8 percent. In fact, 27 percent of the reduction of wage earners in France came from immigrants, 4.5

Table 24 A Comparison of French and Immigrant Economic Status, 1931–1936

Economic status	French	Immigrant	% Immigrant in class
1931			
Employer	6,082,483	154,095	2.4
Self-employed	2,597,527	156,485	5.7
White-collar	3,024,885	150,167	5.0
Unemployed	396,331	58,484	12.8
Blue-collar	8,063,557	1,079,993	11.8
1936			
Employer	5,743,585	177,865	3.0
Self-employed	2,620,593	156,341	6.0
White-collar	2,854,373	123,146	4.3
Unemployed	765,944	98,226	12.8
Blue-collar	7,030,485	689,898	9.8

Source: France, *Résultats statistiques du recensement général de la population*, 1, no. 5 (1936), 57.

Table 25 Occupational Changes among French and Immigrant
Workers, 1931–1936

Occupation	% Change		Foreign worker decline in excess of French (%)
	French	*Immigrant*	
Forestry, agriculture	−12	+ 4	
Mining	−25	−39	56
Quarrying	−17	−29	71
Foods	− 1	−30	290
Chemicals	−14	—45	221
Rubber, paper	−17	—45	165
Printing	−10	—32	350
Textiles	−26	—45	73
Clothing	−15	—23	53
Leather	−22	−36	64
Wood	−32	−44	38
Metallurgy	−24	−54	125
Metal work	−21	−56	167
Construction	−31	−56	81
Glass, brick	−36	−58	59
Transport, goods handling	−11	−14	27
Commerce, banking	− 6	−21	250
Free professions	+21	+ 2	950
Domestic service	− 7	− 9	29
Government	+ 5	−36	414
Total	−12.8	−36	87

Source: France, *Résultats statistiques du recensement général de la population*, 1, no. 4 (1931), 64–65; 1, no. 5 (1931), 121–123; 1, no. 4 (1936), 66–67; and 1, no. 5 (1936), 121–123.

times greater than their share of the laboring population. Most of those who lost jobs repatriated (thus the relatively low increase of immigrant unemployment); some, however, chose to remain in France rather than return to the insecurity of the home they left. These people sought a living from petty trade, handicraft industries, or farming, activities which government did not control. This trend is revealed in the slight increase of foreign born employers and a stable number of self-employed immigrants. These survival tactics, of course, aroused the ire of French merchants and artisans (see p. 211).

Immigrants in some sectors of the economy fared much worse than in others. As Table 25 indicates,[83] those industries which had the sharpest contractions of French manpower also eliminated the highest proportions of immigrant wage earners (note: metals, building materials, construction, and mining). The rate of decline of the foreign wage-earning class was 81 percent higher than for the French. Yet there were substantial deviations from this mean rate of discrimination. Government, commerce, food, and printing industries showed extraordinary rates of discrimination against foreign employment. By contrast, because of their dependence upon immigrants,

Table 26 Occupational Distribution of Immigrant Workers, 1931–1936

	1931		1936	
Occupation	No.	% immigrant	No.	% immigrant
Forestry, agriculture	150,921	7	157,558	8
Mining	145,382	42	88,382	34
Quarrying	18,029	28	12,718	24
Foods	30,252	10	21,108	7
Chemicals	32,666	18	17,961	11
Rubber, paper	16,653	12	9,195	8
Printing	5,089	4	3,438	3
Textiles	62,598	7	34,563	6
Clothing	26,156	10	20,099	6
Leather	15,445	10	9,841	7
Wood	33,332	9	18,797	7
Metallurgy	58,363	38	26,995	23
Metal work	138,277	13	60,782	7
Construction	189,225	30	83,718	19
Glass, ceramics	46,985	24	19,942	16
Transport, goods handling	21,466	4	18,377	3
Commerce, banking	33,822	10	26,735	8
Liberal professions	4,763	6	4,847	5
Domestic service	57,492	8	52,352	8
Government	41,650	0.9	2,666	0.6

Source: France, *Résultats statistiques du recensement de la population*, 1, no. 4 (1931), 64–65; 1, no. 5 (1931), 121–123; 1, no. 4 (1936), 66–67; and 1, no. 5 (1936), 121–123.

other industries were less able to discriminate against the foreigner. In agriculture, for example, there was a slight increase of immigrant labor (4 percent) compared to a decrease of French farm workers of 12 percent. Government toleration of continued immigration into agriculture and the shift of unemployed immigrants from industrial to farm jobs may explain this exceptional pattern. We also observe lower rates of discrimination in such activities as mining, woodworking, quarrying, domestic service, goods handling, and glass and brick making. Comparatively few Frenchmen would seek the jobs of immigrants in these arduous and low-status occupations. The textile and garment industries also showed a low rate of discriminatory layoffs of foreigners, probably because a foreign workforce had been well-entrenched in these industries even before World War I (especially in Paris and the Nord) and thus there was an insufficient pool of skilled French workers to replace them.

The differences in the rates of discrimination are difficult to explain because of our inability to break down the data further to isolate salient factors. Yet it seems clear that, although immigrants fared worse than the French in the shrinking economy, discrimination was limited by French dependence on the foreign worker in many critical occupations. This becomes obvious when we look at the percentages of immigrants employed in important industries (Table 26).[84] Despite large decreases in the proportion of immigrants, they remained over ten percent of the labor force in six industries.

These data document that the immigrant bore a vastly disproportionate share of the economic cost of the depression. As intended by policy makers, systematic discrimination may have placated French workers who saw many more alien workers discharged than their own countrymen. While the data cannot tell us whether Frenchmen were hired to replace dismissed foreigners, surely without the immigrants to fire many more French workers would have suffered unemployment. Yet was the dismissal of immigrants really a solution to French unemployment? Even if all the foreigners had been discharged, still this would have been insufficient to absorb the decline of employed workers in France in the first five years of the depression (a shortfall of 343,169). This was impossible, for the French economy remained dependent on foreign labor, even in the depths of the economic crisis. Despite the cushion that an expendable foreign workforce provided

French leaders during economic downturns, France would never again be able to function without the immigrant workers.

The Popular Front and the Moderation of Immigrant Policy

In June of 1936 the French elected a parliament of the left. The new government, headed by the socialist Léon Blum, was supported by an uneasy coalition of socialists, radicals, and communists. It was preceeded by a unification of the two major trade union confederations—the CGT and the CGTU, who in the summer of 1936 gained unprecedented victories in organizing French labor. The Popular Front government would usher in a year of social and economic experimentation and would remain in office with diminishing power until March of 1938.

Despite the significant changes which the Popular Front brought to France, immigration policy was modified only slightly. With the trade union offensive of the summer of 1936, many immigrant workers doubtlessly were swept into the CGT. In 1935, the CGT estimated that only 50,000 foreign workers were CGT members. However, by mid-1937 the CGT claimed a membership of 350,000 to 400,000 aliens, mostly due to the growth of unionism in the textile, mining, metal goods, and construction industries where many immigrants were concentrated. This claim seems rather inflated, however, considering that it represents 58 percent of the immigrant workers recorded in the 1936 census. Moreover, the entry of immigrants into the union movement did not change the policy of the CGT. Indeed, after the CGTU joined the CGT in 1935, the newly unified CGT largely affirmed the policy of the old "reformist" leadership rather than the radical support of immigrant rights which the CGTU had at least formally espoused. The unity congress of the CGT, held in September of 1935, announced its intent to prevent arbitrary expulsions and its support for a new statute for the foreign worker which would have guaranteed immigrants equal pay and rights to the benefits of French social legislation—goals which both of the old confederations had approved. It also, however, supported the government regulation of immigrants and reaffirmed Jouhaux's long-established plan for a National Labor Office under parity control. Not only had the policy of the "reformist" wing of the labor movement won, but the CGT offered no further resolutions on the question of immigration in its next three congresses (1936, 1937, and 1938). This issue of foreign labor had been swept under the rug.[85]

The left had shown little quarrel with the economic aspects of the immigration policies of the right-leaning governments of 1934–1936. In fact, the executive committee of the CGT in March of 1935 supported the program of the Committee for the Protection of National Labor as an effective means of "ventilating the labor market." CGT chief Léon Jouhaux particularly supported efforts to force immigrants out of the urban centers, where French workers suffered most of the unemployment. The placement offices should channel foreign labor into rural jobs and thus:

> ventilate the centers which suffer from unemployment to the benefit of the regions in which there are public works projects. The places left free in the urban industries will go to the French workers who reside and have families in these towns.[86]

Furthermore, the socialists, especially those with rural constituencies, demanded stricter controls over farmers importing foreign workers. Of course, the CGT opposed the repressive polices of the conservative governments of 1934–1936, alleging that they arbitrarily expelled foreigners, denied refuge to political exiles, and unfairly rejected petitions for naturalization. While the left was more willing to grant immigrants some basic civil liberties, their social base in the French working class obviously prevented their taking a liberal view toward immigrant economic rights.

Given these positions the left held before assuming power, one should not be surprised that the left in office would make few substantial changes in immigration policy. The socialist minister of the interior, Roger Salengro, did eliminate some repressive measures: in October of 1936 he revoked the rule that immigrants had to obtain authorization to move out of their department and requested the prefects not to expel immigrants simply because they were temporarily unemployed.[87] Yet the Labor Ministry of the Popular Front took a strong stance against hiring foreign farm workers and redoubled efforts to shift immigrants out of urban job markets.

In July 1936 the government announced that only in exceptional cases would farmers be allowed to recruit foreign labor. This was clearly designed to prevent farmers from replacing French workers, especially those belonging to a union, with cheap and docile immigrants. As labor minister Lebas warned in March of 1937:

> employers who hope to use [immigrants] to fight improved social conditions for farm workers ought to know that all their requests for new foreign labor will be refused.[88]

In December 1937 a new labor minister, Philippe Serre, claimed that many farmers hired foreign workers in order to depress wages. In order to frustrate this effort, he required employers to verify that farms were sufficiently large to employ the number of workers which were requested.[89]

In a similar effort to protect French workers in the cities, the Popular Front government sought to remove the unemployed foreign competition to the countryside: this goal became somewhat feasible when, after the introduction of the forty-hour week in the fall of 1936, more jobs became available in rural industry. Although the placement services attempted to persuade French workers who were unemployable in their own districts or occupations to accept work elsewhere,[90] few would migrate. As an alternative to this "very delicate" problem of finding French volunteers, Lebas instructed the placement offices to call on foreign workers, "even to use a certain pressure to induce them to move." He claimed that this discrimination was justified because immigrants were more mobile and often lacked family ties.[91] The placement offices also discouraged immigrants from seeking higher paying or less arduous jobs. In January 1938 Serre recognized that this "attempt to force immigrant workers to remain indefinitely in the same occupation . . . would formally contradict the most simple principles of individual liberty and would constitute, in addition, a flagrant violation of the principle of equality between French and foreign labor." He justified controls on their occupational mobility, however, because many immigrants entered France under false pretenses, with plans to move from farm and other undesirable work to better jobs.[92]

Parliamentary spokesmen of agricultural interests, of course, resented these policies of the Popular Front, complaining that they denied employers (especially sugar beet growers) irreplaceable labor. Industrialists also often failed to cooperate with the placement services and their policy of shifting foreigners to the countryside, preferring to hire workers on the spot rather than through the bureaucracy.[93] Nevertheless, these policies were merely slight modifications of the previous foreign labor policies, and they soon would be reversed as the government in 1938 passed again to the conservatives. On balance, the Popular Front, in its efforts to defend French labor, was as hostile to the economic (if not civil) freedom and equality of immigrant workers as were the governments of the right.

The Final Repressive Phase: 1938–1939

With the passing of Blum's second cabinet in March 1938, the short-run interests of agriculture and industry again took command in a conservative government. At the same time, the relatively loose job market, which was related to the forty-hour week, ended with a return to the forty-eight hour week. The government's rightward shift also led to more repressive forms of control. The new labor minister, Paul Ramadier, pacified farmers by eliminating restrictions on hiring foreign workers.[94] Another boon to industry was a decree of May 17, 1938, which allowed labor inspectors to suspend quotas for individual enterprises.[95]

The new government also abandoned the Popular Front's attempt to mobilize foreign labor to fill the gaps in the workforce. Instead, a decree of May 2, 1938 restored the geographical restrictions on immigrant mobility which had been abrogated in October 1936. This new rule limited the holder of the identity card to work in a single department. To assure greater observance of these regulations, the law made employers legally responsible for hiring workers only in the department and profession mentioned on their cards.[96] These efforts of 1938 to stabilize the immigrants, like those to "ventilate" them in

1936–1937, were designed primarily to assure their subservience to the requirements of the changing economy.

Furthermore, the impulse to discriminate against the foreigner was not restricted to workers. As government controls pushed immigrants out of jobs, a number became self-employed artisans and merchants. The inevitable hostility of French merchants to immigrant peddlers[97] led to a decree in 1935 which denied licenses to aliens lacking a five-year residence in France.[98] In the same year, French artisans pressured the state into requiring an identity card[99] for immigrant artisans, which was granted only after the approval of the local artisans' council.[100] This tide of restrictive decrees culminated in June of 1938 when the chambers of commerce won the same privilege to vote on whether foreigners could do business in France.[101] Opposition to foreign competition overrode traditional laissez-faire values and fears that restrictions would lead to reprisals against French business abroad.[102]

Still, the demographic problem also played its part in the late 1930s. With this final revision of immigration policy before the Second World War, a new system of privileged classes was to be established. Immigrants with up to ten years' residence could be granted only a short-term identity card (valid one month to three years). The card restricted them to work in a single profession and department. Residents of ten to fifteen years were allowed to move without restriction and were entitled to a card valid for three years, while residents for more than fifteen years were granted full occupational mobility.[103] The scale of privilege, designed to reward the most assimilated immigrants, made mobility the prize. What defined the status of foreigners was the denial of complete freedom of movement. Although this decree was implemented only slowly and probably never completely, it represented still another compromise between a policy of manipulation and one of assimilation.[104]

After mid-1938 the state also intensified the policing of the immigrant population. By January 25, 1939, 8,405 immigrants had been imprisoned for violations of the decree of May 2, 1938. In November 1938 frontier police were increased by 1,500 men to better control the entry of illegal immigrants. In April 1939 the Interior Ministry again encouraged the prefects to recommend the expulsion of undesirables even if they had broken no law.[105] The mass-circulation newspaper,

Le Petit parisien, praised the Prefecture of Police in March 1939 for its work of "rapidly and almost automatically cleansing" Paris of unwanted immigrants.[106] When 240,000 to 260,000 refugees flooded into France during the decline and fall of the Spanish republic in 1938 and 1939, the cry for police control over foreigners grew more shrill. Although this was a political migration, mostly of Spanish leftists fleeing from the armies of Franco, the threat of their competing with the French for jobs was an element in the hostile response which they received.[107] As in 1934–1935, the arbitrary treatment of immigrants again became a dominant policy.

During the 1930s the desire to displace the costs of the depression onto the non-citizen was zealously promoted by the far right but it also extended across the political and class spectrum. Only the communists remained the exception (at least until 1936, when their denunciations of the class collaboration of the reformist CGT ceased). The structural inflexibility of the labor force restrained the rigors of regulation. So did the French demographic policy. The effort to shift the costs of national economic failure onto the non-citizen is perhaps an inevitable by-product of capitalist democracy. Yet, as the French and other Europeans have discovered since the early 1970s, foreign workers are not expendable and the burden of economic decline cannot be fully shifted to them.

X   Conclusion

DESPITE the decline of immigration in the 1930s, foreigners did not disappear from the French labor force. Native workers never returned to the mines, docks, construction sites, and farms in such proportions as before the First World War. The regulated flow of alien labor became a permanent feature of the economies of France and later of Western Europe. Foreign labor became a vital tool with which to finely tune an economy subject to uneven growth and sharp cyclical swings. Immigrants became pawns who were shifted to and fro in order to compensate for alternating surpluses and shortages in the job market.

A permanent reserve army of laborers emerged, defined less by their social, educational, or racial characteristics than by their legal status as immigrants. Assimilation was only an individual experience; the group status of immigrants remained. Even if the sons of immigrant Polish miners became schoolteachers or merchants in France, still other immigrants would replace their fathers in the mines. Although they performed work essential to economic growth, immigrants were denied the legal and moral rights to equal opportunity and seniority in the French labor force. When opportunity was expanding, they were channeled into jobs and regions which French workers avoided, then laid off first whenever the job market shrank.

Regulated immigration served the interests of a variety of economic groups in France, who otherwise were often in conflict. French farmers, both big and small, building contractors, mine operators, petty garment makers, and heavy industrialists in steel, autos, chemicals and other products obtained the aliens which they wanted. At the same time, by the simple fact of their birth, French workers gained the privilege of job choice and relative security. To be sure, immigration was a mixed blessing: probably slowing wage rises and impeding improvements in working conditions in some industries. Yet without controlled immigration fewer French workers could have moved into the tertiary sector or into preferred industrial jobs. Despite the significant conflicts between labor and management as well as between various business groups, the immigrant question became a pole of coalescence: each class and economic group had an interest in maintaining the immigrants' legal status as an outsider, which deprived them of the democratic rights of the French citizen.

An Emerging Foreign Labor System

This pattern of regulated migration emerged clearly only after the First World War. Before 1914, alien workers, while denied political rights, had much more economic freedom than they would have in the 1920s. Until the war, the French were sharply divided over government control of immigration. Employers generally favored an unregulated migration, whereas labor organizations were divided between those adhering to international class solidarity and those demanding labor tariffs or quotas. Because of the political impotence of labor and the ambiguities of labor policy, government controls were few. When employers found political and economic roadblocks slowing the flow of alien workers, however, they abandoned laissez-faire and turned to the state for diplomatic aid. A reformist section of French labor shifted strategy from either labor tariffs or inter-nationalism to cooperating with business and the state in a planned labor market. These trends coalesced during the Union Sacrée of the First World War when government, business, and labor leaders set aside traditional disagreements and cooperated under the aegis of the state. Because of the labor shortages caused by the mobilization for war, employers supported government efforts to recruit foreign workers for the war economy. Conceding defeat on a policy of exclusion and abandoning the ideals of class solidarity, reformist labor began to identify with the national economic interest: these labor leaders accepted immigration and only sought priority for the French worker in the job market. Most important, a policy goal came from this coalescence: a regulated and channeled immigration which simultaneously filled the different needs of each labor market and minimized its impact on French labor. Potentially, it could mollify competition for labor between different employer groups and reduce tensions between captial and French unions.

After the war, no capital political opposition to immigration emerged and many parties favored foreign labor as a tool to compensate for the demographic losses of the war and to aid economic growth. Yet consensus was never realized. The breakdown of the Union Sacrée and the election of the Bloc National in 1919 assured the failure of a policy of class conciliation. The subsequent split of the opposition guaranteed the impotence of the parliamentary left in shaping government immigration policy and the inability of the reformist wing of the labor movement to bargain with management over the size and placement of the foreign workforce. The potential role of government as an official broker and mediator between the classes disappeared with the failure of legislation to regulate alien labor. Agriculture abandoned a centralized immigration program and opted for a separate network for recruiting labor (aided by the Ministry of Agriculture). Heavy industry, especially mining, joined with a portion of agriculture to create the General Immigration Society, which, acting essentially independent of state control, controlled much of the new immigration from Eastern Europe. In the absence of a political counterforce, the economically dominant employer groups exercised a commanding influence over immigration policy. While there was a return to "private initiative" after 1920, employers did not entirely dispense with the state.

After the war, French employers were no longer able to dominate the international labor market. They required the assistance of the Foreign Affairs Ministry to negotiate with the foreign labor suppliers. To a degree, the fate of immigrants depended upon the relative strength of their nations vis-à-vis their employers and the French state. In the case of the Poles, the French held the winning hand. Despite the cultural cohesion of the Poles, the French had the irresistible advantage of organization and economic power, especially in the General Immigration Society and the coal operators. The Polish state and Polish interest groups in France were not only relatively weak but often cooperated with the employers. In contrast, the Italians came close to a draw: the General Commissariat of Emigration and later the fascist state frustrated French employers by channeling Italian emigrants into advantageous jobs. Finally, the North Africans and refugees, who lacked governments to protect or manipulate them, held no cards at all. They became a subproletariat among the foreign workers, hired in temporary jobs at the lowest levels of the occupational ladder. While the labor market obviously played a role in allocating foreign labor in the French economy, the external political factor was a new and important input. No longer was the skill and motivation of the individual migrant the key to his fate. From the 1920s, he became increasingly an object manipulated by organized business, the French state, and his home government.

The picture is further complicated by the survival of prewar patterns of unorganized migration, especially from the bordering nations (Spain, Belgium, and Germany). Furthermore, despite the efforts of the organizers of immigration, powerful economic interests in France prevented a rigidly rationalized foreign manpower system: many enterprises, especially in construction, urban crafts, and some heavy industries relied on a pool of foreign labor, allowed to seep spontaneously into France, to grease the gears of the labor market. As a result, through a subtle pattern of organization, regulation, and laissez-faire, the various markets for alien labor were served.

Employers' needs dominated immigration policy in the 1920s. Yet state policy was not simply an instrument of the immediate interests of capital. The state's responsibility for social order and political legitimization required a longer view, one which considered the socially disruptive impact of immigration. Aliens frequently broke their contracts, fled the low-paying onorous jobs into which they were recruited, converged on the urban and skilled job markets, and, like the French, sought better jobs. During the economic downturns in 1921, 1925, and 1927, they competed with unemployed Frenchmen and became a source of labor unrest. No longer could the state treat this threat to labor peace as simply a police problem as it had before the war. Immigration was no longer an isolated localized phenomenon. Despite its fragmentation after 1921, organized labor had grown substantially since 1914, and the threat of Bolshevism loomed in the minds of conservative policy-makers. Furthermore, the government had learned the rationality of avoiding violence-breeding competition between French and alien labor. Finally, although French labor had been excluded from the commanding heights of the policy-making ministries in Paris, it had staked a claim (albeit a weak one) to participate in the local placement offices. For these reasons, the state (largely through the Ministry of Labor) chose to accommodate French labor.

Departmental placement offices and the Foreign Labor Service attempted to confine job competition to manageable proportions. When French unions had a significant influence, as they did in Paris, these placement offices became miniature versions of the corporatism which had failed. The Foreign Labor Service anticipated the flood of immigrants, controlled the flow at the border, and irrigated the French landscape with them roughly according to the needs of the economy. Finally, a surrogate for the national labor office emerged in a National Manpower Council, which served as a sounding board for government policy. From the council emerged the Law for the Protection of National Labor in 1926, the only immigration legislation in the 1920s.

This massive influx of foreign labor upset more than labor peace. The manpower bias of the immigration system contributed to numerous social problems. Alien enclaves of homogeneous foreigners, which the SGI had often imported, threatened the dominant French culture. The floating population of underemployed aliens spawned crime and public health hazards. Both business and government had encouraged temporary migration but ignored the potential contribution of aliens to France's permanent population growth. Elements within the French state (public health officials and some police, for example) as well as some politicians, especially from the Radical Party, advocated a deliberate social policy based on the American model of ethnic selection and assimilation. Despite token support for this policy (as witnessed, for example, by the new naturalization law of 1927), there was no consistent political support for massive assimilation. Such a goal was inconsistent with the subordinate economic role which employers (as well as many French workers) desired that the immigrants play. This function was contingent upon aliens remaining non-citizens, subject to a separate legal order. Another social policy had to be devised in order to reinforce the economic imperatives of immigration. This policy stressed social control through the use of residence permits (identity cards) and extrajudicial police measures. By these means the "bad apples" could be tossed out of the barrel. The inferior economic status of the aliens was augmented by their political subjugation. The social solution to the problem of immigration in the 1920s was largely reduced to legal manipulation and discretionary repression.

The new immigration of the 1920s worked reasonably well. At the expense of the economic and political freedoms of aliens, it contributed to French prosperity and social stability. In contrast to the laissez-faire pattern of migration before the war, the new immigration relegated the foreigners to the lower rungs of the occupational and class ladders. There, they provided a cheap and flexible workforce necessary for capital accumulation and economic growth; at the same time, aliens allowed the French worker a degree of economic mobility— although probably at the price of a lower labor standard than would have been possible if immigration had not occurred. This system, however, would be seriously undermined when the era of prosperity ended in 1931.

The economic crisis of the 1930s stimulated the kind of anti-immigrant opinion in France which had been dormant for a generation. This led to the quota law of 1932 and to numerous campaigns to repatriate unwanted foreigners. Despite the frequent hardships that these discriminatory actions brought to foreigners, nothing changed the fundamental dependence of key French industries on alien workers. The state's policy mediated between the political imperative of minimizing French unemployment at the expense of foreigners and the irrepressible demand for immigrant labor.

Immigration in the growth period of the 1920s served to compensate for the inadequacies of the French work force; in the thirties it attenuated and provided a scapegoat for the economic crisis. This was possible because the legal status of the immigrants linked their freedom in France to their serving in a secondary labor market, which the French avoided. To the extent that they failed to do so, either because they exercised their own economic imperatives or became superfluous during economic crises, their freedom was curtailed. Because of their legal status, immigrants became less threatening to French labor exactly as they became more useful to business. In the interwar period immigration performed a stabilizing role, similar to the one it would play after World War II.

The foreign labor system which the French created in the interwar period was hardly a temporary response to the demographic hole caused by World War I. Rather it was a consequence of advanced industrial capitalism—one area in which France was a leader. Industrialization inevitably dried up the wellsprings of the labor supply necessary for an industrial economy. The factory was fed by the young of the countryside. Not only did industrialization lead to urbanization—reducing the flow of cheap rural labor—but it produced a decline in fertility. Industrialization created expectations of social mobility and improved material standards, which caused the working classes to withdraw from the onerous and low paying jobs which even an advanced industrial economy requires. This phenomenon occurred in France a generation ahead of the rest of industrial Europe.

In the face of these difficulties either French capital could be exported or labor imported. There were obvious costs and benefits to both approaches for business. Capital export gave the employer the use of an often totally unorganized labor force. Yet, as the French showed in their failure to exploit their own colonies, there were significant drawbacks to imperialism: the expense of the social and economic infrastructure, the lack of a disciplined and productive colonial workforce, and ultimately the threat of nationalism. "Internal colonization" or immigration had a decided advantage: it required few infrastructural investments (transportation, security etc.). Just as important, immigrants could be more efficiently selected from the semi-industrialized nations. These workers, who during the interwar period came from Poland, Italy, and Spain, required little training and already were acclimated to industrial work discipline. With relatively little cost and even less public debate and accountability, they could be channeled into specific labor markets. This was a necessary but rather successful adaptation of the market economy.

If the French foreign labor system was an outgrowth of advanced industrial capitalism, it was also a culmination of trends in capitalist democracy. One of the live questions of contemporary political economy is that of the relationship between the state and social classes in capitalist democracies: is the state an instrument of the most economically powerful classes or is it autonomous?[1] Governmental immigration policy surely was not controlled by one "leading sector" of capital: the Comité des forges and Comité des houillères (through the SGI) exercised significant influence, especially in their ability to exclude the state from regulating their migratory labor streams. Yet the state did not simply reflect the desires of big business—it mediated between various employers. Immigration contributed to the profitability of large and often expanding industries—keeping wages low, weakening labor demands for costly improvements in working conditions, and supplying the necessary unskilled labor necessary during upturns in the business cycle. At the same time, the state encouraged immigration to protect the backward (and largely small-scale) sectors of the economy—in effect prolonging the life of small business and agriculture. These employers found in the alien an alternative to costly innovation: the availability of cheap foreign workers allowed marginal or backward enterprises (for example, in the garment, leather, and textile industries) to compete without costly investments to improve productivity. As is the case today in the United States, immigrants—especially those without legal status—were a key to the survival of shoestring business or those in highly competitive and labor-intensive industries. Immigrants also provided a substitute for French youth who were no longer willing to remain on the farm filling the traditional role as farm servants and sharecroppers.

Government policy not only cushioned employers from the costs of competing for labor, which without immigration would have been scarce; it also channeled specific ethnic groups into different job markets. The government's policy was neither to use immigrants to advance mechanization and productivity nor to shield uncompetitive industry (although the effect of policy probably went in both directions). The government was controlled neither by the growth sector nor the less vital employers or industries. France was still a relatively split economy. For example, neither agriculture nor industry (to use a crude indicator of traditional and innovative sectors) held a commanding position in population or production. Thus the state reflected a wide spectrum of employer interests; it helped to resolve one potential source of conflict between them—a shortage of labor. One indicator of the success of French democracy was its ability to mollify potentially antagonistic sectors of capital and thus to avoid the social and political dislocations which would otherwise be produced by the cost of uneven economic development. How different was the German and Italian experience between the wars!

The French state was not, however, simply the "executive committee of the bourgeoisie." French labor had conquered a piece of the policy-making turf, however small and distant from the command center. The impact, however, of immigration policy was the opposite of what it was for capital: it tended to divide the working class into citizen and noncitizen sectors. The rights of citizenship may have had relatively little impact on the living standards of French workers in the interwar period and certainly citizenship did not reduce the economic and social distance between wage labor and capital; nevertheless, citizenship provided a privileged status for native labor vis-à-vis the immigrant—a fact which divided the working class and weakened its economic and political bargaining power.

The Legacy: Labor Immigration After World War II

Through the storm of war, France largely unlearned the experience of the interwar period. With a few notable exceptions, the immigration before 1940 was left unstudied and forgotten just as France launched still another massive program of importing labor. In 1945, as in 1919, government officials recognized that immigration was necessary for France's growth. It became part of the plan of the National Demographic Institute for repopulating a nation which was both aging and infertile. Immigration was also an integral element of the manpower program of the General Commissariat of the Plan (Monnet Plan of 1946). Like the policy makers after World War I, the French government in 1946 favored European migration, hoping that many would settle permanently. With the closure of Eastern Europe to the capitalist west in 1947–1948 and the return of thousands of Poles to their homeland, Slavs were no longer available. Planners looked to Italy to fulfill France's unmet needs.[2]

Yet Italy proved to be, as it had in the 1920s, an inadequate supplier. The inflow of Algerians filled some of the gap after 1947 when restrictions on Algerian entry into France were removed. They remained a vital source of unskilled labor until 1964 when, after Algerians gained their independence, France placed restrictions on their migration. Furthermore, as happened in the 1920s, the dominance of Italians among European aliens gradually gave way to other nationalities which had even greater numbers of unemployed: by 1960 Spaniards became the leading immigrants, to be followed in 1966 by the Portuguese. As older streams of migration dried up, France was compelled to draw on ever more distant sources of labor. Between 1963 and 1965, she signed bilateral migration treaties with a number of North African states, as well as Senegal, Turkey, and Yugoslavia. Thus by the mid-1960s the government's hope of encouraging an exclusively European migration had failed. Non-Europeans and peoples of vastly different cultures increasingly filled the ranks of the alien work force.[3]

In the immediate post-war period, the French state recognized the value of consensus on immigration policy. For a second time, the government attempted to fashion a working compromise between French labor and the *patronat*. Briefly this was achieved when the Fourth Republic established the Office national d'immigration (ONI) in 1946. It centralized all recruitment of foreign labor, in effect nationalizing the functions of the old SGI. The office also channeled alien labor into jobs and regions which lacked sufficient French labor. The ONI functioned much as the CGT had proposed in the 1920s. Moreover, it was administered by a tripartite commission which included the CGT, management representatives and the bureaucracy. The CGT representative, A. Croziat, adhered to a program of regulated immigration much as Jouhaux had during the interwar period. This final realization of the old dream of tripartitism lasted only until 1948, when it became a victim of the cold war. With the isolation of the communist-dominated CGT from French institutions, the commission broke up and the ONI became an agency of the Ministry of Labor. It functioned without and largely against the will of the largest union group, the CGT.[4] The result of this second failure of corporatist policies was similar to what happened in the 1920s—a return to less regulated immigration. Gradually the ONI lost control over recruiting most alien labor.

Employers bypassed it by recruiting their own foreign workers either abroad or at the factory gate, where immigrants came as false tourists seeking jobs. The government tolerated this circumvention of the law by "regularizing" these workers—granting work permits and identity cards (residence permits) after immigrants had been hired. Although these "immigrants from within" were subject to a review of their work contracts, similar to the system established in the interwar period, the government was very lenient. By 1968, 82 percent of the immigrants working in France found jobs outside of the ONI.[5]

Yet this tacit government acceptance of employers' free access to alien workers ended by the close of the 1960s. What happened should sound familiar to readers of this book: the economic boom, which had made this liberal policy acceptable, came to an end and the social costs of an unrestricted immigration became evident: immigrant-dominated slums (bidonvilles), riots against Arab and black aliens, and signs of labor militance among foreigners. In an effort to reduce the economic and social impact of spontaneous migrations, the government severely restricted regularization. Employers henceforth had to recruit alien labor through the ONI. In turn, the ONI redoubled its efforts to channel foreign labor into the secondary labor market and sought to reduce the numbers of non-European immigrants allowed to enter France. During the recession of 1973, immigration was suspended. Although the government made token efforts to improve the housing and social services of aliens in France, the main thrust of the new policy was to abandon permanent for temporary migration.[6] Despite trade union efforts to organize foreign workers and to defend them against discrimination, in the 1970s they too accepted a regulated guest worker program.[7]

Patterns of labor migration very similar to those in France appeared throughout Western Europe, especially in Switzerland, West Germany, and Great Britain. During the boom of the 1960s immigrants from southern Europe, Turkey, North Africa and, in the case of Britain, from Commonwealth nations, flooded into Western Europe to fill unskilled and unstable jobs. By the early 1970s, aliens constituted from 10-20 percent of the work forces of these countries. With the partial exception of Britain, these industrial democracies from the beginning treated alien workers as temporary and controlled their access to the job market. Paralleling events in France, these nations became even more restrictive in the 1970s. In 1970 and 1974 the Swiss set quotas on new migration and in 1973, the Federal Republic closed its frontiers and encouraged massive repatriation. These governments used the non-citizen status of alien workers to shape labor immigration to fit the exigencies of the 1970s—economic stagnation and a perceived threat of ethnic minorities.[8]

Despite these efforts immigrants have hardly disappeared from the scene. Just as was true for France in the 1930s, guest workers today cannot be dispensed with. Western European societies have become dependent upon them to fill the jobs in the secondary labor market which show no signs of disappearing. Aliens, who have resided for long periods in Europe, have been able to bring in their families and settle permanently. Their children will become an important part of the labor force of the next generation. Furthermore, some have gained access to trade unions, political parties, and even have participated on government advisory committees in an effort to advance their interests. Democracy is contagious and efforts to permanently marginalize the non-citizen worker are bound to fail in the modern welfare state. As we have seen in the case of Italy, external pressure from sending nations will also check any policy of discrimination and exploitation of emigrant citizens of these nations.[9]

From all this are we to assume that in the long run, perhaps in a generation, the immigrants will become assimilated? Many, as individuals and families, may naturalize and join their adopted societies (although this remains difficult). Yet this will hardly remove the structural need for a foreign labor system: this study has stressed the vital economic and social functions that non-citizen labor played in one advanced capitalist democracy. It has shown that a nation like France in the interwar period required peoples from less developed nations in order to assure economic growth without social disruption. As native workers struggled for new social entitlements and as they sought social mobility, they surmounted the insecurity and dependence which characterized the lives of their 19th century ancestors. Yet without a fundamental transformation of the social order, capital still required labor willing to accept those traditional labor standards. The foreign labor system, which emerged in France in the 1920s and which has continued to the present, fitted that need. Ironically, by its very denial of democratic entitlements to the non-citizen worker, this system lessens the pressure of elites to withdraw these rights from the native citizen, especially in periods of economic decline. In the short run this stabilizes capitalist democracy in the West. In the long run, however, it subverts international stability by perpetuating inequities between the advanced industrial nations and the poor countries which supply immigrants. It also undermines democracy and social progress in Europe by creating a divided laboring class, an important part of which is denied full equality and freedom.

ABBREVIATIONS

AS	*Annuaire statistique de la France*
BR	Archives départementales, Bouches-du-Rhône
CDeb	Chambre des députés, *Annales, Débats parlementaires*
CDoc	Chambre des députés, *Annales, Documents parlementaires*
CH	Archives des Charbonnages de la France
CS	Commissaire spécial
F^7, F^{10}, F^{22}, F^{33}	Archives nationales de la France
Gard	Archives départementales, Gard
Isère	Archives départementales, Isère
JO	*Journal officiel de la République française, Lois et décrets*
Moselle	Archives départementales, Moselle
MOA	*Main-d'oeuvre agricole*
MM	Archives départementales, Meurthe-et-Moselle
N	Archives départementales, Nord
PC	Archives départementales, Pas-de-Calais
PP	Archives de la Préfecture de Police
SDeb	Senat, *Annales, Débats parlementaires*
SDoc	Senat, *Annales, propositions du loi*
SO	Archives départementales, Seine-et-Oise

Notes

I: Introduction

1. Good introductions to this immense literature are Stephen Castles and Godula Kosack, *Immigrant Workers and Class Structure in Western Europe* (London: Oxford University Press, 1973), Gary P. Freeman, *Immigrant Labor and Racial Conflict in Industrial Societies* (Princeton: Princeton University Press, 1979), and Georges Tapinos, *L' immigration étrangère en France* (Paris: Presses universitaires de France, 1975).

2. For example, see Centre des études anti-imperialistes, *Les immigrés* (Paris: Stock, 1975), p. 32, and Colin Dyer, *Population and Society in Twentieth-Century France* (London: Hodder and Stoughton, 1978), p. 71.

3. For a recent discussion of U.S. immigration policy options see *International Migration Review*, 5 (Winter 1978).

4. The best study of intercontinental migrations is Brinley Thomas, *Migration and Economic Growth* (Cambridge, Eng.: Cambridge University Press, 1973).

5. Adolphe Landry, *La révolution démographique* (Paris: Recueil Sirey, 1934), p. 11.

6. Jacques Bertillon, *La dépopulation de la France* (Paris: F. Alcan, 1911), p. 2. Bertillon claims that 90 of 106 doctors interviewed in 1893 attributed the low reproduction rate to the "crime of Onan." See p. 97.

7. Landry, *Révolution*, pp. 30–31.

8. Bertillon, *Dépopulation*, p. 110.

9. Jean Mesnaud de St. Paul, *De l'immigration étrangère en France consideré au point de vue économique* (Paris: A. Rousseau, 1902), p. 80.

10. Charles Gide, *La France sans enfants* (Paris: 1914), p. 373.

11. Alfred Sauvy, *The General Theory of Population* (New York: Basic Books, 1969), p. 484.

12. Paul Leroy-Beaulieu, "La question des étrangers en France au point de vue économique," *Journal de droit international privée* (1888), p. 175.

13. Sauvy, *Population,* pp. 445–446.

14. Kenneth Willis, *Problems in Migration Analysis* (Lexington: Lexington Books, 1974), p. 50.

15. T. H. Marshall, *Class, Citizenship and Social Development* (Garden City: Doubleday, 1964).

16. Daniel Bell, *The Cultural Contradictions of Capitalism* (New York: Basic Books, 1976).

17. Examples of anti-Malthusian organizations are J. Bertillon's L'Alliance nationale pour l'accroissement de la population française and Le Comité français pour le rélévement de la natalité. See Bertillion, *Dépopulation,* pp. 249–250, and Archives nationales (hereafter cited with "F" numbers) F⁷ 13955.

18. Sauvy, *Population,* p. 47.

19. F⁷ 13955.

20. See Joseph Spengler, *France Faces Depopulation* (New York: Greenwood Press, 1968).

21. James O'Conner, *The Fiscal Crisis of the State* (New York: St. Martin's Press, 1973) develops this theme.

22. The literature which deals with migration theory is immense. A good summary is in Georges Tapinos, *L'économie des migrations internationales* (Paris: Fondation nationale des sciences politiques, 1974), and *Migration and Urban Development* (London: Methuen, 1972). For recent studies see James McDonald, "Toward a Typology of European Labor Migration," *International Migration,* 7 (1969), 6–24; E. Lee, "A Theory of Migration," *Demography,* 2 (1966), 45–57; and "Migration Models and their Significance of Population Forecasts," *Milband Memorial Fund Quarterly,* 13 (January 1963), 56–76.

23. Gaeton Piou, "La main-d'oeuvre étrangère en France," *Revue socialiste,* 51 (May 15, 1912) 413.

24. France, Statistique générale, *Résultats statistiques du recensement général de la population* (hereafter cited as *Recensement*), 1 (1906), 140.

25. For a discussion of this problem see A. Souchon, *La crise de la main-d'oeuvre agricole en France* (Paris: A. Rousseau, 1914).

26. See Peter Stearns, *Lives of Labor* (New York: Holmes and Meier, 1975).

27. Jean Gravier, *Paris et le désert français* (Paris: Flammarrion, 1972), p. 52.

28. Leroy-Beaulieu, "La question des étrangers," p. 176.

29. Paul Gemahling, *Travailleurs au rabais, la lutte syndicale contre les sous-concurrences ouvrières* (Paris: Bloud and Cie, 1910), p. 14.

30. Piou, "La main-d'oeuvre," p. 445.

31. Charles Kindleberger, *Europe's Post War Growth* (Cambridge: Harvard University Press, 1967).

II: State, Society, and Supplemental Labor

1. France, Statistique générale, *Résultats statistiques du recensement géneral de la population* (hereafter cited as *Recensement*), 1, no. 5 (1936), 41.

2. For recent discussions of corporatism see Martin Fine, "Toward Corporatism" (Ph.D. diss., University of Wisconsin-Madison, 1973); Charles S. Maier, *Recasting Bourgeois Europe: Stabilization in France, Germany, and Italy in the Decade after World War One* (Princeton: Princeton University Press, 1975); F. B. Pike and T. Stretch, eds., *The New Corporatism* (Notre Dame: University of Notre Dame Press, 1974); and Nicos Poulantzas, *Political Power and Social Classes* (London: Sheed and Ward, 1973).

3. Henri Bunle (Institut national des études économiques), *Mouvements migratoires entre la France et l'étranger, Études et documents*, 4 (Paris: Presses universitaires de France, 1943), 67. cf. *Recensement*, 1, no. 2 (1921), 55.

4. Henry Wilcox, *International Migrations*, 2 (New York: National Bureau of Economic Research, 1931), 223.

5. *Recensement*, 1, no. 1 (1936), 36.

6. Ibid, 1, no. 1 (1906), 140.

7. Maurice Hollande, *La défense ouvrière contre le travail étranger* (Paris: Bloud, 1912), p. 179. See also M. de Bryas, *Les peuples en marches, les migrations politiques et économiques en Europe depuis la guerre mondiale* (Paris: A. Pédone, 1926), p. 13; M. Ronse, "L'émigration saisonnière en Belgique," *Bulletin de l'Association internationale pour la lutte contre le chômage* (October–December 1913).

8. Archives de la Préfecture de Police (hereafter cited as PP), 67, untitled report, April 17, 1907.

9. Numa Raflin, *Le placement et l'immigration des ouvriers agricoles polonais en France* (Paris: Imprimerie nationale, 1911), p. 8.

10. M. Sorre, *Les réssources, l'outillage et la production de la région du Nord* (Lille: 1927), p. 99.

11. Philippe Ariès, *Histoire des populations françaises* (Paris: SELF, 1948), p. 103.

12. Georges Hottenger, *Le pays de Briey hier et aujourd'hui* (Nancy: Berger-Levrault, 1912), p. 90.

13. Stephane Wlocevski, "La main-d'oeuvre polonaise en France," *Pologne*, 14 (November 1933), 63.

14. Louis Poszwa, *L'émigration polonaise agricole en France* (Paris: Gebethner et Wolff, 1930), p. 50.

15. *Main-d'oeuvre agricole* (hereafter cited as MOA) (July 1915), p. 11.

16. Edouard Payen, "Les étrangers en France," *Économiste française*, 38 (March 19, 1910), 200. See also Poszwa, *L'émigration polonaise*, p. 54.

17. Raflin, *Le placement et l'immigration*, pp. 8–15. See also, MOA (July 1915), p. 12.

18. Wlocevski, "La main-d'oeuvre polonaise en France," p. 64.

19. Ibid., p. 68.

20. Hottenger, *Le pays de Briey*, p. 94.

21. Claude Woog, *La politique d'émigration de l'Italie* (Paris: Presses universitaires de France, 1930), pp. 197–198; Hollande, *La défense ouvrière*, pp. 139–140; Comte de Canisy, *La question ouvrière dans le bassin de Briey* (Paris, 1919), pp. 33–34.

22. Woog, *La politique d'émigration*, pp. 200–205; Bertrand Nogaro and Lucien Wiel, *La main-d'oeuvre étrangère et colonial pendant la guerre* (Paris: Presses universitaires de France, 1926), p. 33. Cf. E. Lemonon, *L'après-guerre et la main-d'oeuvre étrangère en France* (Paris: F. Alcan, 1918), pp. 28–29, 45–46.

23. Lemonon, *L'après guerre*, p. 74. A. Landry in *Chambre des députés, Annales, Débats parlementaires* (hereafter cited as CDeb), of December 28, 1915, opposed direct government hiring of immigrant workers as contrary to employer prerogatives but favored government action to prevent an excessive number of recruitment organizations from competing in the same labor market.

24. Paul Gemahling, *Travailleurs au rabais, la lutte syndicale contre les sous-concurrences ouvrières* (Paris: Bloud 1910), p. 219. See also Hollande, *La défense ouvrière*, pp. 205–208; and Jean Delevsky, *Antagonismes sociaux et antagonismes prolétariens* (Paris: M. Giard, 1924), p. 258.

25. In the case of the entertainment and food industries, foreigners frequently went to France to learn the tricks of the trade in much the same way as provincial apprentices had gone to Paris to learn a skilled craft in the nineteenth century. German and Swiss hotel workers were often preferred because of their knowledge of languages. Hollande, *La défense ouvrière*, p. 208; Gemahling, *Travailleurs au rabais*, p. 219; Delevsky, *Antagonismes sociaux*, p. 257, and Confédération générale du travail (CGT), *Congrès du Bâtiment* (1914), p. 464.

26. See an interesting report on CGT construction unions' attempts to organize unions of migratory workers in the Alpes-Maritimes, which were immigrant-dominated. CGT, *Congrès du Bâtiment* (1914), pp. 69–78.

27. Gemahling, *Travailleurs au rabais*, p. 198.

28. *Chambre des députés, Annales, Documents parlementaires* (hereafter cited as CDoc) (1903), p. 1761. See also Hollande, *La défense ouvrière*, p. 185.

29. CGT, *Congrés des travailleurs de l'agriculture* (1920), p. 181.

30. Ibid., and Gemahling, *Travailleurs au rabais*, p. 218.

31. Delevsky, *Antagonismes sociaux*, p. 257.

32. Hollande, *La défense ouvrière*, pp. 205–208.

33. Paul Frezouls, *Les ouvriers étrangers en France* (Montpellier: Imprimerie G. Fermin, 1909), pp. 253–307.

34. J. Didion, *Les salaires étrangers en France* (Paris: M. Giard, 1911), p. 23.

35. Archives départementales, Pas-de-Calais (hereafter cited as PC) M 2774. See also Delevsky, *Antagonismes sociaux*, p. 253 and Gemahling, *Travailleurs au rabais*, p. 218. M. Perrot in *Les ouvriers en grève*, I (Paris: Mouton, 1974), pp. 170–177, counts 89 "xenophobic" riots between 1867 and 1893, 58 of which were between 1882 and 1889.

36. Archives départementales, Seine-et-Oise, 16 M 19, Ministry of Interior circular, September 13, 1893.

37. Charles Tilly et. al., *The Rebellious Century, 1830–1930* (Cambridge: Harvard University Press, 1975), pp. 48–61.

38. Delevsky, *Antagonismes sociaux*, p. 290.

39. At a convention of construction workers (CGT) held in 1912, a union organizer from Marseilles admitted that it was impossible to unionize Spanish and Portuguese workers because no French member could speak their languages. He complained that strikebreaking Belgian brick workers in the Nord were isolated from the union because they worked all of their non-sleeping hours. CGT, *Congrès du Bâtiment* (1912), pp. 39–40.

40. CGT, *Congrès des travailleurs de l'agriculture* (1920), pp. 66–8, 196.

41. Perrot, *Les ouvriers en grève*, I, pp. 169–177.

42. Office du Travail, *Associations professionales ouvriers*, pp. 2, 310, 320, 420–421, 771. See also, *Bulletin de l'office du travail*, 11 (1904), 332, 598, and Delvesky, *Antagonismes sociaux*, p. 282.

43. For example, see Paul Louis, *La guerre économique* (Paris: Éditions de la Revue blanche, 1900).

44. D. I. Ferenczy, *Rapport sur le chômage et les migrations internationales des travailleurs* (Paris: 1913), pp. 48, 68.

45. Didion, *Les salaires étrangers*, pp. 75–77.

46. For a complete list of restrictionist bills see Didion, *Les salaires étrangers*, p. 75; also Emile Mas, "La main-d'oeuvre étrangère en France," *Revue politique et parliamentaire*, 11 (March 1904), 474 and P. Pic, *Traité élémentaire de législation industrielle* (Paris: A Rousseau, 1902), pp. 160 ff.

47. Hollande, *La défense ouvrière*, pp. 190–194; Didion, *Les salaires étrangers*, pp. 75–79.

48. CDoc, 1902, p. 538; Didion, *Les salaires étrangers*, p. 77.

49. Jean Mesnaud de Saint-Paul, *De l'emigration étrangère en France* (Paris: A. Rousseau, 1902), p. 12.

50. CDeb, (November 19, 1931), p. 11, 897.

51. PP 67, Interior to Prefect of Police, June 8, 1916.

52. Lucien Wiel, *La main-d'oeuvre étrangère et coloniale pendant la guerre* (Paris: Presses universitaires de France, n.d.) p. 7.

53. F¹⁴ 11331, "Rapport, Conférence interministérielle de la main-d'oeuvre" (hereafter, CIMO), July 7, 1917; Wiel, *La main-d'oeuvre étrangère*, p. 9.

54. F¹⁴ 11331, Report on the Mission Truptil to China, January 17, 1917.

55. F¹⁴ 11334, CIMO, January 27, 1917, April 14, 1917.

56. Wiel, *La main-d'oeuvre étrangère*, pp. 19–21.

57. PP 67, Interior Ministry to Prefect of Police, June 8, 1916; F¹⁴ 11334, "Cahiers des chargés pour les travailleurs chinoises" (1916).

58. So much a problem was the "run-away" colonial that in December 1917 a bounty of 10 francs was offered police for each captured runaway. Officials were anxious to prevent their gravitation to Paris, where they could easily hide. Archives départementales, Bouches-du-Rhône (hereafter cited as BR) 6 M 1520, War Ministry Circular, December 12, 1917; *Usines de guerre*, January 8, 1918.

59. "Migration," *International Labour Review*, 2 (October 1922), 599.

60. F¹⁴ 11334, CIMO, May 1, 1917.

61. Ibid., July 7, 1917.

62. Ibid., May 19, 1917.

63. Wiel, *La main-d'oeuvre étrangère*, p. 21.

64. F¹⁴ 11331, Instructions of P. Famin, Directeur général des troupes coloniales, September 26, 1916.

65. Archives des Charbonnages de France (hereafter cited as CH) 40, CIMO, November 25, 1916, and PP 67 Ministry of War circulars, November 24, 1917, and February 27, 1918.

66. F¹⁴ 11331, Correspondence between the Ministry of Public Works and the port authorities, July 1917 to December 1918.

67. Office national de la main-d'oeuvre agricole (ONMA), "Placement et immigration de la main-d'oeuvre agricole" (a pamphlet dated August 25, 1918). See also MOA 16 (October 10, 1919), 7; 11 (August 10, 1914), 6; and 12 (May 1915), 7.

68. MOA, 12 (June 1915), 4.

69. MOA, 15 (August 25, 1918), 7.

70. Michel Augé-Laribé, *L'agriculture pendant la guerre* (Paris: Presses universitaires de France, 1925), pp. 73, 81, 83, and 87.

71. MOA, 13 (May 1916), 3.

72. Augé-Laribé, *L'agriculture*, p. 69.

73. Ibid., pp. 81, 83, and 87.

74. MOA, 15 (May 1918), 4.

75. Until the spring of 1918 militarized French workers were paid only 1.9 francs per day, while POW's received only fifty centimes. Foreigners were not

only expensive to import but cost roughly the same as free French workers (3.5 francs per day in 1916). See Office national de la main-d'oeuvre agricole, "Placement et immigration," p. 3.

76. MOA, 14 (May 14, 1917), 34.

77. Office national de la main-d'oeuvre agricole, "Placement et immigration," p. 5.

78. A study by the ONMA found that only 100 of 215 Algerians hired in September of 1915 at the sugar beet farms of the Beauce remained more than one week. The study attributed this turnover to a combination of factors: they received the meager wages of 3.5 francs per day; they often had only pork meat to eat (religiously objectionable); and they had to sleep on beds of straw. Those who quit also had job options. They went mainly to the war factories of Lyons, St. Etienne, Rouen, and Paris where they could earn up to one franc per hour. MOA, 13 (April 1916), 4.

79. Office national de la main-d'oeuvre agricole, "Placement et immigration," pp. 4, 11.

80. B. Nogaro, "La main-d'oeuvre étrangère pendant la guerre," *Revue d'économie politique* 44 (1920), 720. See also *Usines de guerre* (May 5, 1916), pp. 37–38 and (March 19, 1917), p. 373.

81. Nogaro, "La main-d'oeuvre", pp. 731–722.

82. *Bulletin du Ministère du travail*, 27 (January–February 1920), pp. 19–20.

83. F[14] 11332, Report of Service de la main-d'oeuvre étrangère to Commission interministérielle de la main-d'oeuvre, December 6, 1917.

84. Nogaro and Wiel, *La main-d'oeuvre étrangère*, pp. 52–55.

85. *Bulletin de l'Association internationale pour la lutte contre le chômage* (November 1917), p. 6; Peyerimhoff claimed turnover in the mines jumped from 25–30 per cent before the war to 200 per cent in 1916. CH 40, CIMO, May 20, 1916.

86. Nogaro, "La main-d'oeuvre étrangère," *Revue d'économie politique* (1920), 730.

87. Ibid., p. 725. *Usines de guerre* (March 4, 1917), p. 373, and (September 25, 1916), p. 172.

88. PP 67 Interior Circular, June 16, 1916.

89. Ibid., June 8, 1916.

90. CH 40, *Compte rendu de l'Association national d'expansion économique* (November 7, 1916), and Lemonon, *L'aprés guerre*, p. 18.

91. *Journal officiel de la République de France, Lois et décrets* (hereafter cited as JO) (April 22, 1917), p. 3186.

92. Members of the Commission included the main government manpower chiefs (L. Wiel, F. A. Brancher, and B. Nogaro), as well as Arthur Fontaine and Charles Picquenard from the Ministry of Labor. It also included representatives from key employer groups (Robert Pinot from the Comité des

forges and G. de Peyerimhoff from the Comité des houillères). Joining them infrequently was Léon Jouhaux, chief of the CGT, and Auguste Keufer from the printers union. See F¹⁴ 11334, CIMO, March 1917.

93. Ibid., February 10, 1917.

94. F¹⁴ 11332, CIMO, October 22, 1917.

95. Ibid., November 1, 1917.

96. F¹⁴ 11334, CIMO, April 14, 1917.

97. Ibid., January 20, 1917.

98. F¹⁴ 11332, CIMO, January 26, 1918.

99. *Compte rendu de la deuxième Conférence des Offices régionaux, départementales, et munipicaux du placement* (January 9–11, 1919).

100. F¹⁴ 11334, Circular of the Office central de placement, December 26, 1916; CH 40, Henri Cheron, "Rapport sur la loi du placement," December 15, 1916.

101. *Bulletin du Ministère du travail*, 22 (March 1915), p. 50.

102. Henri Sellier and Emile Deslandres, "La constitution de l'office départemental du placement: rapport au Conseil général de la Seine," October 30, 1918.

103. F¹⁴ 11334, CIMO, June 9, 1917, and July 7, 1917.

104. CH 40, "Procès verbal, Commission administratif de l'office central de placement," November 16, 1916. It is significant that de Peyerimhoff of the Coal Committee opposed this resolution on the ground that the offices were not competent to pass a decision on the labor needs of big industries. At this same meeting, Jouhaux proposed that foreigners not be expelled. His proposition was tabled due to the opposition of several business representatives who held that expulsion was a purely administrative matter.

105. F¹⁴ 11334, CIMO, July 7, 1917.

III: Organizing Immigration after the First World War

1. Association nationale d'expansion économique (ANEE), *Enquête sur la production française et la concurrence étrangère* (Paris: Lib.-imp. réunies, 1917). The Agricultural Commission of the ANEE included key representatives of big farming such as Ferdand David, F. I. Brancher, Henri Hetier, and Albert Souchon. The Industrial Commission included Henri Hauser, Paul de Rousiers (Comité des armateurs), and Robert Pinot (Comité des forges).

2. A. Souchon in Ibid., p. 451. On the opposition to the continuation of colonial immigration, see "La main-d'oeuvre après la guerre," *Réforme social*, 28 (1917), 127–128.

3. P. de Rousiers in *Enquête sur la production*, p. 175.

4. See Main-d'oeuvre agricole (hereafter cited as MOA), 15 (April 1918), 4–5, and 15 (June 5, 1918), 3 for reports on French fears that foreign governments would interfere in their efforts to recruit Portuguese and Irish farm workers.

5. Souchon, in *Enquête sur la production*, p. 453.

6. MOA, 14 (October 9, 1917), 7.

7. Ibid., 13 (October 1916), 6 and (May 1916), 2–3.

8. Not surprisingly, when Gaston Treigner of the Agricultural Commission of the Chamber of Deputies surveyed 4,000 farm societies on the question of whether the farm placement offices should be joined to the industrial labor exchanges, only 4 per cent approved. MOA, 15 (June 5, 1918), 6.

9. Brancher claimed in 1919 that 250,000 farm workers were lost to industry during the war. *Bulletin de l'Association internationale pour la lutte contre le chômage* (March 1920), p.4.

10. Souchon in *Enquête sur la production*, p. 453.

11. For Meline's ideas on farm worker unions see MOA, 13 (August 1916), 2–3.

12. Emile Fuster, director of the Paris Placement Office, Arthur Fontaine, Director of Labor in the Ministry of Labor, and Charles Picquenard, often Minister of Labor, were active in this association. Founded in 1900 as the *Association pour la protection légale des travailleurs*, this organization had long strived for ameliorative labor legislation in Western European countries as well as cooperation between labor, business, and the state. See *Bulletin de l'Association internationale pour la lutte contre le chômage* (January 31, 1919), p. 1.

13. Ibid. (November 1917), p. 5.

14. Ibid. (March 15, 1918), p. 11.

15. Léon Jouhaux, "Le Marché du travail," *Europe nouvelle*, 13 (August 6, 1917), 1041.

16. *La vie ouvrière*, 4 (December 1922), 767 and CGT, *Questions ouvrières*, pp. 9–10.

17. For details on postwar politics in France, see Arno Mayer, *Politics and Diplomacy of Peacemaking: 1918–1919* (New York: Knopf, 1967), chapter 19; Charles Maier, *Recasting Bourgeois Europe* (Princeton: Princeton University Press, 1975), pp. 53–87, 91–108, 458–480; and Georges Bonnefous, *Histoire politique de la Troisième République* (Paris: Presses universitaires de France, 1956), vols. II and IV.

18. The best source on the split of the left remains Annie Kriegel, *Aux origines du communisme français, 1914–1920* (Paris: Mouton, 1964), especially pp. 359–547.

19. *Voix du peuple*, 4 (July 1922), 418.

20. French fears of job competition were well-founded. Placement offices

reported French veterans complaining that foreign workers had taken jobs which the soldiers had held before the war. In response, the foreign labor office in Paris channeled foreign workers outside the crowded Parisian labor market. See Archives nationales (hereafter cited with "F" numbers) F²² 2565, Labor Ministry report, March 8, 1919. For further information on colonial repatriation see Henri Bunle (Institut national des études économiques), *Mouvements migratoires entre la France et l'étranger, Études et documents*, no. 4, p. 77, and Michel Huber, *La population de la France pendant la guerre* (Paris: Presses universitaires de France, 1931), p. 509.

21. F¹⁴ 11335, report from the Ministry of Public Works to the Labor Ministry, November 25, 1918. See also F¹⁴ 11334, circular from the Labor Ministry, December 20, 1918. Other sources on early postwar policy are *Bulletin du Ministère du travail*, 27 (January–February 1920), pp. 20, 23. See also Archives départementales, Meurthe-et-Moselle (hereafter cited as MM) 40 M 34, Interior Ministry circular, June 19, 1918.

22. *Journal officiel de la République de France, Lois et décrets* (hereafter cited as JO) (March 4, 1919), p. 2383.

23. Foreign labor continued to be recruited through placement offices at Perpignan, Hendaye, and Marignac for the Iberian migation, at Baisieux for the Belgian, and at Pontailler for the Swiss. Offices at Modane and Menton collected Italians, while the Toul office gathered in Poles, other eastern Europeans, and a few Germans. See JO (October 24, 1919), p. 11799 and (August 6, 1919), p. 8221.

24. Ibid. (June 27, 1919), p. 1844. See also *Bulletin du Ministère du travail* (January–February, 1920), p. 21.

25. Copies of these treaties can be found in Ibid., pp. 7–10, and for Poland in JO (February 4, 1920), p. 1844 and for Italy in Chambre des députés, *Annals, Documents parlementaires* (hereafter cited as JDoc) (annex number 1036, 1920), pp. 1607–1608.

26. MOA, 17 (January 25, 1920), 2.

27. Robert Stahl, *L'organisation du relèvement économique dans le Nord libéré, un an de reconstruction* (Lille: 1920), p. 30. See also Huber, *La population française*, pp. 501–504.

28. Stahl, *L'organisation du relèvement économique*, p. 84, and *Bulletin quotidien* (June 23, 1920).

29. *Le Bâtiment* (August 8, 1919).

30. "Notes on Migration," *International Labour Review*, 2 (April 1922), 542.

31. Of these 135,044 immigrants involved in the reconstruction in September of 1922, 79,493 were Italian; 26,665 Belgian; 10,431 Portuguese; 64,470 Spanish; 6,202 Polish; 1,634 Czech; and 4,146 from various nationalities. William Oualid, "The Occupational Distribution and Status of

Foreign Workers in France," *International Labour Review*, 9 (August 1929), 178.

32. Alfred Morain, *La réconstitution du Nord dévasté: au 1ᵉʳ septembre 1923* (Lille: Impr. Martin-Mamy, 1923).

33. Between 1920 and 1924, French officials recorded 649,611 immigrants entering non-agricultural employment and 362,399 hired as farm workers. See *Bulletin du Ministère du travail*, 33 (July–September 1926), p. 267. While all of these workers entered France under a work contract, an undetermined additional number entered as tourists later finding jobs. Furthermore, the government had only a perfunctory role in recruiting 210,601 eastern Europeans. See note 52.

34. Bunle, *Mouvements migratoires*, p. 18.

35. Archives départementales, Meurthe-et-Moselle, 10 M 37, Interior Ministry circular, November 13, 1919.

36. Ibid., prefect's report to the Interior Ministry, March 15, 1920.

37. Ibid., report of J. Baches, Director of the foreign labor depot at Toul to the Labor Ministry, October 23, 1920.

38. Chambre des députés, *Annales, Débats parlementaires* (hereafter cited as CDeb), July 7, 1920, pp. 2825–2826.

39. *Informations sociales*, 12 (April 14, 1922), 6. See also JO (August 4, 1920), p. 11184 and MOA 18 (June 1920), 2 and 19 (November 1921), 9.

40. MOA, 19 (November 1921), 9.

41. Ibid., 18 (July 1920), 2.

42. Ibid., 19 (January 1921), 708.

43. The Ministry of the Liberated Regions provided CARD a subsidy of 500,000 francs in 1920–1921. See CDeb, March 16, 1923, p. 1324.

44. "Notes on Migration," *International Labour Review*, 4 (May 1924), 744.

45. *Revue d'immigration*, 2 (January 1928), 1.

46. *Industrial and Labour Information*, 4 (March 31, 1924), 484.

47. "Notes on Migration," *International Labour Review*, 4 (May 1924), 744.

48. *Revue d'immigration*, 2 (August 1928), 23.

49. CH 109, SGI meeting notes, May 17, 1924. Included among the SGI's clients were a number of metal-mechanical firms, construction materials companies, Alsatian textile mills, Lyons silk factories, hydro-electric plants in the French Alps, paper mills in the Dauphiné, and glass works in the Vosges. CH 109, SGI report, May 31, 1927.

50. Ibid.

51. International Labour Office, *Studies and Reports*, Series O, no. 5 (1925), p. 95.

52. Bunle, *Mouvements migratoires*, p. 91 and *Revue d'immigration*, 6 (April 1932), 26.

53. *Revue d'immigration*, 6 (April 1932), 32.

54. Ibid., 5 (April 1931), 17.

55. "Notes on Migration," *International Labour Review*, 4 (May 1924), 741.

56. International Labour Office, *Studies and Reports*, Series O, no. 5 (1925), p. 135.

57. *Revue d'immigration*, 6 (April 1932), 26.

58. For a graphic description of the SGI's recruitment practices by an author who, with the co-operation of the SGI, followed a Pole through the immigration process, see G. Le Fevre, *L'Homme travail* (Paris, 1929), pp. 43–74; *Le Peuple* (January 16, 1930).

59. The SGI usually received requests from French employers through their employers' *syndicats*. These requests were sent to the Foreign Labor Services of the Labor or Agriculture Ministries and then to the departmental placement offices for summary approval. In the cases of job offers in agriculture and mining, this last step was not required. The centrality of the SGI can be seen in the accompanying diagram of how the immigration process worked. In its advertising, the SGI claimed that any effort to bypass

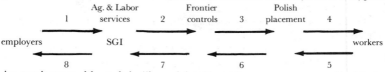

its services would result in "long delays" and "numerous contacts" with the Labor Ministry. *Revue d'immigration*, 3 (February 1929), 16.

60. *Le Tribune des mineurs*, October 10, 1933.

61. These impressions of Polish immigrants were gathered by the Institut national d'études démographiques between 1950 and 1952 in a study of long-term assimilation. The institute interviewed 94 Polish miners, as well as similar numbers of Polish farmworkers (Aisne), Italian construction workers and artisans (Seine), and Italian farmers (Lot-et-Garonne).

These interviews are limited to long-term residents (a sample biased in the Polish case because of the repatriation of leftist Poles during the depression and especially in 1946–1948); still they are one of the few sources available which present the immigrants' viewpoint. See Alain Girard and Jean Stoetzel (Institut nationale des études démographiques) *Français et immigrés: l'attitude française, l'adaptation des italiens et des polonais, Travaux et documents*, Cahier no. 19 (Paris: Presses Universitaires de la France, 1953), pp. 456, 386–387.

62. CH 48, SGI, report, July 1, 1926, CH 109, SGI, reports, March 16, 1927, and May 15, 1927.

63. By 1932, of the 25, 202, 219 francs held by the SGI, this finance company represented 18.8 million francs. The SGI grew from an initial capital investment of 5 million francs in 1924. CH 109, SGI reports, May 10, 1933, March 16 and December 28, 1927, as well as September 2, 1926.

64. CH 107, SGI report, December 9, 1929.

65. As early as September 1928, de Warren noted that the Poles had just demanded more control over the immigration of farm workers, but doubted that the Polish government could "close the doors" because "Yugoslavia ought to be able to give us what we want." CH 48, September 4, 1928. See also the archival reports of M. Paon on his complex maneuverings to limit the SGI in Poland. Paon supported a group of distillers seeking to recruit Poles outside the SGI. In response to de Warren's complaint about this new competition, Paon noted that farmers were critical of excessive SGI profits, F^{10} 2754, Paon to the Ministry of Foreign Affairs, October 17, 1930.

66. René Martial, *Traité de l'immigration et de la greffe inter-raciale* (Cuesmes-lez-Mons: Imprimerie fédérale, 1932), pp. 50–52.

67. *Revue d'immigration*, for example, was a monthly newsletter published by the SGI to advertise its ideas and to provide its customers with information on immigration. It was sponsored by the Comité des houillères, Union des industries métallurgiques et minières, Association de l'immigration des forges et mines de fer de l'Est de la France, Union des industries chimiques, Comité central des fabricants de sucre, and the Office central de la main-d'oeuvre agricole.

68. Jean-Charles Bonnet, *Les pouvoirs publics français et l'immigration dans l'entre deux guerres* (Lyons: Centre d'histoire économique et sociale de la région lyonnaise, 1976), pp. 100–101.

69. See Maier, *Recasting Bourgeois Europe*, pp. 458–480, 494–510 for an account of the Cartel des Gauches.

70. See Archives départementales, Pas-de-Calais (hereafter cited as PC) M 2382, Report of Commissiare spéciale of Carvin, March 8, 1920, for an account of a short strike of reconstruction workers against the hiring of immigrants.

71. For example, see Confédération général du Travail, *Congrés national corporatif: compte rendu des travaux* (1918), pp. 22–23.

72. For the opinions of public health officials, see the entire issue of *La Revue d'hygiène*, 48 (November 1926), which was devoted to the problem of immigration and public health. For police fears of Polish enclaves, see Archives départementales, Nord (hereafter cited as N) M 208–135, Report of Procureur of Douai to the Justice Ministry, May 10, 1922.

73. Charles Lambert, *France et les étrangers* (Paris: Delegrave, 1928).

74. Jean-Charles Bonnet, *Les pouvoirs publics français*, pp. 71–79.

75. See Italy, Commissariato generale dell'emigrazione, *L'emigrazione italiana, 1910–1923* and *1923–1925* (Rome: Edizione del commissariato generale dell'emigrazione 1924 and 1926), for the official position of the Italian government on emigration. Attilio Oblath reviews Italian policy in the late

1920s in "Italian Emigration and Colonialization Policy," *International Labour Review*, 11 (June 1931), 805–834.

76. Among the proponents of de Warren's bill were the Union des industries métallurgiques et minières, the Fédération national du bâtiment, and the Fédération des employeurs industriels et commercials. See *Industrial and Labour Information*, 4 (March 31, 1924), 486. This bill appears in the *Chambre des députés, Annales, Documents parlementaires* (hereafter cited as CDoc) (Annex number 2343, 1921), pp. 1444–1446.

77. For a discussion of the CGT's position, see Confédération général du travail, *Congrès national corporatif: compte rendu des travaux*, 19 (1923), 116–118. See also *Le Peuple* (September 9, 1924).

78. See "Notes on Migration," *International Labour Review*, 3 (July 1923), 109, *Industrial and Labour Information*, 3 (May 4, 1923), 216, and *Le Temps* (December 8, 1924).

79. B. Nogaro was a veteran administrator from the Ministry of Labor and in charge of negotiations during the war for procuring European immigrant workers. As Deputy from Gers and a *rapporteur* of the Commission du travail, he inserted his proposal for an immigration office into the budget request of the Ministry of Labor for 1925. It can be found in CDoc (Annex number 517, 1924), p. 1995. Parliamentary discussion of this proposal appears in CDeb (December 17, 1924), pp. 4383–4386, 4602.

80. For an overview of the debate on Nogaro's proposal, see Louis Pasquet, *Immigration et la main-d'oeuvre étrangère en France* (Paris: Rieder, 1927), p. 108. The CGT's response appears in *Le Peuple* (November 12, 1924, and March 17, 1925). The criticisms of agricultural organizations and parliamentary representatives appear in MOA, 20 (January 1925), 16 and 20 (May, 1925), 16.

IV: Farms, Mines, and Poles

1. Data on French economic development in this period are found in Alfred Sauvy, *Histoire économique de la France entre les deux guerres* (Paris: A. Sauret, 1969), especially volume 2, chapter 5; Jean Jacques Carré, ed., *French Economic Growth* (Stanford: Stanford University Press, 1975), pp. 41, 169; and William Ogburn and William Jaffe, *The Economic Development of Post-War France* (New York: Columbia University Press, 1929).

2. *Annuaire Statistique de la France* (1910), p. 152; (1928), p. 128.

3. Henri Bunle (Institut national des études économiques), *Mouvements migratoires entre la France et l'étranger, Études et documents*, no. 4, p. 96.

4. France, Statistique générale, *Résultats Statistiques du recensement général de la population* (hereafter cited as *Recensement*), 1, no. 5 (1931), 65.

5. *Main-d'oeuvre agricole* (MOA), 20 (March 1922), 5.

6. A. Fontaine, *L'industrie française pendant la guerre* (Paris: Presses universitaires de France, 1925), p. 58.

7. *Annuaire statistique* (1910), p. 153; (1928), p. 128.

8. The mean daily wage in industry rose from four francs (10-hour day) in 1911 to 33.8 francs (8-hour day) in 1930; by contrast, the daily wage in agriculture rose only from 3.3 francs in 1911 to 24.7 in 1930 (high in comparison to other sources see note 25). Thus, while in 1911 farm workers earned 83.5 per cent of industrial wages, by 1930 they earned only 73 per cent of industrial wages and worked for a much longer day (often twelve or more hours). See *Annuaire statistique* (1966), pp. 422, 424–425. See also Michel Augé-Laribé, "Labour Conditions in French Agriculture," *International Labour Review*, 12 (January 1932), 38–39, and *Bulletin du Ministère du travail*, 29 (April–June 1922), 177.

9. MOA, 20 (March 1922), 4–5.

10. See Michel Augé-Laribé, *Le paysan français après la guerre* (Paris: Garnier frères, 1923), chapters 1–3, and Confédération général du travail (CGT), *Le Congrès de travailleurs de l'agriculture* (1920), pp. 37–39.

11. Augé-Laribé, "Labour Conditions," p. 33.

12. *Bulletin du Ministère du travail*(1929–1931).

13. In 1931, 50 per cent of the aliens working in agriculture and fishing were employed in the 25 departments directly on the frontier. *Recensement*, 1, no. 5 (1931), 234, 236.

14. Bunle, *Mouvements migratoires*, p. 96.

15. Michel Huber, *La population de la France* (Paris: Hachette, 1937), pp. 780–781.

16. CGT, *Congrès de travailleurs de l'agriculture* (1920), pp. 181, 195, and Augé-Laribé, *Le paysan*, p. 461.

17. Chao Ying Li, *Le mouvement de la main-d'oeuvre étrangère en France* (Dijon: Langres, 1940), pp. 25–26.

18. MOA, 20 (April 1922), 5.

19. See Bunle, *Mouvements migratoires*, p. 96, and *Annuaire statistique* (1929), pp. 54* and 84*, which show that the number of sugar beet workers increased from about 20,000 in 1922 to 29,700 in 1930.

20. Chambre des deputés (CDeb), *Annales, Débats parlementaires* (November 29, 1927), pp. 335–337.

21. International Labour Organization, *Monthly Record of Migration*, 1 (April 1926), 172–174.

22. Augé-Laribé, "Labour Conditions," p. 33.

23. Ibid. See also CGT, *Congrès de travailleurs de l'agriculture* (1920), pp. 180–195.

24. René Martial, *Traité de l'immigration et de la greffe inter-raciale* (Cuesmes-lez-Mons: Imprimerie fédérale, 1930), p. 230.

25. Zdzislaw Ludkiewicz, "Agrarian Structure of Poland and France from the Point of View of Emigration," *International Labour Review*, 10 (August 1930), 173–176.

26. MOA, 18 (November 1920), 2. See also Albert Demangeon and Georges Mauco, *Documents pour servir à l'étude des étrangers dans l'agriculture française* (Paris: Hermann, 1939), p. 128.

27. Archives des Charbonnages de France (CH) 109, Société général d'immigration report, May 15, 1927.

28. *Recensement*, 1, no. 5 (1931), 258–328.

29. CH 109, Société général d'immigration report, May 15, 1927.

30. MOA, 20 (October 1922), 4. Note that between 1921 and 1926, 37 percent of the Polish farm workers entering France were women (29,549). In comparison, for the immigrant population as a whole the figure was only 27 percent (1931) and for the same period as that of the Poles, only 18 percent of the Italians, 4 percent of the Belgians, and 31 percent of the Spanish were women. Huber, *Population*, p. 816, and *Recensement*, 1, no. 3 (1926), 181.

31. Louis Poszwa, *L'émigration polonaise agricole en France* (Paris: Gebethner and Wolff, 1930), pp. 97, 100–101.

32. CDeb, November 29, 1927, p. 3258. Marcel Paon, chief of the labor service of the Agricultural Ministry, admitted that farmers paid foreign workers below the French rate because farmers had no guarantee of the immigrants' "professional value" when they were first hired. Seldom, however, did the French raise their pay. *Le Peuple* (February 15, 1927).

33. Poszwa, *L'émigration polonaise*, p. 116.

34. MOA, 20 (October 1922), 5.

35. Augé-Laribé, *Le paysan*, p. 102.

36. This at least was the claim of deputy Eugen Raude, CDeb, December 21, 1931, p. 822.

37. André Pairault, *L'immigration organisée et l'emploi de la main-d'oeuvre étrangère en France* (Paris: Presses universitaires de France, 1926), p. 213.

38. Huber, *Population*, p. 831.

39. Martial, *Traité*, p. 215.

40. Archives départementales, Pas-de-Calais (hereafter cited as PC) M 3210-11, passim.

41. *Revue d'immigration*, 6 (April 1932), 8.

42. MOA, 18 (July 1920), 3.

43. See "L'Opieka d'Amiens," *Les Dossiers de l'Action populaire* (September

15, 1925), pp. 770–777, and "Un noyau polonais dans le département de l'Aisne," *Les Dossiers de l'Action Populaire* (October 25, 1925), pp. 841–845.

44. For an example of this belief that rural proprietorship would instill petty bourgeois attitudes, see *Le Temps* (September 27, 1924). See also "La valeur de la terre et l'immigration," *Moniteur des intérêts materials* (June 23, 1926), for this notion of land acquisition as a solution to the problem of immigrant instability.

45. In 1927, there were 4,797 Belgium, 14,719 Italian, 8,045 Spanish, and 3,413 Swiss landowners. However, there were only 109 Polish, 68 Hungarian, and 27 Czech landholders. See Ministère de l'Agriculture, *Enquête sur les étrangers* (Paris: Imprimerie nationale, 1929), pp. 46–47.

46. Robert Lafitte-Leplace, *L'économie charbonnière de la France* (Paris, 1933), chapters 1–2.

47. "Situation de personnel employé dans les etablissements sinistrés," *Réconstitution industriel*, 4 (January 1, 1923), 12. Stephane Wlocevski, "La main-d'oeuvre polonaise en France: enquête dans le bassin houille du Nord et du Pas-de-Calais," *Pologne*, 14 (November 1933), 537.

48. Miners in 1922 earned about 19 francs per day while masons' assistants could earn 30 or more francs. *Annuaire statistique* (1938), pp. 173* and 200*.

49. CH 7, Report to the General Assembly of the Comité des houillères, March 26, 1920. On January 1, 1918, there were only 5,734 non-militarized French miners in the mining population of 145,721, a fact that helps explain the problem of reconstituting a free labor force after the war. F^{14} 13423, Report of the Ministère du travaux publics, January 1, 1918.

50. *Conseil général du Pas-de-Calais*, 3 (1920), Report of Ingenieur des mines, 437.

51. Ibid., pp. 430, 438; see also *Annuaire statistique* (1966), p. 229.

52. *Bulletin quotidien* (January 26, 1920), and *Le Temps* (August 31, 1920).

53. The birth rate in the mining town of Bully, for example, dropped from 400 annually per 10,000 in the period of 1901–1911 to 280 per 10,000 in the decade 1921–1931. Phillipe Ariès, *Histoire des populations françaises* (Paris: SELF, 1948), pp. 228, 249–262.

54. Hans Urig-Wehren, "Die Polen im Ruhrgebiet bis 1918," in *Moderne Deutsche socialgeschichte*, ed. Hans Urig-Wehren (Cologne: Kiepenheur, 1968), pp. 437–455.

55. Czeslaw Kaczmarek, *L'émigration polonaise en France après la guerre* (Paris: Berger, 1928), p. 131, for the years 1922 to 1925, and Lafitte-Laplace, *L'économie charbonnière*, pp. 197–198 for 1919–1921 and 1926–1929.

56. M. Georges, "Le développement de la production en 1923 dans les mines du Nord et du Pas-de-Calais," *Revue de l'industrie minérale*, 4 (January 8, 1924), 345.

57. *Reveil du Nord* (April 18, 1923).

58. *Annuaire statistique* (1932), p. 62*.

59. When one uses the census figures for 1911 and 1931, which include the entire mining class (no figures for coal only), 95 per cent of the growth in the mining work force is a result of immigration. *Recensement*, 1, no. 3 (1931), 19, and 1, no. 5 (1931), 122.

60. CH 7 Report of the Comité des houillères, 1920.

61. *Annuaire statistique* (1931), p. 62*.

62. Jean Condevaux, *Le Mineur du Nord et du Pas-de-Calais* (Lille, 1928), pp. 10, 15.

63. *Conseil général du Pas-de-Calais*, 3 (1924), Report of the Ingenieur des mines, 133. In December of 1934, foreigners comprised 42 percent of the underground miners in the Pas-de-Calais mines and 46 percent of those in the Nord. This involved 87 per cent of the foreigners employed by the mines. PC 1 Z 501 subprefect of Douai report, February 3, 1935.

64. M. Georges, "Renseignements statistiques sur les mines du Pas-de-Calais en 1924," *Revue de l'industrie minérale* 4 (August 1, 1924), 396.

65. PC M 2384, M 6679, passim.

66. *Conseil général du Pas-de-Calais*, 3 (1925), Report from Ingenieur des mines, 118. One police report claimed that the mines eliminated unmarried foreign workers "with the slightest pretense" in order to lower production costs. The operators expected no serious opposition as "no one cares about them." PC M 382, Report of Commissaire de Police of Bruay, March 13, 1928.

67. Kaczmarek, *L'émigration polonaise*, p. 224.

68. PC M 8213, mine company correspondence with prefect, May 28, 1929. In some cases labor-hungry construction companies sent agents to the mines to hire directly at the canteens and barracks. Despite pledges not to pirate the immigrants of other mines, some operators in the Loire induced Poles to leave their jobs in the mines of the north. See PC M 6857, Labor Ministry report to the prefect, May 34, 1923, and PC M 3213, report of (Commissaire spécial) of Lens, June 22, 1929.

69. For example, Alfred Morain, the prefect of the Nord, required that the name of the importing employer be placed on the identity card of the immigrant to discourage job-hopping. Alfred Morain, *La réconstitution du Nord devasté au 1ᵉʳ septembre 1923* (Lille: Martin-Mamy, 1923), p. 127.

70. PC M 3213 contains numerous examples of state aid for employers suffering contract ruptures for the years 1929–1930. However, in the case of thirty-two Poles who the mines of Ostricourt had identified as runaways in 1929, only four could be found from forwarding addresses left at the mine.

71. Archives départementales, Nord (hereafter cited as N) M 208-135, Report of *procureur* of Douai to the prefect, May 10, 1922.

72. Ibid., Report of CS of Lille, March 21, 1923.

73. *Conseil général du Pas-de-Calais,* 3 (1924), Report of the Ingenieur des mines, 193.

74. N M 208-135, Prefect's report to subprefects, March 2, 1923.

75. For descriptions of coal mining housing, see Ariès, *L'histoire des populations françaises,* pp. 249–262, and Rolande Trempé, *Les mineurs aux Carmaux: 1848–1914* (Paris: Les éditions ouvrières, 1971), passim.

76. One could easily exaggerate the role of housing, for there were higher proportions of workers per house in the 1920s than before the war, a fact which may have contributed less to stability than to the inexpensive maintenance of the new miners. See M. Georges, "Les mines du Pas-de-Calais en 1924," p. 346.

77. Morain, *La réconstitution du Nord,* p. 74, and N M 208-135, subprefect at Valenciennes to the prefect, March 16, 1927.

78. Stephane Wlocevski, "Le Scoutisme," *Pologne,* 13 (November 1933), 52.

79. PC M 6689, Circular from the Ministry of Labor, March 16, 1930, and October 23, 1928.

80. Calculated from *Recensement,* 1, no. 5 (1931), 168–172, 158–161.

81. In the Commune of Lens (17 percent foreign in 1926) the birth rate was double that of Cambrai (2 percent foreign). Georges Mauco, *Les étrangers en France* (Paris: A. Colin, 1932), p. 185.

82. N M 208-135, Report of the subprefect of Valenciennes to the prefect, March 16, 1923.

83. Ibid., Letter of the prefect of the Nord to the subprefects, March 2, 1923. Note also that the General Immigration Society advocated that Polish assimilation in France should be delayed for two generations. *Documents du Travail* (March–June 1930), p. 57.

84. Morain, *La réconstitution du Nord,* p. 77.

85. Archives diplomatiques, Poland, 283, (November 1924), 38.

86. Chambre des députés, *Annales, Documents parlementaires* (hereafter cited as CDoc), Annex number 607 (1928), p. 1579.

87. The commissaire spécial (CS) of Lens noted the "precious aid in the purification of the Polish colony of the principal extremists" provided by a Polish journalist. PC 1Z 501, April 20, 1926.

88. Kaczmarek, *L'émigration polonaise,* pp. 280, 287, 294.

89. In the period between March 1923 and January 1925, some 31,527 Westphalian Poles passed through the depot at Toul; of these, 5,260 were men (i.e., mostly miners) or 32 percent of the total; 7,540 were women or 24 percent; and 13,904 were children (under 16 years old) or 44 percent. In contrast, between April and December 1924, the Poles who migrated directly from Poland were distributed as follows: 15,121 men (47 percent), 6,677

women (21 percent), and 10,099 children (32 percent). MM 10 M 37, reports of prefect of Meurthe-et-Moselle to the Ministry of Hygiene, April 10, 1923 to February 15, 1925.

90. PC M 6857, reports of the Procureur of Arras, 1929; Kaczmarek, *L'émigration polonaise,* p. 367; and Alain Girard and Jean Stoetzel, *Francais et immigrés: l'attitude française, l'adaptation des italiens et des polonais* (Cahier 19, Institut national des études démographiques) (Paris: Presses universitaires de France, 1953), p. 459.

91. Bunle, *Mouvements migratoires,* p. 100.

92. There were, of course, problems of adjustment. The Westphalian Poles had been accustomed to German mines, which were more modern and provided better safety and hygienic standards. Their coming to France often resulted in a drop in status and position in the occupational hierarchy since they were not given seniority. Kaczmarek, *L'émigration polonaise,* pp. 280–294. See also E. Gogolewski, "Les polonaises en France avant la seconde guerre mondiale," *Revue du Nord,* no. 242 (1979), 649–663.

93. Ibid., p. 118.

94. PC M 3231, report of the CS of Lens, February 8, 1923.

95. R. Poignant, " L'immigration polonaise dans le Pas-de-Calais," (Arras: unpublished MS.), pp. 18, 22.

96. PC 1Z 501, report of the CS of Lens, February 12, 1924.

97. N M 208-135, report of the CS of Douai, November 24, 1924, and PC 1Z 501, report of the CS of Lens, February 24, 1926.

98. For information on the ZRP, see R. Poignant, "L'émigration polonaise," pp. 44–45, and Stephane Wlocevski, "Chronique de l'émigration polonaise en France," *Pologne* 13 (December 1933), 112.

99. PC M 3229, report of the CS of Bethune, September 12, 1925.

100. PC 1Z 501, report of the CS of Bethune, October 23, 1924.

101. Ibid., report of the Commissaire de police of Bethune, June 29, 1924.

102. Ibid., Report of the CS of Lens, January 17, 1926.

103. Archives nationales (hereafter cited with "F" numbers), AN F⁷ 13269, Correspondence between the CGT and the ZRP, January 1927.

104. In the mines of Anzin (Nord), Martial reported that contract ruptures for the entire work force dropped to 5 percent by 1925 from a prewar figure of 19 percent. Martial, *Traité de l'immigration,* p. 257.

105. *Revue d'immigration,* 5 (January 1931), 17; *Recensement,* 1, no. 5 (1931), 57.

106. *Informations sociales,* 13 (June 5, 1933), 374, and AN F⁷ 14369, Interior Ministry correspondence with the Ministry of Foreign Affairs, March 10, 1928.

107. *Recensement,* 1, no. 5 (1931), 317, 299; 1, no. 3 (1931), 172–173.

108. PC M 6857, report of the CS of Bethune, September 30, 1929.

109. PC 1Z 501, *Narodowiec*, February 13, 1926 (French translation).

110. Ibid., report of the CS of Lens, January 4, 1925, and April 27, 1925.

111. N M 208-135, report of the CS of Douai, September 30, 1925.

112. Archives diplomatiques, Pologne, 271 (February 1927), 83–87.

113. AN F⁷ 13469, report of the prefect of the Nord, October 1, 1925.

114. N M 208-135, report of the CS of Douai, September 30, 1925.

115. Ibid., report of the CS of Lille, September 30, 1926, and translations of *Wiarus Polski*, November 17, 1927, and April 11, 1929.

V: The Fascist State and Italian Emigration

1. France, Statistique générale, *Résultats statistiques du recensement général de la population* (hereafter cited as *Recensement)*, 1, no. 3 (1911), 146–147. See also Comte de Canisy, *La question ouvrière dans le bassin de Briey* (Paris: 1919); G. Hottenger, *Le Pays de Briey* (Nancy: Berger-Levrault, 1912); G. Reynaud, "La colonie italienne d'Homecourt," *Le musée social*, 15 (October 1910), 205–241; Serge Bonnet, C. Santini, and H. Barthelemy, "Les Italiens dans l'arrondissement de Briey avant 1914," *Annales de l'Est*, 35 (1962); and Jean-Baptiste Duroselle and E. Serra, *L'immigrazione italiana in Francia prima de 1914* (Milan: F. Angeli, 1978).

2. Commissiarato generale dell'emigrazione (CGE), *Annuario statistico dell' emigrazione italiana* (Rome: Edizione del CGE, 1925), pp. 375–376.

3. Istituto centrale di Statistica, *Sommario di statistische storiche dell'Italia, 1861–1965* (Rome: ISSN, 1966) pp. 28–29.

4. See Anne Marie Faidutti, *L'immigration italienne dans le sud-est de la France* (Gap: Editions Ophrys, 1964), for a description of the origins and distribution of Italian labor in France before the war, especially pp. 1–50. *Annuario statistico dell'emigrazione italiana*, pp. 275–276.

5. For background on international migrations in Europe in the 1920s, see John W. Brown, *World Migration and Labor* (Amsterdam: International Federation of Trade Unions, 1926); Donald Taft, *Human Migration* (New York: Ronald Press, 1936); and Louis Varlez, *Les migrations internationales et leur réglementations* (Paris: Recueil des cours, 1929).

6. In 1925, 34 percent of the Italian immigrants originated from Venetia, 18 percent from Piedmont, 12 percent from Lombardy, 9 percent from Tuscany, and 7 percent from Emilia—all northern provinces. The other 20 percent came from central and southern Italy. Data derived from Opera Bonomelli, *Vadecum dell'emigrante* (Milan), p. 100.

7. CGE, *L'emigrazione italiana, 1910–1923*, p. 70.

8. John W. Brown, *World Migration and Labour* (Amsterdam: International Federation of Trade Unions,1926), p. 80.

9. P. Armenjon and G. de Fonclare, "L'immigration italienne dans la région des Alpes françaises," *Revue économique internationale: Bruxelles*, 21 (May 1929), 285.

10. Gérard Walter, *L'évolution de problème de la main-d'oeuvre dans la métallurgie de la Lorraine* (Maçon: J. Buguet-Comptour, 1935).

11. *Recensement*, 1, no. 2 (1931), 149–155 and 1, no. 1 (1931), 76.

12. Ibid., 1, no. 3 (1931), 149–155 and 1, no. 5 (1931), 76.

13. CGE, *L'emigrazione, 1910–1923*, pp. 95–96. See also Guiseppe de Michelis, *La corporazione del mondo* (Milano: V. Bompiani, 1934), for details on his philosophy of labor exchanges.

14. CGE, *L'emigrazione, 1910–1923*, pp. 102–103.

15. CGE, *L'emigrazione italiana, 1924–25*, pp. 408–409.

16. Ibid., pp. 342–349, 425–432.

17. Ibid., pp. 342, 344.

18. Ibid., pp. 55–56, 349–351, 336–340.

19. CGE, *L'emigrazione, 1910–1923*, p. 110.

20. CGE, *L'emigrazione, 1924–1925*, pp. 358–360, 374.

21. CGE, *L'emigrazione, 1910–1923*, chapter 4. See also CGE, *L'emigrazione, 1924–1925*, pp. 66–67.

22. In 1924, French employers recruited 18,293 emigrants under individual contracts, while the Italian state recruited 38,463 Italian workers anonymously for the French under collective contracts. Ibid., pp. 349–351, 336–340. See also CGE, *L'emigrazione, 1910–23*, pp. 364, 356.

23. Quoted in E. Albonico, *Saggio di una prima inchiesta sulla emigrazione italiana in Europa* (Milan: Lanzani, 1921), p. 10.

24. Serge Bonnet, "Italian Immigration in Lorraine," *Journal of Social History*, 2 (Winter 1968), 137.

25. CGE, *L'emigrazione, 1910–23*, pp. 602–632.

26. Opera Bonomelli, *Vadecum*, pp. 65–66. See also André Pairault, "La politique italienne d'émigration," *Revue Politique et parlementaire*, 10 (October 12, 1927), 468; for details about the foundation of this religious mission, see Carlo Bello, *Geremia Bonomelli* (Rome: Bescia, 1961).

27. "Notes on Migration," *International Labour Review*, 2 (August 1922), 268.

28. Archives départementales, Meurthe-et-Moselle (hereafter cited as MM), 10M 34, report of Commissaire spéciale (CS) of Briey, August 2, 1924.

29. Archives nationales (hereafter cited with "F" numbers), F⁷ 13453, Report of CS of Strasbourg, December 9, 1921.

30. Albonico, *Saggio*, p. 13.

31. *Recensement*, 1, no. 5 (1931), 76–78, and 1, no. 3 (1931), 96.

32. Raoul Blanchard, "L'électrométallurgie et l'électrochimie dans les Alpes françaises, II," *Les alpes économiques*, 5 (October 1924), 204.

33. F⁷ 13456, undated Interior Ministry report.

34. In *Le Peuple* (May 10, 1921), for example, H. Cordier complained that anti-union Italians moved into the old CGE stronghold of St. Claude in Jura under the tutelage of the Opera Bonomelli. *Le Peuple* (September 9, 1923) reports that Italian clergy and fascists spied on those Italians at St. Claude who participated in a leftist demonstration, leading to their expulsion.

35. Archives diplomatiques, Italie, Volume 85, letter from Robert Pinot, December 2, 1920, pp. 3–28.

36. CGE, *L'emigrazione, 1910–23*, pp. 148–151.

37. G. F. Rosoli, ed., *Un secolo di emigrazione italiana* (Rome: CSER, 1978), p. 37.

38. CGE, *L'emigrazione, 1910–23*, p. 119.

39. Philip Cannistraro and Gianfausto Rosoli, "Fascist Emigration Policy in the 1920s: An Interpretive Framework," *International Migration Review*, 13 (Winter 1979), 683. See also C. Noble, "Politicia migratoria evicende dell'emigrazione durante il fascismo," *Il Ponte* (November–December 1974), pp. 1325–1333.

40. Cannistraro and Rosoli, "Fascist Emigration Policy," p. 675.

41. For the fascist demographic program, see B. Mussolini, "Il problema demografico italiano," *Bollettino dell'emigrazione*, no. 6 (1927), 10, and M. Appelius, "L'emigrazione italiana e il fascismo," *Bollettino dell'emigrazione*, no. 5 (1925), pp. 40–42.

42. Archives diplomatiques, Italie, Volume 185, report of the French consul at Ventimille, January 25, 1928, p. 199.

43. *Corriere della sera* (July 23, 1926), clipping in F⁷ 13458.

44. See speech of Dino Grandi, Italy, *Camera dei Deputati, Atti parlemetarii*, March 31, 1927, quoted in Attilio Oblath, "Italian Emigration and Colonization Policy," *International Labour Review*, 11 (June 1931), 808.

45. For background on Mussolini's colonization program, see Oblath, "Italian Emigration," pp. 831–832. For recent studies of internal colonization see A. Treves, *Le migrazioni interne nell'Italia fascista* (Turin: Einaudi, 1976), and E. Scarzanella, "L'emigrazione veneta nel periodo fascista," *Studi Storici*, 18 (1977), 171–199. For Mussolini's imperialist alternative to emigration, see R. Cantalupo, *L'Italia Mussulmana* (Rome: La Voce, 1928), Denis Mack Smith, *Mussolini's Roman Empire* (New York: Longman, 1976), and Esmonde M. Robertson, *Mussolini as Empire Builder* (New York: Macmillian, 1977).

46. Cannistraro and Rosoli, "Fascist Emigration," pp. 679–681.

47. International Labour Office, *Monthly Record of Migration*, 3 (December

1928), 433.

48. For details of the new decrees, see Ibid., 3 (September 1928), 313. See also the following articles in the *Bollettino dell'emigrazione:* B. Mussolini, "Spiriti e forma della nuova politica dell'emigrazione," no. 5 (1927), 10; Dino Grandi, "La soppressione del Commissariato generale dell'emigrazione nei documenti parlamentari," no. 6 (1927), 38–40; and B. Mussolini, "La nuova politica dell'emigrazione," no. 7 (1927) 75–77. For another interpretation of fascist change of policy in 1927, see Cannistraro and Rosoli, "Fascist Emigration," pp. 686–689.

49. Archives départementales, Isère, 165 M-2 prefect's report to the Ministry of Labor, March 24, 1928.

50. International Labour Office, *Monthly Record of Migration*, 3 (September 1928), 314.

51. Archives diplomatiques, Italie, Volume 185, report of Consul of Vintimille, January 25, 1929, p. 199.

52. Italy, *Atti Parlamenti: Camera di Deputati* (May 26, 1927), p. 7617. See also, Claude Woog, *La politique d'émigration de l'Italie* (Paris: Presses universitaires de France, 1930), pp. 127 ff.

53. International Labour Office, *Monthly Record of Migration*, 3 (September 1928), 314.

54. *Conseil générale de Bouches-du-Rhône* (1929), pp. 429–430, and *Conseil général de l'Isère* (1928), pp. 121–122.

55. Archives départementales, Isère, 165 M-2, report of prefect to the Interior Ministry, March 4, 1928.

56. F⁷ 13458, Interior Ministry report, October 13, 1926; International Labour Office, *Monthly Record of Migrations*, 1 (April 1926), 130–133 and 3 (December 1928), 399. See also Woog, *Politique d'émigration*, p. 109; Armenjon and de Fonclare, "L'immigration italienne," p. 300; and Oblath, "Italian Emigration," pp. 805–834.

57. "Notes on Migration," *International Labour Review*, 3 (February 1923), 649.

58. International Labour Office, *Monthly Record of Migration*, 2 (February 1927), 65.

59. Ibid., 1 (February 1926), 47–48.

60. *Congrès du Bâtiment* (Independent) (1925), p. 146.

61. *L'Humanité* (August 6, 1926) and (January 4, 1927).

62. Archives de la Préfecture de Police (hereafter cited as PP) 67, "Main d'oeuvre" report, 1924.

63. F⁷ 13456, Interior Ministry reports to the Ministry of Foreign Affairs, May 20, 1925, August 22, 1926.

64. F⁷ 13458, report of the CS of Lyons, October 7 and 17, 1926.

65. F⁷ 13458, report of the prefect of Loire-Atlantique (Nantes), November 9, 1926.

66. Archives départementales, Bouches-du-Rhône (hereafter cited as BR), 6 M 10895, passim.

67. F⁷ 13458, report of the CS of Toulouse, June 8, 1926.

68. F⁷ 13454, report of the CS of Menton, December 9, 1922.

69. F⁷ 13454, report from the prefect of the Drome, December 9, 1925.

70. Archives diplomatiques, Italie, Volume 185, internal report, December 23, 1925.

71. Archives départementales, Gard, M 130, report of the prefect to the Interior Ministry, January 19, 1939.

72. CGE, *L'emigrazione, 1924–25*, p. 259.

73. F⁷ 13461, Interior Ministry report to the Ministry of Foreign Affairs, May 12, 1928.

74. PP 283, report of the Prefect of Police to the Interior Ministry, August 19, 1928.

75. F⁷ 13460, report of CS of Toulouse, January 2, 1927.

76. Archives diplomatiques, Italie, Volume 185, undated report (about 1924), p. 226.

77. For example, sixteen Italian organizations, eight language schools, and a vigorous fascist press functioned at Lyons in the early 1920s. Ibid., pp. 241–242.

78. For the demands of French employers for more labor see *Revue d'immigration*, 2 (October 1928), 24; 3 (January 16, 1929), 3; and 3 (September 8, 1929), 30–31. See also *Le Nord industriel* (August 10, 17, and 31, 1929) and *Informations sociales*, 10 (April 7, 1930), 139.

79. *Revue d'immigration*, 3 (February 1930), 18.

80. Ibid., 2 (October 1928), 39. This source reported that the unemployed in Poland decreased from 250,000 in 1927 to only 100,000 by mid-1928.

81. *Informations sociales*, 10 (January 6, 1930), 118, and 9 (July 22, 1929), 33.

82. Polish authorities complained that Polish women worked at men's jobs for "female pay" and frequently were sexually exploited by their employers. *Revue d'immigration*, 3 (January 6, 1929), 7.

83. Ibid.

84. The French Ambassador to Poland quoted a Mr. Stemler who, at a meeting of the "Assembly of Poles Living Abroad," claimed that miners in France contributed to unemployment in Poland for they competed with Polish coal. Archives diplomatiques, Poland, Volume 271, report dated July 18, 1929, p. 141.

85. CH 48, report of an agent of the Societé générale d'immigration, December 16, 1929.

86. *Le Temps* (April 27, 1926).

87. International Labour Office, *Monthly Record of Migration*, 1 (May 1926), 161; 1 (September 1926), 332–333; and 3 (January 1928), 173.

88. *Revue d'immigration*, 3 (January 1929), 7.

89. *Informations sociales*, 10 (March 10, 1930), 467; and 10 (November 3, 1930), 508. See also International Labour Office, *Studies and Documents*, Series O, no. 5 (1925), p. 80.

90. Derived from H. Bunle (Institut national des études économiques), *Mouvements migratoires entre la France et l'étranger, Études et documents*, no. 4 (Paris: Presses universitaires de France, 1943), p. 91.

VI: Foreign Labor in a Period of Growth

1. France, Statistique générale, *Résultats statistiques du recensement général de la population* (hereafter cited as *Recensement*) 1, no. 5 (1931), 74. It is not the purpose of this work to describe in detail the various nationalities which comprised the immigration of the 1920s nor their occupational or regional distribution. For an encyclopedic treatment of these topics, see G. Mauco, *Les étrangers en France* (Paris: A. Colin, 1932).

2. The cartons Archives de la Préfecture de Police (hereafter cited as PP) 67 and Archives départementales Bouches-du-Rhône (hereafter cited as BR) 6M 6262 contain reports of these efforts to flush the North Africans out of Paris and Marseilles.

3. Norbert Gomar, *L'émigration algérienne en France* (Paris: Les presses modernes, 1931), p. 21.

4. BR 14 M 23-21, Arab petition to the prefect, January 22, 1921, and prefect's report to the Ministry of the Interior, January 20, 1921.

5. Ibid., undated (1924) departmental placement office report, pp. 21 and 24.

6. Gomar, *L'émigration*, p. 71, and chapter II. Most colonial immigrants originated from a few districts in Algeria: of the 37,499 Algerian immigrants in 1923, 18,096 came from the department of Tizi-Ouaou, 11,861 from Bougie (Constantine), 3,108 from Selif, and 2,354 from Algiers. See France, *La Situation générale de l'Algérie* (Paris: Imprimerie nationale, 1923), p. 536.

7. M. Huber, *La population de la France pendant la guerre* (Paris: Presses universitaires de France, 1931), p. 793.

8. BR 14 M 23-20, undated departmental placement office report, pp. 4–5.

9. In a study (1924) of 258 metal works employing 60,000 immigrants, only 15 percent of the Arabs were considered by the employers to be "good workers," compared to 85 percent of the Belgians, 70 percent of the Italians,

65 percent of the Poles, and 50 percent of the Portuguese, Spanish, and Russians. See André Pairault, *L'immigration organisée et l'emploi de la main-d'oeuvre étrangère en France* (Paris: Rieder, 1927), p.273.

10. Gomar, *L'émigration*, p. 39.

11. Louis Chevalier, *Le problème démographique Nord-Africain* (Institut national des études démographiques, Cahier no. 6) (Paris: Presses universitaires de France, 1947).

12. *Recensement*, 1, no. 5 (1936), 66.

13. BR 14 M 23-2, undated departmental placement office report, p. 24.

14. *Recensement*, 1, no. 5 (1931), 78.

15. For details on French controls over Algerian migration, see "Notes on Migration," *Industrial and Labour Information*, 12 (October 6, 1924), 47, and International Labour Office, *Monthly Record of Migration*, 2 (April 1927), 114; 2 (November 1927), 421; and 3 (September 1928), 307.

16. Moroccans and Tunisians had to place a deposit of 1,000 francs. BR 6 M 9097, report from the Résidence générale de Maroc to the prefect, October 17, 1931.

17. BR 6 M 8410, 9119, 9117, and 9097 for police reports on clandestine North African immigration.

18. See BR 6 M 9097, 9117, 4949, 6363, and 5582 as well as BR 14 M 23–4 for details on the importation and distribution of refugees. See also G. Mauco, *Les étrangers*, pp. 168 and 172.

19. "Statistics," *International Labor Review*, 10 (February 1930), 275.

20. Mauco, *Les étrangers*, pp. 97–104.

21. For example, Marseilles, as early as 1911, had 97,057 Italian residents (110, 421 total foreigners). A survey by the Italian consul claimed that Italians constituted 45 percent of the coopers (770), 80 percent of the cabinet makers (400), 40 percent of the carpenters (1,400), 40 percent of the stone masons (500), and 30 percent of the painters (660). They also comprised a large share of the employees of heavy industries such as chemicals, olive oil, and gas. See G. Selli, *Marsiligilia a la sua colonia italiana* (Marseilles, 1913).

22. *Recensement*, 1, no. 5 (1936), 66.

23. Jean Gravier, *Paris et le désert français* (Paris: Flammarrion, 1972), p. 52.

24. Mauco, *Les étrangers*, p. 312.

25. *Recensement*, 1, no. 5 (1931), 59, 61.

26. Mauco, *Les étrangers*, p. 312.

27. Ibid., pp. 286–309, and Commissariato generale dell'emigrazione, *L'emigrazione italiana, 1910–1923* (Rome: Edizione del CGE, 1924), p. 39.

28. For the suburbs the alien work force rose from 5 percent to 12.3 percent in the 1920s, whereas it rose in Paris from 6.5 percent to 9.5 percent. *Recensement*, 1, no. 5 (1931), 50.

29. *Recensement,* 1, no. 1 (1931) 62.

30. Ibid., 1, no. 5 (1931), 206–207, 59 and 1, no. 3 (1931), 174–177.

31. Ibid., 271.

32. Ibid., 324.

33. Ibid., 317.

34. Ibid., 315.

35. Between 1921 and 1931, there was a 7 per cent decrease in the proportion of the foreign population living in the border regions. Ibid., 9–10.

36. Commissariato generale dell'emigrazione, *L'emigrazione italiana, 1924–25,* p. 388.

37. Mauco, *Les étrangers,* p. 256.

38. Archives nationales (hereafter cited with "F" numbers) F⁷ 3528, report of Commissaire spéciale of Albi, May 26, 1925. See also Confédération générale du travail *Congrès nationale de la Fédération nationale des travailleurs de l'industrie du bâtiment* (April 1914), pp. 181–192.

39. *L'Humanité* (November 11, 1925), and N M 595-46, trade union poster from Armentières, January 1924.

40. F⁷ 13518, report of the prefect of the Somme, March 12, 1925.

41. *Congrès du Bâtiment* (Independent) (1925), p. 142.

42. PP 314, internal police reports, July 7, 1927, and December 12, 1930.

43. Paul Maurin, *La main-d'oeuvre immigré sur la marché du travail en France* (Paris, 1933), p. 66.

44. *Le Peuple* (April 2, 1930).

45. Archives départementales, Pas-de-Calais (hereafter cited as PC) M 6857, Service de la main-d'oeuvre étrangère (Préfecture), letter to the Ministry of Labor, June 28, 1929.

46. BR 14M 22-5 contains a file of reports from departmental labor inspectors (1928) which show numerous cases of clothing shops and tanneries employing illegal immigrants who worked in crowded and unsafe conditions.

47. Archives départementales, Nord (hereafter cited as N) M 208-135, Labor Ministry to Prefect, December 18, 1927.

48. Mauco, *Les étrangers,* p. 274. See also BR 14M 23-3, "Conférence régionale des Offices du placement," 1923.

49. For details on immigrants in the iron and steel industries, see William Oualid, "Foreign Workers in France," *International Labour Review,* 9 (August 1929), 177; Mauco, *Les étrangers,* p. 256; and Georges Daulatly, *La main-d'oeuvre étrangère en France et la crise économique* (Paris: Loviton, 1933), p. 58. For the Alpine industries, see Raoul Blanchard, "L'électrométallurgie et l'électrochimie dans les Alpes françaises, II," *Les alpes économiques,* 5 (October 1924), 204; P. Armenjon and G. de Fonclare, "L'immigration italienne dans la région des Alpes françaises," *Revue économique internationale: Bruxelles,* 21

(May 1929), 285.

50. Some of the business and trade union descriptions of these industries indicate the rudiments of a program designed to stabilize immigrant workers. There were family housing projects at the Belleviller potash works, for example. See *L'Humanité* (May 24, 1930). Similar projects were undertaken by several plants in the Alpine hydro-electric district (Blanchard, "L'électrométallurgie," p. 205) and in the Lorraine steel centers (Martial, *Traité de l'immigration* (Cuesmes-lez-Mons: Imprimerie fédérale, 1930), p. 251). Yet reports of overcrowded barracks predominated. *L'Humanité* (May 28, 1930) and Blanchard, "L'électrométallurgie," p. 205.

51. *Le Peuple* (December 1 and 4, 1928) for reports on government studies of the immigrant in the Moselle iron and steel industry. For additional background, see Compte de Canisy, *La question ouvrière dans le bassin de Briey* (Paris, 1919), pp. 55–75, and Serge Bonnet, *L'Homme de fer: mineurs de fer et ouvriers sidérurgistes lorrains, 1889–1930* (Nancy: Centre lorraine des études sociologiques, 1976), p. 281.

52. Mauco, *Les étrangers*, p. 275.

53. Blanchard, "L'électrométallurgie," p. 205, and Armenjon and de Fonclare, "L'immigration," p. 285.

54. *Le Peuple* (December 26, 1929) reported that only 10 percent of the international coal and metallurgical regions, which included French Lorraine, the German Saar, and Luxembourg, were unionized. This was partially attributed to the fact that 60 percent of the workers of this district were not citizens of the countries where they worked.

55. F^{14} 11334, Ministry of War circular, "Instructions relatives à l'emploi de main-d'oeuvre algérienne, tunisienne, morocaine, et chinoise," 1917.

56. André Paircault, *L'immigration organisée*, p. 177.

57. Blanchard, "L'électrométallurgie," p. 205.

58. Armenjon and de Fonclare, "L'immigration italienne," p. 285.

59. *L'Humanité* (March 28, 1930).

VII: Acceptance without Integration

1. General background on CGT immigration policy is found in Leon Gani, *Syndicats et travailleurs immigrés* (Paris: Éditions sociales, 1972), pp. 20–24. See also CGT, *Congrès confédéral, compte rendu* (1919), pp. 46–47. For efforts of the construction unions of the northern region, see PC M2373 and M2382, reports of the Commissaire spécial of Lens, November 1921 to March 1924.

2. PC M 2372, report of the Commissaire spécial (CS) of Lens, December 12, 1923. See also CGT, *Voix du peuple*, 20 (September 1938), 26–27.

3. N 599-43, report of the CS, December 10, 1929. See also Georges Kletch, "L'organisation syndicale des travailleurs étrangers" (unpublished in A.D. Pas-de-Calais), pp. 4–5.

4. Annie Kriegel, *La Croissance de la CGT: 1918–21* (Paris: Mouton, 1966), p. 29; Antoine Prost, *La C.G.T. à l'époque du Front populaire* (Paris: A. Colin, 1964), pp. 102, 182; and France, Statistique générale, *Résultats statistiques du recensement général de la population* (hereafter cited as *Recensement)*, 1, no. 5 (1931), 53. When calculating the percentages for "industry," we included the following industries: metals, textiles, garments, construction, mines, chemicals, stone-ceramics, glass, leather, and docks. For a liberal estimate of trade union membership, see David Saposs, *The Labor Movement in Post-War France* (Columbia University Press, 1931), pp. 118, 137.

5. CGTU, *Congrès de la Fédération unitaire des ouvriers et ouvrières sur metaux* (1925), pp. 111–112, and *Congrès de la Fédération nationale unitaire des travailleurs du sous-sol et similaires* (1926), p. 123.

6. Alain Girard and Jean Stoetzel (Institut national des études démographiques), *Français et immigrés, Travaux et documents,* Cahier no. 19 (Paris: Presses universitaires de France, 1953), pp. 191, 461.

7. CGT, *Congrès national de la Fédération du bâtiment* (1929), p. 36.

8. For example, see CGT, *Congrès national de la Fédération des metaux* (1921), pp. 26–27 and (1927), p. 111. See also CGT, *Congrès national de la Fédération du bâtiment* (1929), p. 36. These sources also reveal persistent French displeasure over the continued membership of Belgians in their unions back home, which provided them with emergency benefits unavailable from French unions.

9. Girard and Stoetzel, *Français et immigrés,* pp. 329, 365, 389–390, 421, 456–458.

10. Ibid., pp. 448–449, 466, 475–477.

11. One hundred construction workers struck briefly in 1921 over the hiring of foreign workers; textiles workers from the Nord also demanded priority over Belgian commuters in a meeting with employers from the Roubaix-Tourcoing region. See PC M 2382, report for the Commissaire de police of Carvin, March 8, 1921, and N M 599–43, report of the CS of Lille, January 10, 1921.

12. Archives de la Préfecture de Police (hereafter cited as PP) 67, unsigned internal police report, September 24, 1924, and CGT, *Congrès des travailleurs de l'alimentation* (1919), pp. 53–54. For additional information on anti-immigrant unions, see G. Mauco, *Les étrangers en France,* pp. 476, 481; René Martial, *Traité de l'immigration et de la greffe inter-raciale* (Cuesmes-lez-Mons: Imprimerie fédérale, 1930), p. 154; and Jean-Charles Bonnet, *Les pouvoirs publics français et l'immigration dans l'entre deux guerres* (Lyons: Centre d'histoire économique et sociale de la région lyonnaise, 1976), p. 86. Note also another center of anti-immigrant sentiment, a fraction of the CGTU's construction workers,

which became independent in 1924. Dominated by anarcho-sydicalists from Lyons, this group expressed a deep hostility to immigrants. A report at its congress in 1925 declared that immigrants came "to France only for a short time and accepted any working conditions. Their ambition is to get as much money as possible; their appetite for money makes them enemies of all social development and makes them go against us." The report warned them to respect the eight-hour day, refuse to work on the piece rate, and to adhere to the French union. If they did not, they "placed themselves outside the French workers movement. Anyone who fights the proletariat with or without knowledge exposes himself to its wrath. . . ." This "friendly warning" was distributed throughout the worksites in which this union had influence. See *Congrès du bâtiment* (Independent) (1925), pp. 139–149.

13. David Saposs, *The Labor Movement in Post-War France* (New York: Columbia University Press, 1931), pp. 155–163.

14. *L'Humanité* (September 22, 1924, March 3, 13, and 16, 1926, and August 17, 1927).

15. Ibid. (January 7, 1927, September 28, 1927, and January 9, 1928). See also CGTU, *Congrès national, compte rendu des débats* (1927), p. 478.

16. Ibid. (1925), p. 392.

17. CGTU, *Congrès de la Fédération nationale unitaire des travailleurs du sous-sol et similaires* (1926), p. 54.

18. PP 300, untitled internal report, February 21, 1929.

19. CGTU, *Congrès de la Fédération nationale des travailleurs du bâtiment* (1927), p. 152.

20. Prost, *La C.G.T.,* p. 202.

21. Especially construction and taxi driver unions affiliated with the CGTU resisted the policy of solidarity with foreigners. See CGTU, *Congrès . . . des travailleurs du bâtiment,* pp. 179–180, where a delegate admitted that there were strong nationalist sentiments against immigrants in the building trades unions of Paris and doubted that immigrants would be organized into these unions as a result.

22. See M. Huber, *La population de la France pendant la guerre* (Paris: Presses universitaires de France, 1931), p. 509, and Henri Bunle (Institut national des études économiques), *Mouvements migratoires entre la France et l'étranger, Études et documents,* no. 4 (Paris: Presses universitaires de France, 1943), p. 77.

23. *Main-d'oeuvre agricole,* 17, no. 9 (January 25, 1920), 2.

24. For example, the subprefect of the Vienne in Isère asked textile manufacturers to lay off colonial and foreign workers before the French. Archives départementales, Isère, M 165-2, subprefect's report, November 23, 1920.

25. Data for this figure was derived from the *Bulletin du Ministère du travail,* 43

(January–March 1936), p. 25; 43 (July–September 1936), p. 290; and 45 (January–March 1938), p. 17.

26. For an official description of the powers of the Foreign Labor Service, see "Organisation du placement," an unpublished internal report of the Service (1930?) found in Archives départementales, Bouches-du-Rhône (BR) 14 M 22-23.

27. Derived from *Bulletin du Ministère du travail* (1921–1931).

28. In 1928, some 32,136 immigrants requested regularization, of which 68 percent were approved. This was 33 percent of the 97,742 immigrants who entered France in 1928 with a work permit and under the control of the Foreign Labor Service. Mauco, *Les étrangers,* pp. 131, 135.

29. *Le Temps* (February 28, 1927), and International Labor Office, *Monthly Record of Migration,* 2 (March 1927), 95–96. See also Archives nationales (hereafter cited with "F" numbers) F⁷ 13423, Interior Ministry circular, January 21, 1927.

30. *Le Peuple* (January 7, 1927).

31. Ibid. (December 11, 1929).

32. F⁷ 13527, Prefect of Police report to the Interior Ministry, November 7, 1927, and Prefect of Police report to the Labor Ministry, November 12, 1927. See also International Labor Office, *Monthly Record of Migration,* 2 (March 1927), 96, and 2 (April 1927), 114.

33. Unemployment funds were restricted to those workers who fulfilled a residence requirement (six months to a year depending on the commune or township), a qualification that many of the transient foreigners could not meet. Also, because communes were required to give aliens this aid by treaty rather than general law, only the nationals of Italy, Poland, Czechoslovakia, and Belgium had a legal right to unemployment funds. As a general indication of how few immigrants obtained relief benefits, only 37 of the 2,942 beneficiaries of these funds in St. Etienne in 1927 were immigrants. The figure was only 18 of the 377 recipients in Meurthe-et-Moselle. F⁷ 13423, reports of the prefects to the Labor Ministry, and return directives, September 1927.

34. F⁷ 13427, Prefect of Police report to the Labor Ministry, November 14, 1927.

35. *Le Temps* (March 4, 1927).

36. See, for example, the editorial of the CGT leadership, *Le Peuple* (July 11, 1925).

37. BR 14 M 23-20, departmental placement office report, 1920.

38. In many cases, according to the CGT, these commissions met only biannually, functioning primarily as window dressing for an otherwise bureaucratic operation. See *Le Peuple* (November 4, 1930).

39. For example, the director of the placement office of the Isère claimed

that during the recession of 1921 he tried to prevent a flood of cheap foreign workers from affecting prevailing wage levels. Archives départementales, Isère, 169 M 1, placement office report July 21, 1921, pp. 368–369. The director of the placement office of the Bouches-du-Rhône frequently investigated whether employers seeking to hire immigrants were offering them substandard wages. BR 14M 23–24 letter from the placement office director to the Foreign Labor Service, March 28, 1926.

40. Even in 1924, a year of economic prosperity, the placement office director of the Seine declared that he treated any immigrant's request for a work permit to be an "offer of employment for a French worker." Office départemental de placement de la Seine, *Rapport au Conseil général* (1924), p. 147.

41. In the Gard, for example, the parity commission was composed of eight workers, five of which were identified by profession; a carpenter, rope maker, an accountant, mason, and mechanic. The employers' representatives included a candy manufacturer, two bakers, a construction contractor, a local "industrialist," and three farmers. Archives départementales, Gard 14 M 1174, report of the departmental placement office, September 4, 1922.

42. BR 14 M 23–20, report of the departmental placement office, 1920. See also Henri Sellier and Emile Deslandres, "La constitution de l'Office départmental du placement et de la statistique du travail de la Seine" (1918), p. 2.

43. Office départemental de placement de la Seine, *Rapport au Conseil général* (1930), p. 59.

44. See *Le Peuple* (May 14, 1924), and *L'Humanité* (April 5, 1924) for evidence of fears of immigrants flooding the construction industry of Paris.

45. Office départemental de placement de la Seine, *Rapport au Conseil général* (1930), p. 59, and Archives départementales Isère, M 162–2, report of the departmental placement office, 1929.

46. See Charles Tilly et al., *The Rebellious Century* (Cambridge: Harvard University Press, 1975), pp. 48–55.

47. The National Manpower Council included six members from each of the following groups: the CGT, employer associations (including the Comité de forges and the SGI), parliament, and the government bureaucracy. See *Voix du peuple* (March 27, 1927), 1, and *Revue d'immigration*, 1 (October 28, 1927), 2.

48. *Le Peuple* (June 25, 1925).

49. M. Labe, a CGT delegate to the National Manpower Council and secretary of the metal workers, had high hopes of the council's becoming a tool with which to organize the national labor market. He expected it to frame government policy, to lead to the elimination of private manpower offices, and

to more effectively control immigration. He was convinced that allies of the CGT from the chamber (e.g., B. Nogaro) that were also on the council would help to realize these goals. See CGT, *Congrès de la Fédération des ouvriers des metaux* (1925), pp. 196–197.

50. The Agricultural Ministry, which was to control farm labor immigration, never exercised any controls in the interests of local labor, according to the CGT. The same was true of the departmental placement offices in mining regions. See *Le Peuple* (May 21, 1926).

51. Ibid. (August 18, 1925, May 3, 1926, and May 21, 1926). See also *Revue d'immigration*, 2 (May 1928), 24, and 3 (June 1929), 18.

52. For example, see *Information sociale et ouvrière*, 6 (July 1923), 8.

53. *Le Peuple* (July 11, 1925).

54. *Journal officiel de la République de France, Lois et décrets*, August 10, 1926, p. 9171 for the text of the law. Note that even though employers could be fined for infractions of this law, the "harmed employer" had to make a complaint. The investigative resources of the Ministries of Labor and Agriculture were inadequate; they had to rely on local police for information. For more details, see *Revue d'immigration*, 3 (January 7, 1929), 8.

55. Only 440 cases of violations of this law were prosecuted in 1928. *Revue d'immigration*, 3 (June 1929), 17.

56. See Ibid., 5 (April 1931), 2–3.

57. *Recensement*, 1, no. 5 (1936), 58.

58. Ibid., 51.

59. Ibid., 1, no. 5 (1931), 59.

60. Ibid., 1, no. 5 (1931), 52.

61. The scales were derived from ibid., 107. *Annuaire statistique de la France* (1909), pp. 126–129 and (1935), pp. 188–190. The percentages were calculated from the following equation: where economically active French in each industry in 1906 equals FA 6, total economically active population in 1906 and 1931 equal TA 6 and TA 31, the expected French actives in 1931 equal FE 31 and actual French actives in 1931 equal FA 31, the rate of displacement is calculated as follows: $\dfrac{FA\,6}{TA\,6} = \dfrac{FE\,31}{TA\,31}$,

$$FE\,31 = \frac{FA\,6\,TA\,31.}{TA\,6} \qquad \text{Displacement rate} = \frac{FA\,31 - FE\,31.}{TA\,31} \qquad \text{These displace-}$$

ment rates, calculated for each industry, were then corrected to discount the effect of French war losses and population decline and to isolate the factor of occupational migration. The correction is the displacement rate for the entire French workforce in 1931 or 4.4 percent. The corrected displacement rate for each industry involved subtracting 4.4 percent from each of the rates.

VIII: Limits of Assimilation

1. Jean Charles Bonnet, *Les pouvoirs publics français et l'immigration dans l'entre deux guerres* (Lyon: Centre d'histoire économique et sociale de la région lyonnaise, 1976), pp. 13–45.

2. France, Statistique générale, *Resultats statistiques du recensement général de la population* (hereafter cited as *Recensement*), 1, no. 1 (1931), 41.

3. Ibid., 1, no. 2 (1931), 57 and 81.

4. *Le Reveil du Nord* (June 28, 1924).

5. René Martial, "Le Problème de l'immigration," *Revue politique et parlementaire*, 22 (December 10, 1926), 401.

6. Georges Dequidt, *La Revue d'hygiène*, 48 (November 1926), 1000 and 1019; see also *Information sociale et ouvrière* (July 10, 1926), and G. Dequidt, "Assistance aux étrangers" (report for the Ministry of Interior, 1929), p. 140.

7. Archives départementales, Nord (N) M 208-135 (the entire file contains reports relating to police reaction to the influx of Poles into the mines of this department).

8. Archives diplomatiques, Italie, 185, note from the Ministry of Interior to the Ministry of Foreign Affairs, 1926, p. 130.

9. Georges Marcel-Remond, *L'immigration italienne dans le sud-ouest de la France* (Paris: Dalloz, 1928), p. 22.

10. Archives diplomatiques, Italie, Volume 185, French Ambassador to the United States letter to the Ministry of Foreign Affairs, March 21, 1924, p. 134, and N M 605-19 Ministry of Foreign Affairs circular to the prefects, November 1, 1926.

11. Louis Chevalier, *Laboring Classes and Dangerous Classes in Paris during the First Half of the Nineteenth Century* (New York: H. Fertig, 1973).

12. N M 6857 (B), prefectural report to the Ministry of Interior.

13. *L'Homme libre* (April 6, 1926).

14. Paul Geuriot, "Politique d'immigration," *Revue politique et parlementaire*, 20 (June 10, 1924), 434.

15. *Le Tribune du mineur* (October 16, 1926).

16. Ibid. (October 24, 1924).

17. Archives de la Préfecture de Police (hereafter cited as PP) 335 police report on the CGTU, 1927.

18. PP 67; internal report entitled, "Rapport sur la main-d'oeuvre étrangère," 1923. See also Archives nationales (hereafter cited with "F" numbers) F⁷13455, internal report entitled, "Au sujet de l'activité politique des italiens résidants en France," October 15, 1924. This report notes that Italians had twenty-four of the thirty-five comités intersyndicaux (foreign language organizations) of the CGTU.

19. PP 300, Internal report on the CGTU, May 1930, pp. 66–67.

20. See CGTU, *Congrès de la Fédération nationale des travailleurs du bâtiment*, 5 (1927), 152, and Georges Kletch, "L'organization syndicale des travailleurs étrangers" (unpublished in A.D. Pas-de-Calais), p. 4.

21. William Oualid, "La France deviendra-t-elle un pays de minorités nationales?" *Le Musée social*, 34 (May–June 1927), 125–159.

22. For a discussion of the American policy of assimilation and preselection see Maurice Davie, *A Constructive Immigration Policy* (New Haven: Yale University Press, 1923); Roy L. Garis, *Immigration Restrictions: a Study of the Opposition to and Regulation of Immigration in the U.S.* (New York, 1927); William Bernard, ed., *Americanization Studies*, 10 volumes (Montclair, N.J.: Paterson Smith, 1971).

23. *La Volonté* (May 9, 1926). See also *Information sociale et ouvrière* (July 10, 1926), René Martial, *Traité de l'immigration et de la greffe interraciale* (Cuesmes-lez-Mons: Imprimerie fédérale, 1930), chapters 19–20, and G. Dequidt, *Revue d'hygiène*, 48 (December 1926), 1035, 1048.

24. Charles Lambert, *France et les étrangers*, p. 183.

25. Marcel Paon, *L'immigration en France* (Paris: Delagrave, 1928), pp. 140–157. Note also that William Oualid, head of the Immigration Committee of the conservative business study group, Redressement français, also advocated the formation of a "Commission nationale de l'immigration" with employer, worker, and philanthropic membership. It was to plan for an improved government control of immigration, to prevent the formation of autonomous ethnic concentrations, and to improve the selection process. See *Redressement français*, Cahier 23 (1927), pp. 34–35.

26. *Bulletin du Ministère du travail*, 33 (January–March 1927), p. 15.

27. Archives départementales, Bouches-du-Rhône (hereafter cited as BR) 14 M 1174, Labor Ministry circular, March 4, 1928.

28. Bonnet, *Les pouvoirs publics français*, pp. 91–94.

29. *La Volonté* (September 5, 1926) declared that the French "must choose to assimilate the foreigners or be colonized by them." For a review of French acceptance of assimilation, see International Labour Office, *Monthly Record of Migration*, 2 (February 1927), 73–74.

30. Oualid, "La France deviendra-t-elle," p. 173.

31. Eugen Weber, *Peasants into Frenchmen* (Stanford: Stanford University Press, 1976).

32. Czeslaw Kaczmarek, *L'émigration polonaise en France après la guerre* (Paris: Berger, 1928), pp. 280–294, and Alfred Morain, *La réconstitution du Nord devasté au 1ᵉʳ septembre 1923* (Lille: Martin-Mamy, 1923), p. 740.

33. Chambre des députes, *Annales, Documents parlementaires* (hereafter cited as CDoc), February 11, 1931, Annex Number 4511, p. 187. See also *Le Foyer*

français, compte rendu, Ire année: 1924–25, and Paul Raphael, "Le Problème des étrangers," *Grande revue,* 29 (August 1926), 213–214.

34. Archives départementales, Nord (hereafter cited as N), M 484–3, undated declaration of the Comité de protection polonaise.

35. Ibid., circulars from the Central Farm Labor Service (Ministry of Agriculture), January 19, 1929, and April 4, 1929. See also prefectural reports on the Comité de protection polonaise, December 12, 1929, May 9, 1931, June 30, 1931, and general report for 1933.

36. Martial, "Le Problème de l'immigration," *Revue politique et parlementaire,* 22 (December 10, 1926), 400. See also *Voix du peuple,* 11 (February 1929), 86.

37. The CGT claimed that only 1,991 Polish families joined their working heads of families in 1927 before the protocol, but 2,808 joined them in 1928 after the protocol was signed. Ibid.

38. *Recensement,* 1, no. 5 (1931), 31.

39. As a result of depopulation during World War One (a loss of 126,761, or 9 percent of the population), four departments in the southwest (Gers, Haute-Garonne, Tarn-et-Garonne, and Lot-et-Garonne) suffered a farm-labor shortage. Landowners responded by attracting Italian and Spanish settlers to the region as sharecroppers and tenants. The number of Italians in the region rose from 917 in 1921 to 37,113 by 1931. Throughout the interwar period, this peasant immigration was glorified as the proper way of assimilating foreigners in contrast to the unstable and alien urban immigration. See M. Huber, *La population de la France* (Paris: Hachette, 1937), pp. 834–888, and Alfred Sauvy, *The General Theory of Population,* (New York: Basic books, 1969) p. 462. Nevertheless, this ideal immigrant to the southwest constituted only 1.3 percent of the immigrant population (1926) and immigrants in the agricultural sector remained a small part of the foreign influx. *Recensement,* 1, no. 2 (1931), 112–113. For more information about migration to the southwest, see Georges Marcel-Remond, *L'immigration italienne dans le sud-ouest de la France* (Paris: Libraire Dalloz, 1928). See also the recent local study, Rosa Dalla, "L'immigration étrangère dans le Lot-et-Garonne," *96e Congrès de la Société des savantes, Toulouse, Section geographique* (1975), pp. 217–237.

40. For a summary of the laws on naturalization, see Pierre Depoid, *Les naturalisations en France,* in Institut national des statistiques et études économiques, *Études et documents,* no. 3 (Paris: Presses universitaires de France, 1942), p. 16.

41. For a review of sentiment in favor of a revision of naturalization laws, see "Migrations," *International Labour Review,* 3 (September 1923), 424, and *Le Peuple* (October 31, 1925, February 27, 1927).

42. *Congrès de la natalité* (Marseilles: Éditions de la cité chrétienne, 1926), p. 35. See also Louis Escasaut, *Pour la plus grande France* (Paris: A. Colin, 1932),

pp. 117–118, for the expression of similar themes.

43. Attilio Oblath, "Italian Emigration and Colonization Policy," *International Labor Review*, 11 (June 1931), 805–834.

44. *Journal officiel de la République de France, Lois et décrets* (hereafter cited as JO), August 14, 1927, p. 8702.

45. *Congrès de la natalité* (1926), p. 35.

46. JO, August 14, 1927, p. 8702 for a text of the law. See also Depoid, *Les naturalisations,* pp. 16–19, and Bonnet, *Les pouvoirs publics français,* pp. 150–170. With the revised naturalization law of 1927, children born in France to a foreign father, but who had a French mother, automatically became French at 21 years of age; formerly they had the option of adopting their father's nationality. The new law also eliminated the need of foreign parents of children born in France to request their naturalization when they became 21 years old. Finally, the law removed the possibility of children of naturalized parents renouncing their automatic naturalization. Given the fact that there were in 1925 426,500 children of immigrant fathers, the unfettered "francification" or automatic naturalization of this group was important for French population growth. See Depoid, *Les naturalisations,* p. 100.

47. Ibid., pp. 24–31, 47–48.

48. Ibid., p. 51, and *Recensement,* 1, no. 5 (1931), 59.

49. Ibid.

50. Bureau of the Census, *Historical Statistics of the U.S.A.,* 1 (Washington: U.S. Government Printing Office, 1975), 114, and *Recensement,* 1, no. 2 (1931), 55.

51. Temporary immigration is difficult to document because of poor government counting procedures, especially regarding repatriations of foreigners. Government statistics indicate that repatriations accounted for 34 percent of entries between 1921 and 1930, based on 571,770 controlled repatriations and 1,666,474 controlled entries of foreign workers. Both figures probably greatly undercount the true numbers. Henri Bunle (Institut national des études économiques), *Mouvements migratoires entre la France et l'étranger, Études et documents,* No. 4 (Paris: Presses universitaires de France, 1943), p. 91.

52. Alain Girard and Jean Stoetzel (Institut national des études démographiques), *Français et immigrés: nouveaux documents sur l'adaptation, Travaux et documents,* Cahier no. 20 (Paris: Presses universitaires de France, 1954), pp. 525–526. For recent studies of naturalization, see Jean-Charles Bonnet, "Naturalisation et revisions de naturalisation de 1927 à 1944: l'exemple du Rhone," *Mouvement social,* 98 (January–March 1977), 43–74, and Louis Köll, "Immigration italienne et integration française à Auboue (M et M.) (1901–1939), "*Annales de l'Est,* 5e serie 30e année (1978), 231–265.

53. Data derived from Archives départementales, Pas-de-Calais (hereafter cited as PC) M 2412, 6677, and 6846.

54. PC 1Z 306, identity card reports 1920–1926. PC 1Z 311, identity card reports 1927–1931. See also PC M 3198, identity card correspondence 1927–1931; N M 605-19, identity card correspondence 1920–1931.

55. M. Auzemat (Interior Ministry), *Rapport presenté par l'inspection générale de Services administratives, 1932: Réglementation du séjour des étrangers en France* (Paris: Imprimerie nationale, 1932), pp. 42–44.

56. Alexis Martini, *L'expulsion des étrangers* (Paris: L. Larose, 1959). See also PP 65, "Rapport sur les étrangers dans la Seine," no date.

57. PC M 2412, Interior Ministry circular, October 5, 1926. See also PP 64, Interior Ministry circular, December 3, 1930.

58. JO, January 12, 1933, p. 5718. Note also that of 13,230 expulsions between July 1926 and February 1927, 11,675 followed imprisonment for criminal convictions. Only 1,565 immigrants were expelled administratively, i.e., without judicial condemnation. F^7 13230, Interior Ministry report, no date. This group of administrative expulsions was proportionally larger in the Seine: 481 compared to 880 judicial expulsions in 1927, and 398 to 427 in 1929. Of these administrative expulsions, in these two years, 152 and 172 were for political reasons. PP 65, Statistics on expulsions, 1927 and 1929.

59. Only about 20 percent of the immigrants sentenced for violation of the criminal code were expelled, according to an estimate of the Interior Ministry. F^7 13518, Interior Ministry circular, 1927. *Le Journal* (September 23, 1925), and *L'Humanité* (September 24, 1925).

60. F^7 13469, report of the Commissaire spécial (CS) of Douai to Interior Ministry, August 24, 1925, and November 7, 1929. PC M 2412, CS of Arras, June 8, 1925, N M 154-202B. CS of Valenciennes, March 21, 1927: all these reports contained examples of police singling out "leaders" among the Poles that spoke out in CGT meetings. A similar pattern occurred in the south in police action against Italian CGTU members. F^7 13458, CS of Toulouse, July 5, 1926.

61. CGTU, *Congrès des ouvriers et ouvrières sur metaux*, 3 (1925), 70–73, 113.

62. PP 67, Reports on P. Maurin, CGTU foreign labor organizer, August 12, 1931. See also CGTU, *Congrès des travailleurs du sous-sol*, 2 (1923), 47, and *l'Humanité* (October 23, 1931).

63. *Conseil général du Pas-de-Calais* (1924), 3 (Report of the Ingenieur des mines), 193. During a mine strike in April 1931, foremen warned Poles that they would be expelled if they participated; *L'Humanité* (April 11, 1931). This threat was easily carried out for companies did not hesitate to provide police with the names of "subversives." For example, in PC M 8865 there is a list of 78 "extremists" provided by the Mines de Lens to the Prefecture for expulsion

or non-renewal of the identity card (March 29, 1935).

64. These newspapers included: *Robotnik Polski* (outlawed in December 1923), *L'Émigrant* (August 1925), *Information Zycie Polski* (October 1925), *Robotnik Polski we Francji* (November 1925), *Robotniczy* and *Trybuna Robotnicz* (August 1926), *Na Tulaczce* (September 1926), *Glos Pracy* (April 1928), *Nasza Gazeta* (November 1928), *Trybuna Emigranta* (September 1929), *Nova Gazetta* (December 1929), *Nasza Obona* (May 1931), *Nasza Pomoc* (March 1931), *Porzeglad Robotinczy Wiezieme* (March 1932), *Mysa Robotnicza* (April 1932), *Wiadomosi* (June 1932), *Jednosc Robotnicza* (July 1932). AN F⁷ 13469–70. See Andrzek Packowki, "La presse des émigres polonais en France: 1920–1940," *Revue du Nord*, 60 (January 1978), 151–162.

65. F⁷ 13453–5 reports on repression of Italian communists.

66. F⁷ 13469–70, The CS of Lille used the lists of subscribers which police seized from the offices of banned foreign language newspapers to identify "subversives." N M 154–202B, CS of Lille, June 26, 1928.

67. N M 154–202A, report of CS of Valenciennes, August 14, 1925.

68. Quoted in S. Bonnet, *L'Homme de fer*, 1 (Nancy: Centre lorraine d'études sociologiques, 1976), 195.

69. Girard and Stoetzel, *Français et immigrés*, pp. 284, 306, 513, 525.

IX: Regulating the Immigrant Worker during the Depression

1. See Michael Piore, *Birds of Passage* (Cambridge: MIT Press, 1979).

2. *Informations sociales*, 11 (April 7, 1931), 320.

3. *Le Peuple* (June 1, 1930), and Chambre des députés, *Annales, Débats parlementaires* (hereafter cited as CDeb), February 13, 1931, p. 571.

4. From early 1928 until the spring of 1930, the French placement offices tolerated and even encouraged illegal Italian entry into France over the Alps. By mid-1930, as Italians anticipated restrictions, the offices reported with alarm a flood of irregular entries. *Conseil général du Isère*, 3 (1931), placement office report, p. 515, and Archives départementales, Bouches-du-Rhône (hereafter cited as BR) 6 M 9096, *Commissaire de police* (Marseilles), March 1, 1930.

5. The prefect of the Nord noted in a letter to the Ministry of Labor that the entry of *frontaliers* should be restricted because their lower cost of living in Belgium allowed them to compete unfairly with the French. Archives départementales, Nord (hereafter cited as N) M 208–135, prefect letter to Ministry of Labor, 1932. A series of six articles in the popular *La Reveil du Nord*

from January 17 to 28, 1932, made the same point. See also Archives départementales, Moselle, 10M 142–3 for reports on opposition to *frontaliers*.

6. The Italians were famous for their skilled masonry, cabinet making, and ornamental stone crafts. For complaints against the cost-cutting practices of Italian sub-contractors, see *Le Peuple* (September 11, 1930, and April 30, 1931).

7. Archives nationales (hereafter cited with "F" numbers) F⁷ 13541, Prefect of Police report to Interior Ministry, November 14, 1931.

8. *Le Peuple* (February 13 and 14, 1931).

9. Ibid. (November 30, 1931).

10. F⁷ 13541, Prefect of Police report to the Labor Ministry, January 14, 1931.

11. *Informations sociales*, 10 (November 11, 1930), 516. See also *Voix du peuple*, 12 (November 1930), 838. The CGT also published leaflets in Italian that warned of the futility of immigrants seeking work in Paris. They were distributed within the provincial construction trades. F⁷ 13541, Prefect of Police report to the Interior Ministry, January 14, 1931.

12. For example, in the Bouches-du-Rhône, the number of regularizations (work permits granted immigrants who entered France as tourists) dropped from 623 of 783 requests in the first three months of 1930 to 618 of 1,178 for the same period of 1931. See *Conseil général de Bouches-du-Rhône*, 3 (1931), 518. A Labor Ministry circular of December 1, 1930, demanded stricter control over regularization. In the cartons, F²² 669–670, prefects from twenty departments reported that they complied with this and other new regulations intended to restrict the access of immigrants to jobs.

13. The Prefect of Police in Paris, C. Chiappe, promised in January of 1931 to expel any immigrant who lacked the prescribed identity card. His prosecutions of delinquents rose from 511 for the first eleven months of 1930 to 557 for December alone. *Informations sociales*, 11 (February 16, 1931), 258. See also Jean-Charles Bonnet, *Les pouvoirs publics français et l'immigration dans l'entre deux guerres* (Lyons: Centre d'histoire de la région lyonnaise, 1976), p. 269.

14. *Informations sociales*, 10 (November 3, 1930), 335–336.

15. *Le Peuple* (March 21, and 23, 1931) and CGT, *Congrès confédéral* (1931), p. 63.

16. CDeb. February 13, 1931, p. 569, and December 22, 1931, pp. 808, 836.

17. F⁷ 13541 report of the Prefect of Police to the Interior Ministry, January 17, 1931. The same pattern of veteran support for native labor appeared in Marseilles; see BR 14 M 23–20, prefect's report, October 17, 1931. Note also that a veterans' group in Paris led a group of 300 unemployed musicians to confront a proprietor of a music hall who employed an all-Russian band; shortly thereafter they distributed leaflets in the Montmartre district which

denounced the faddish enthusiasm "for black and other exotic music as only a sign of snobbery." See F⁷ 13541, Report of the Prefect of Police to the Interior Ministry, October 1, 1930, and November 30, 1930.

18. Ibid., January 9, 1931.

19. *La Victoire* (November 14 and 17, 1931).

20. F⁷ 13541, Prefect of Police report to the Interior Ministry, February 6, 1931, and December 10, 1931.

21. *La Victoire* (December 5, 1931).

22. For a summary of this literature, see *Informations sociales*, 12 (April 21, 1931), 7, and *Revue d'immigration*, 5 (January 1931), 36, and 5 (January–March 1931), 18.

23. *Revue d'immigration*, 5 (March 1931), 28. See also *Informations sociales*, 12 (July 30, 1931), 135, and *Revue d'immigration*, 5 (September 1931), 22.

24. *La journée industrielle* (November 14, 1931). For a review of the big-business press on immigration policy in 1931, see *Revue d'immigration*, 5 (November 1931), 38–39, and 5 (December 1931), 20.

25. *Le Tribune des mineurs* (April 20, 1934).

26. See *Le Populaire* (November 16, 1931) for the view of the socialists on the necessity of immigration. See also Leon Gani, *Syndicats et travailleurs immigrés* (Paris: Éditions sociales, 1972), p. 17.

27. CGTU, *Congrès confédéral* (1933), pp. 307–316, and 593–595. Information on immigrant sections of communist "unemployment committees" is found in F⁷ 13527, and details of communist involvement in expulsion cases (including the expulsion of the former chief of the Polish state, E. Giereck, in August of 1933 from Leforest) are in Archives départementales, Pas-de-Calais (hereafter cited as PC) M 5006.

28. *Chambre des deputés, Annales, Documents Parlementaires* (hereafter cited as CDoc), March 25, 1928, Annex no. 7393, pp. 674–675 and January 17, 1924, Annex no. 6948, p. 177.

29. Ibid., November 26, 1931, Annex no. 1561, p. 244, and November 12, 1931, Annex no. 5557, p. 142; see also CDeb, February 28, 1931, pp. 1261–1262, and February 28, 1931, p. 572.

30. CDoc, November 17, 1931, Annex no. 5658, pp. 191–192.

31. *Le Populaire* (December 1, 1931).

32. CDoc, November 17, 1931, Annex no. 5566, p. 146.

33. CDeb, December 21, 1931, p. 821.

34. Ibid., pp. 810–815.

35. CDeb, December 21, 1931, pp. 821 and 824–825.

36. *Journal officiel de la République de France, Lois et décrets* (hereafter cited as JO), August 10, 1932, p. 8818. In the final vote both the Socialists and Communists abstained, the former because farm workers were excluded from

the bill and the latter because they opposed quotas and wanted instead an equal pay law. See CDeb, December 21, 1931, pp. 801, 841.

37. See Jean-Charles Bonnet, *Les pouvoirs*, pp. 211–212.

38. Pierre Laroque, "Rapport sur l'organisation des Services de la main-d'oeuvre étrangère en France" (unpublished report in PC, 1937), p. 809. This report was made for the Labor Ministry and emphasized the need for greater administrative autonomy and less interference in labor market regulation from "personalities," "local interests," and other organizations.

39. Lists of requests for quota decrees were published weekly in the JO, from October 22, 1932, p. 11348, to October 31, 1934, p. 10932. For the evidence of CGT initiation of many of these decrees, see *Le Peuple* (August 6, 1932), and *Congrès de la Fédération des travailleurs de l'alimentation* (1932), p. 152.

40. Stephane Wlocevski, "Y a-t-il trop de travailleurs étrangers en France?" *Revue d'économie politique*, 49 (1935), 340.

41. *Revue d'immigration*, 7 (March 1933), 29–30.

42. Derived from Henri Bunle (Institut national des études économiques), *Mouvements migratoires entre la France et l'étrangers, Études et documents*, No. 4 (Paris: Presses universitaires de France, 1943), p. 96.

43. Ibid.

44. See *Bulletin du Ministère du travail*, 39 (January–March 1932), 30–32. The Comité central de fabricants de sucre promised the government to repatriate all their alien workers at the end of their contracts, which lasted from September to January. PC M 8865, Labor Ministry circular, October 23, 1934.

45. *Bulletin du Ministère du travail*, 39 (January–March 1932), 30.

46. Office départemental de placement du Seine, *Rapport au Conseil général* (1932), p. 194, and (1933), p. 141.

47. F²² 669 includes fifteen reports written by the prefects to the Labor Ministry on the measures which they undertook to overcome unemployment. All listed stiffer investigation of requests for work permits, especially of irregular immigrants, who had entered France without previous authorization to work.

48. Between January of 1931 and 1932, the farm labor section of the SGI, the Office central de la main-d'oeuvre agricole, also persuaded 7,098 immigrants who had been employed in industry and mining to "return to the land," mostly as sharecroppers and often on land owned by the SGI. *Revue d'immigration*, 7 (March–May 1933), 32.

49. Ibid., 6 (July 1932), 194.

50. A decree of May 1932 required hotel and apartment owners to report all foreign residents as a means of flushing out illegal foreigners. The League for the Rights of Man complained about a wave of expulsions which followed the

appearance of this decree. Archives de la Préfecture de Police (hereafter cited as PP), 68, Interior Ministry Circular, May 26, 1932.

51. *Informations sociales,* 16 (January 21, 1935), 97.

52. *Revue d'immigration,* 7 (April 1933), 30.

53. CH 48, Internal report, March 22, 1937. France, Statistique générale, *Résultats statistiques du recensement général de la population* (hereafter cited as *Recensement*), 1, no. 5 (1936), 50, and 1, no. 5 (1931), 52.

54. One index of economic contraction were the monthly reports of the labor inspectors on the decline in man-hours worked in industrial and commercial enterprises from the base year of 1930. While there was a decline of 36.5 percent in June 1933 this figure dropped in June 1934 to 29.4 percent. However by December the decline had reached 32 percent compared to only 25.4 percent a year before. This trend bottomed out in February of 1935 at 36.2 percent compared to 28.5 percent the year before. *Bulletin du Ministère du travail,* 42 (October–December 1935), 404.

55. *Le Peuple* (November 5, 1934, December 2, 1934). See also CGT, *Congrès des travailleurs de l'alimentation* (1933), pp. 18 and 53.

56. F²² 676–678, passim.

57. F²² 676–678, passim.

58. Isère demanded that a 10 percent maximum of foreigners be allowed in all industry and that all immigrant occupational transfers be approved by the placement offices. Seine-et-Oise demanded the exclusion of all immigrants from public contract work. The Conseil général of Alpes-Maritimes requested greater efforts to eliminate Italian competition in skilled building trades, while the Seine-Inferieure found that unacceptably high numbers of foreigners were hired as general laborers. See F²² 672–676.

59. *Informations sociales,* 15 (April 30, 1934), 227; CDoc, March 8, 1934, Annex no. 3212, p. 304; and *Annales du Senat, project de lois,* November 8, 1934, Annex no. 566, p. 864.

60. *Informations sociales,* 14 (December 20, 1934), 1. See also *Revue d'immigration,* 8 (February 1934), 36–37 for review of the new wave of xenophobia.

61. *Informations sociales,* 14 (April 30, 1934), 229.

62. CDeb, November 13, 1934, p. 2787.

63. *Le Temps* (November 21, 1934).

64. Laroque, "Rapport sur l'organisation," pp. 5–6.

65. A list of recommendations from this committee was published in *Le Temps* (November 24, 1934). The following notes list the references to their implementation in *décret-lois, arrêts,* and circulars.

66. J. C. Bonnet, *Les pouvoirs publics français,* p. 303.

67. *Informations sociales,* 16 (June 3, 1936), 324–326. See also BR 6 M 9096, Labor Ministry circular, March 3, 1936.

68. PP 64, Interior Ministry circular, January 18, 1935.

69. Archives départementales, Moselle M 1994, Confidential circular from the Labor Ministry, December 2, 1935.

70. CDeb, November 29, 1935, p. 2297.

71. CDoc, February 28, 1935, Annex no. 4830, pp. 379–380.

72. JO, April 2, 1935, p. 3714.

73. N M 605–21, Labor Ministry letter to the prefect, April 5, 1934. The government asked coal mines to pay half of the costs of repatriating unemployed immigrant miners. See also Alain Girard and Jean Stoetzel (Institut national des études démographiques), *Français et immigrés: nouveaux documents sur l'adaptation, Travaux et documents*, Cahier no. 20 (Paris: Presses universitaires de France, 1954), p. 191.

74. Derived from Bunle, *Mouvements migratoires*, pp. 53, 96.

75. JO, February 8, 1935, p. 1675.

76. N M 605–21, Douai police report, September 5, 1934. See also *Informations sociales*, 13 (April 30, 1934), 183.

77. Ibid., 14 (March 28, 1935), 7. See also PC M 8865, report of the Commissaire spécial of Bethune, January 6, 1937 and Girard and Stoetzel, *Français et immigrés*, p. 513.

78. BR 14 M 22–24, Labor Ministry circulars, May 11, 1935, September 5, 1935, September 24, 1935, January 14, 1936, February 7, 1936, and May 23, 1936, which informed the prefects that the "privileged status" had been granted not only to the Swiss and Belgians but also to Italians, Czechs, Yugoslavs, Poles, and Luxembourgeois.

79. There was a decline in unemployment in 1935. A fairly reliable index of unemployment was the percentage of partial unemployment which peaked at 44.9 percent in February of 1935 and dropped to 32.7 percent by December 1935. This can be compared with rates of 34 percent and 42.3 percent for the same months in 1934. See *Bulletin du Ministère du travail* 42 (October–December 1935), 304. This decline in unemployment in 1935 was paralleled by an increase in economic activity. The drop in production stabilized in December 1934 at an index figure of 93 (1913=100) and rose slowly to 98 by January 1936. See France, *Annuaire statistique* (1936) p. 74. There is no indication that the drop in the unemployment rate was linked to the elimination of foreign labor.

80. See BR 14 M 22–24, Correspondence between the Labor Ministry and the departmental placement office, February 8, 1935, and February 19, 1935.

81. CDeb, February 19, 1935, p. 578. See also Bonnet, *Les pouvoirs publics*, pp. 307–308.

82. *Recensement*, 1, no. 5 (1936), 57.

83. Ibid., 1, no. 4 (1931), 64–65; 1, no. 5 (1931), 121–123; 1, no. 4 (1936),

66–67; and 1, no. 5 (1936), 121–123.

84. Ibid.

85. Gani, *Syndicats,* pp. 23–24, presents this information—without drawing my conclusions.

86. *Voix du peuple,* 15 (March 1935), 147–148.

87. JO, October 24, 1936, p. 11107. *Informations sociales,* 17 (April 30, 1937), 400. See also JO, April 14, 1937, p. 4233, and BR 14M 22–24, Labor Ministry Circular, August 6, 1937. Also note that even before the Popular Front in February 1936, the Interior Ministry liberalized its expulsion policy by granting a two-year probation for most expellees. PP 64, Interior Ministry Circulars, February 3, 1936, and April 28, 1936.

88. The Labor Ministry asked the placement offices to obtain the opinion of local mayors and trade unions before granting requests for work authorizations for newly imported farm workers. BR 14 M 22–24, Labor Ministry circular, March 10, 1937.

89. BR 14 M 22–24, Labor Ministry circular, December 2, 1937.

90. See Alfred Sauvy, *Histoire économique de la France entre les deux guerres,* 2 (Paris: A. Sauret, 1967), 209, 330. Also note that in November of 1936, for example, the Labor Ministry directed the placement offices to advertise for recruits to the Lorraine metallurgical mills and mines (there were about 7,000 openings). Because it was obvious that insufficient numbers of French workers would apply, the Labor Ministry instructed the offices to encourage immigrants to accept these jobs as an alternative to the importation of additional foreign workers. BR 14 M 22–24, Labor Ministry circular, November 27, 1936.

91. Ibid., Labor Ministry circulars, January 14 and 27, 1937.

92. *Senat, Annales, Débats Parlementaires* (hereafter cited as SDeb), March 10, 1937, p. 127, and March 11, 1937, pp. 272–275.

93. BR 14 M 22–24 Labor Ministry circular, February 5, 1937.

94. JO, May 28, 1938, p. 6000.

95. Ibid., May 24, 1938, p. 5830.

96. Ibid., May 28, 1938, p. 6000.

97. For example, see de Tastes' speech condemning Jewish peddlers in Paris and demanding their expulsion. CDeb, November 6, 1934, p. 2254.

98. JO, October 31, 1935, p. 11490.

99. *Voix du peuple,* 13 (November 1933) p. 708–709, which describes how Mme. Lefranc of the Hatmakers Union, with the support of "some employers," petitioned the Labor Ministry to investigate and institute control over these small immigrant artisans. Also *Le Peuple* (August 21, 1934) reported that the Federation of Clothing Workers demanded that the August 10, 1932, law be extended to cover artisans.

100. JO, August 9, 1935, p. 8699. For background, see *Revue d'immigration*, 8 (January 1935), 19–21.

101. JO, June 23, 1938, pp. 7333–7334.

102. See CDoc, November 16, 1933, Annex no. 2, 522, p. 275.

103. JO, May 15, 1938.

104. By June 1939 no unrestricted ID cards had been delivered, according to Bonnet, *Les pouvoirs publics*, p. 347.

105. PP 64, Interior Ministry Circular, April 20, 1939.

106. PP 335, clipping from *Le Petit parisien* (March 25, 1939). Additional anti-immigrant sentiments are found in Prosper Josse and Pierre Rossillion, *L'invasion étrangère en France en temps de paix* (Paris: La Nation, 1938), Raymond Millet, *Trois millions d'étrangers en France* (Paris: Librairie de Medicis, 1938), and René Martial, *Les métis* (Paris: Flammarion, 1942).

107. For details on the Spanish refugee problem, see Bonnet, *Les pouvoirs publics*, pp. 351–56, and especially Louis Stein, *Beyond Death and Exile: The Spanish Republicans in France, 1939–55* (Cambridge: Harvard University Press, 1979).

X: Conclusion

1. Important works in this discussion of the modern state and social classes are Theda Skucpol, *States and Social Revolutions* (Cambridge: Cambridge University Press, 1979), and Nicos Poulantzas, *Political Power and Social Classes* (London: Sheed and Ward, 1973). See also articles by Alan Wolf, Amy Bridges, and Jean-Claude Girardin in *Politics and Society* 4 (Winter 1974), 131–224. For an interesting treatment of the political impact of social discontinuities, see A. F. K. Organski, *The Stages of Political Development* (New York: Knopf, 1965). Note also Michael Piore and Suzanne Berger, *Dualism and Discontinuity in Industrial Societies* (Cambridge: Cambridge University Press, 1980).

2. Two important post-1945 studies of immigration which deal with the interwar period are Louis Chevalier, *Le problème démographique Nord-africain* (Institut national des études démographiques, Cahier no. 6) (Paris: Presses universitaires de France, 1947), and Alain Girard and Jean Stoetzel, *Français et immigrés* (Institut national des études démographiques, Cahier no. 19) (Paris: Presses universitaires de France, 1954).

3. For analysis of post-1945 immigration, see Xavier Lannes, *L'immigration en France depuis 1945* (La Haye: M. Nijhoff, 1953), pp. 3–18, Georges Tapinos, *L'immigration étrangère en France* (Institut national des études démographiques, Cahier no. 71) (Paris: Presses universitaires de France, 1975), pp. 27–36, and

Gary P. Freeman, *Immigrant Labor and Racial Conflict in Industrial Societies* (Princeton: Princeton University Press, 1979), pp. 68–76.

4. Freeman, *Immigrant Labor*, pp. 77–85; Tapinos, *L'immigration*, pp. 47–62.

5. For an analysis of the ONI and its evolution see Tapinos, *L'immigration*, pp. 22–33, Juliette Minces, *Les travailleurs étrangers en France* (Paris: Éditions du Seuil, 1973), pp. 127–128, and especially Leon Gani, *Syndicats et travailleurs immigrés* (Paris: Éditions sociales, 1972), pp. 30–46.

6. Tapinos, *L'immigration*, chapter 3, and Minces, *Les travailleurs étrangers*, pp. 128–129.

7. Daniel Kubat, ed., *The Politics of Migration Policies* (New York: Center for Migration Studies, 1979), pp. 134–138; Tapinos, *L'immigration*, pp. 87–93; and Freeman, *Immigrant Labor*, pp. 85–98. For a description of trade union policy concerning immigration, see Gani, *Syndicats*, especially pp. 74–84. For a communist view of alien labor, see André Vieuguet, *Français et immigrés: le combat du C.P.F.* (Paris: Éditions sociales, 1975). The position of the other major union group, the Confédération français democratique du travail (CFDT), is outlined in Françoise Pinot, *Travailleurs immigrés dans la lutte de classes* (Paris: Éditions du Cerf, 1973). Finally, a left-wing critique of the CGT position on immigrants is found in Bernard Granotier, *Les travailleurs immigrés en France* (Paris: F. Maspero, 1970).

8. A good survey of European immigration after 1945 is Phillip Martin and Mark Miller, "Guest Workers: Lessons from Western Europe," *Industrial and Labor Relations Review*, 33 (April 1980), 315–330. See also Stephan Castles and Godula Kosack, *Immigrant Workers and Class Structure in Western Europe* (London: Oxford University Press, 1973).

9. Martin and Miller, "Guest Workers," pp. 326–327. For an analysis of the contemporary impact of alien labor on advanced capitalist countries, see Michael Piore, *Birds of Passage* (Cambridge: MIT Press, 1979), pp. 86–115. Note also the interpretations of André Gorz, "Immigrant Labour," *New Left Review*, 11 (1970), 11–13, and Anthony Ward, "European Capitalism's Reserve Army," *Monthly Review*, 27 (November 1975), 3–30. For a sensitive description of the lives of guest workers, see John Berger and Jean Mohr, *A Seventh Man* (New York: Viking Press, 1975). For a treatment of the new political impact of immigrants in the 1970s, see Mark Miller, *Foreign Workers in Western Europe: An Emerging Political Force* (New York: Praeger, 1981).

Selected Bibliography

Albonico, Erminio. *Saggio di una prima inchiesta sulla emigrazione italiana in Europa*. Milan: Fratelli Lanzani, 1921.

Ambelouis, Pierre. *L'organisation du marché du travail en France et à l'étranger*. Paris: Association des maîtres-imprimeurs, 1932.

Ariès, Philippe. *Histoire des populations françaises*. Paris: Self, 1948.

Armenjon, Pierre, and Georges de Fonclare. "L'immigration italienne dans la région des Alpes françaises," *Revue économique internationale, Bruxelles* 21 (May 1929): 281–304.

Armonnel, D. E. *L'Office des houillères sinistrées du Nord et du Pas-de-Calais et les charbons de réparations*. Paris: Jouve, 1933.

Association nationale d'expansion économique, *Enquête sur la production française et la concurrence étrangère*. Paris: Libi-imprimerie réunies, 1917.

Auge-Laribé, Michel. *Le paysan français après la guerre*. Paris: Garnier frères, 1923.

———*L'agriculture pendant la guerre*. Paris: Presses universitaires de France, 1925.

———"Labour Conditions in French Agriculture," *International Labour Review* 12 (Jan. 1932): 23–57.

Bell, Daniel. *The Cultural Contradictions of Capitalism*. New York: Basic Books, 1976.

Bello, Carlo. *Geremia Bonomelli con documenti inediti*. Rome: Bescia, Morcelliana, 1961.

Bernard, Léon. "Le problème sanitaire de l'immigration," *Revue d'hygiène* 47 (Sept. 1925): 9–25.

Bertillon, Jacques. *La dépopulation de la France*. Paris: F. Alcan, 1911.

Blanchard, Raoul. "L'électrométallurgie et l'électrochimie dans les Alpes-françaises," *Les Alpes économiques* 5 (Oct. 1924): 204.

Blondel, André. *L'expulsion des étrangers*. Paris: Recueil Sirey, 1930.

Bonnefous, Georges. *Histoire politique de la Troisième République*, vols. 3, 4. Paris: Presses universitaires de France, 1956.

Bonnet, Jean Charles. *Les pouvoirs publics français et l'immigration dans l'entre deux guerres*. Lyon: Centre d'histoire économique et sociale de la région lyonnaise, 1976.

Bonnet, Serge. "Italian Immigration in Lorraine," *Journal of Social History* 2 (1968): 123–55.

————*L'homme de fer: Mineurs de fer et ouvriers siderurgistes lorraines, 1889–1930*. Nancy: Centre lorraine d'études sociologiques, 1976.

Bonnet, Serge, Charles Santini, and H. Barthelemy. "Les italiens dans l'arrondissement de Briey avant 1914," *Annales de l'Est* 15 (1962).

Brizon, Gabriel. "La main-d'oeuvre étrangère en France," *Revue politique et parlementaire* 41 (October 8, 1935): 254–67.

Brown, John W. *World Migration and Labour*. Amsterdam: International Federation of Trade Unions, 1926.

Bryas, Madeline de. *Les peuples en marchés, les migrations politiques et économiques en Europe depuis la guerre mondiale*. Paris: Pédone, 1926.

Bunle, Henri. *Mouvements migratoires entre la France et l'étranger*, INDEE, *Études et documents*, No. 4. Paris: Presses universitaires de France, 1943.

Camera di Commerio Italiana de Marsiglia. *Marsiglia e la sue colonie*. Marseilles: 1911.

Canisy, Comte de. *La question ouvrière dans le bassin de Briey*. Paris: 1919.

Cannistraro, Philip V., and Georgio Rosoli. *Emigrazione, Chiesa e Fasciso: Lo socioglimento dell'Opera Bonomelli, 1922–28*. Rome: Studium, 1979.

————"Fascist Emigration Policy in the 1920s: An Interpretative Framework," *International Migration Review* 13 (1979): 673–92.

Cantalupo, Roberto. *L'Italia Musulmana*. Rome: Casa editrice Italia d'oltremare, 1929.

Carré, Jean-Jacques, ed. *French Economic Growth*. Stanford, Calif.: Stanford University Press, 1975.

Castells, Manuel. "Immigration Workers and Class Struggles in Advanced Capitalism: The Western European Experience," *Politics and Society* 5 (1975): 33–66.

Castles, Stephen. and Godula Kosack. *Immigrant Workers and Class Structure in Western Europe*. London: Oxford University Press, 1973.

Catalogone, Edouard. *La politique de l'immigration en France depuis la guerre de 1914*. Paris: Imprimerie A. Tournon, 1925.

Centre des études anti-imperialistes. *Les immigrés*. Paris: Stock, 1975.

Chassevent, L. *Appel à la main-d'oeuvre étrangère pour l'agriculture française*. Paris: Rousseau et cie, 1919.

Chevalier, Louis. *Le probléme démographique Nord-Africain*, Institut national des études démographiques, Cahier no. 6. Paris: Imprimerie nationale, 1947.

————*Laboring Classes and Dangerous Classes in Paris during the First Half of the Nineteenth Century*. New York: H. Fertig, 1973.

————ed. *Documents sur l'immigration*. Paris: Presses universitaires de France, 1947.

Christian, William, and William Braden. "Rural Migration and the Gravity Model," *Rural Sociology* 30 (March 1966): 73–80.

Chromecki, Thadée. *Le problème de l'immigration polonaise en France*. Paris: Les Presses modernes, 1929.

Cinanni, Paulo. *Emigrazione e imperialismo*. Roma: Editori riuniti, 1968.

Commissariato generale dell'emigrazione. *L'emigrazione italiana, 1910–1923*. Rome: Commissariato generale dell'emigrazione, 1926.

————*L'emigrazione italiana, 1924–1925*. Rome: Commissariato generale dell'emigrazione, 1927.

Condevaux, Jean. *Le mineur du Nord et du Pas-de-Calais*. Lille: 1928.

Confédération générale du travail (CGT). *Les problèmes de la main-d'oeuvre française et étrangère et du placement*. Paris: Confédération générale du travail, n.d.

————*Les questions ouvrières*. Paris: Confédération générale du travail, 1918.

————*Congrès national corporatif: Compte rendu des travaux*. Paris: Confédération générale du travail: 1918, 1919, 1920, 1923, 1925, 1927, 1929, 1931, 1933, and 1935.

Confédération générale du travail unitaire (CGTU). *Congrès national: Compte rendu des débats*. Paris: CGTU, 1923, 1925, 1927, 1929, 1931, and 1933.

————*Contre la xenophobie: La main-d'oeuvre étrangère sur la marché du travail française*. Paris: CGTU, 1931.

Confédération nationale des associations agricoles. *Congrès de l'agriculture: Compte rendu des travaux*. Paris: CNAA, 1919.

Conférence internationale de l'émigration et de l'immigration. *Actes*. Roma: Tipografia de la Camera dei deputati, 1924.

"Congrès d'hygiene," *Révue d'hygiène* 13 (1926): full issue.

Congrès de la natalité. Marseilles: Éditions de la Cité chrétienne, 1926.

Daulatly, Georges. *La main-d'oeuvre étrangère en France et la crise économique*. Paris: Loviton et cie, 1933.

Debré, Robert, and Alfred Sauvy. *Des français pour la France: le problème de la population*. Paris: Gallimard, 1946.

Delage, Jean. *La Russie en exile*. Paris: Delagrave, 1930.

Delevsky, J. *Antagonismes sociaux et antagonismes prolétariens*. Paris: L. M. Giard, 1924.

Demangeon, Albert and Georges Mauco. *Documents pour servir à l'études des étrangers dans l'agriculture française*. Paris: Hermann, 1939.

Depoid, Pierre. *Les naturalisations en France*. INDEE, *Études et documents*, No. 3. Paris: Presses universitaires de France, 1942.

Desrois, Abel. *Les étrangers dans le départment de l'Ain, leur rôle dans l'activité économique*. Bellegarde: Sadag, 1939.

Didion, J. *Les salaires étrangers en France*. Paris: M. Giard, 1911.

Duhamel, Jean. "Les problèmes de l'émigration: systèmes soumis au Bureau international du travail," *Europe nouvelle* 11 (Jan. 11, 1928): 78–82.

Duroselle, Jean-Baptiste, and Enrico Serra. *L'immigrazione italiana Francia prima de 1914*. Milan: F. Angeli, 1978.

Duval-Arnould, Louis. "Les problèmes de l'immigration étrangère en France," *Semaines sociales de France: Le Havre* 18 (1926): 619–38.

————"Immigration agricole dans l'Aisne," *Les dossiers de l'action populaire* 27 (March 30, 1926): 76–89.

————"Enquête sur le problème d'une politique internationale des migrations de travailleurs: Réunions du comité directeur du 30 janvier, 1930 à 20 mars, 1930," *Les documents du travail* 51 (March–June 1930): 28–111.

Dyer, Colin. *Population and Society in Twentieth-Century France*. London: Hodder and Stoughton, 1978.

Escasaut, Louis. *Pour la plus grande France*. Paris: A. Colin, 1932.

Fagnot, François. *Le problème de la main-d'oeuvre étrangère.*Paris: F. Alcan, 1924.

Faidutti, Anne Marie. *L'immigration italienne dans le sud-est de la France*. Gap: Editions ophrys, 1964.

Feblowicz, S., and Philippe Lamour. *Le statut juridique des étrangers en France— Traité—practique*. Paris: Librairie science et litterature, 1937.

Fédération des ouvriers des metaux. *Congrès fédéral*. Paris: CGT, 1925, 1927, 1929, 1931, 1933.

Fédération des syndicats confédérés des travailleurs de l'alimentation. *Congrès fédéral*. Paris: CGT, 1919, 1931.

Fédération nationale des travailleurs de l'agriculture. *Congrès national*. Paris: CGT, 1920, 1937.

Fédération nationale des travailleurs du bâtiment et travaux publics. *Congrès national*. Paris: CGTU, 1923, 1925, and 1927.

Fédération nationale des travailleurs du bâtiment. *Congrès*. Lyons: 1925.

Fédération nationale des travailleurs du sous-sol et similaires. *Congrès national*. Paris: CGT, 1926, 1928, 1929, 1931, and 1933.

Fédération nationale unitaire des travailleurs du sous-sol et similaires. *Congrès national*. Paris: CGTU, 1922, 1923, 1924, 1925, 1926, and 1928.

Fédération unitaire des ouvriers et ouvrières sur métaux. *Congrès national*. Paris: CGTU, 1921, 1923, 1925, 1927.

Fine, Martin. "Toward Corporatism." Doctoral diss., University of Wisconsin–Madison, 1973.

Fontaine, Arthur. *L'industrie française pendant la guerre*. Paris: Presses universitaires de France, 1925.

Freeman, Gary. *Immigrant Labor and Racial Conflict in Industrial Societies.* Princeton, N.J.: Princeton University Press, 1979.

Frezouls, Paul. *Les ouvriers étrangers en France.* Montpellier: G. Fermin, 1909.

Fuster, Emile. "Vers l'organisation nationale du placement," *Avenir* 1 (June 1916): 163–84.

————"L'organisation de la marché du travail," *Revue politique et parlementaire* 11 (Dec. 10, 1915): 321–40.

Gani, Leon. *Syndicats et travailleurs immigrés.* Paris: Éditions sociales, 1972.

Gauthier, E. *Le marché du travail en France: Le problème de la main-d'oeuvre.* Paris: Imprimerie du commerce, 1923.

Gemahling, Paul. *Travailleurs au rabais, la lutte syndicale contre les sous-concurrences ouvrières.* Paris: Bloud et cie, 1910.

Georges, Michel. "Le développement de la production en 1923 dans les mines du Nord et du Pas-de-Calais," *Revue de l'industrie minérale* 4 (Jan. 8, 1924): 345–30.

————"Les renseignements statistiques sur les mines du Pas-de-Calais en 1924," *Revue de l'industrie minérale* 5 (Aug. 1, 1924): 344–48.

Geuriot, Paul. "Politique d'immigration." *Revue politique et parlementaire* 20 (June 10, 1924): 419–35.

Gide, Charles. *La France sans enfants.* Paris: A. Rousseau, 1914.

————*Effects of the War upon French Economic Life.* London: H. Milford, 1923.

Girard, Alain, and Jean Stoetzel. *Français et immigrés,* Institut national des études démographiques, Cahier no. 19. Paris: Presses universitaires de France, 1953–54.

Gogolewski, G. "Les polonais en France avant la Seconde Guerre Mondiale," *Revue du Nord* 242 (1979): 649–63.

Gomar, Norbert. *L'émigration algérienne en France.* Paris: Les Presses modernes, 1931.

Granotier, Bernard. *Les travailleurs immigrés en France.* Paris: F. Maspero, 1970.

Gravier, Jean. *Paris et le désert français.* Paris: Flammarion, 1972.

Hansen, Marcus. *The Atlantic Migration, 1607–1860.* Cambridge, Mass.: Harvard University Press, 1951.

Heide, H. Ter. "Migration Models and Their Significance for Population Forecasts," *Milbank Memorial Fund Quarterly* 41 (January 1963): 56–76.

Hollande, Maurice. *La défense ouvrière contre le travail étranger.* Paris: Bloud et cie, 1912.

Huber, Michel. *La population de la France pendant la guerre.* Paris: Presses universitaires de France, 1931.

————*La population de la France, sa évolution et ses perspectives.* Paris: Hachette, 1937.

Hubert, Lucien. "La main-d'oeuvre coloniale dans l'industrie de la guerre,"

Revue Hebdomadaire 25 (Feb. 10, 1917): 220–32.

International Labour Organization. *International Migration Treaties, Studies and Reports*, Series O, 1, and 5. Geneva: ILO, 1925.

————*International Migration Treaties, Studies and Reports*, Series O, 6. Geneva: ILO, 1936.

Istituto central di statistica. *Sommario di statistiche storiche del l'Italia, 1861–1965*. Rome: ISSN, 1966.

L'Italia, Commissariato generale dell'emigrazione. *L'emigrazione italiana, 1910–23* and *1923–25*. Rome: Edizione del commissariato generale dell'emigrazione, 1924 and 1926.

Izard, Paul. *Le chômage et le placement en France pendant la guerre*. Paris: E. Sagot et cie, 1920.

Josse, Prosper, and Pierre Rossillion. *L'invasion étrangère en France en temps de paix*. Paris: La nation, 1938.

Jouhaux, Léon. "Le marché du travail." *Europe nouvelle* 13 (Aug. 8, 1917): 1041–45.

Joyeux, Maurice. *Le consulat polonais, un roman*. Paris: Calmann-Levy, 1957.

Kaczmarek, Czeslaw. *L'émigration polonaise en France après la guerre*. Paris: Berger, 1928.

Kindleberger, Charles. *Europe's Post-War Economic Growth*. Cambridge, Mass.: Harvard University Press, 1967.

Kirk, Dudley. *Europe's Population in the Interwar Years*. Princeton, N.J.: Princeton University Press, 1946.

Kletch, Georges. *L'organisation syndicale des travailleurs étrangers en France*. Paris: Societé des études et information économique, 1937.

Kriegel, Annie. *Aux origines du communisme française, 1914–1920*. Paris: Mouton, 1964.

————*La croissance de la CGT, 1918–21*. Paris: Mouton, 1966.

Kubat, Daniel, ed. *The Politics of Migration Policies*. New York: Center for Migration Studies, 1979.

Lafitte-Laplace, Robert. *L'économie charbonnière de la France*. Paris: 1933.

Lambert, Charles. *La France et les étrangers*. Paris: Delegrave, 1928.

Landry, Adolphe. *La révolution démographique, études et essais sur les problèmes de population*. Paris: Recueil Sirey, 1934.

Lannes, Xavier. *L'immigration en France depuis 1945*. La Haye: M. Nijhoff, 1953.

Laroque, Pierre. "Rapport sur l'organisation des services de la main-d'oeuvre étrangère en France." Paris: unpublished report, Ministère du Travail, 1937.

Lee, Everett. "A Theory of Migration," *Demography* 2 (1966): 45–57.

LeFevre, Georges. *Homme-travail*. Paris: 1929.

Lemonon, E. *L'après-guerre et la main-d'oeuvre italienne en France*. Paris: F. Alcan, 1918.

Leroy-Beaulieu, Paul. "La question des étrangers en France au point de vue économique," *Journal de droit international privé* (1888): 173–78.

Li Chao Ying. *Le mouvement de la main-d'oeuvre étrangère en France depuis la Grande Guerre*. Dijon: Langres, 1940.

Lorbet, A. *La France au travail: La région du Nord; Nord-Pas-de-Calais-Somme-Aisne*. Paris: P. Roger, 1927.

Lorwin, Val Rogin. *The French Labor Movement*. Cambridge, Mass.: Harvard University Press, 1954.

Louis, Paul. *La guerre économique*. Paris: Éditions de la Revue blanche, 1900.

Ludkiewicz, Zdzislaw. "Agrarian Structure of Poland and France from the Point of View of Emigration," *International Labour Review* 10 (Aug. 1930): 155–76.

Lugand, Joseph. *L'immigration des ouvriers étrangers en France et les enseignements de la guerre*. Paris: Librairies-imprimeries réunies, 1919.

Maier, Charles S. *Recasting Bourgeois Europe: Stabilization in France*. Princeton, N.J.: Princeton University Press, 1975.

————"The Two Postwar Eras and the Conditions for Stability in Twentieth Century Western Europe." *American Historical Review* 86 (April 1981): 327–67.

Marshall, T. H. *Class, Citizenship and Social Development*. Garden City, N.Y.: Doubleday, 1964.

Martial, René. "Le problème de l'immigration," *Revue politique et parlementaire* 22 (Dec. 10, 1926): 391–402.

————"L'immigration et l'avenir de la France," *Mercure de France* (July 15, 1933): 257–92.

————*La race française*. Paris: Mecure de France. 1934.

————*Les métis*. Paris: Flammarion, 1942.

————*Traité de l'immigration et de la greffe inter-raciale*. Cuesmes-lez-Mons, Belgium: Imprimerie fédérale, 1930.

Martin, Phillip, and Mark Miller. "Guest Workers: Lessons from Western Europe," *Industrial and Labor Relations Review* 33 (April 1980): 315–30.

Martini, Alexis. *L'expulsion des étrangers: études de droit comparé*. Paris: L. Larose, 1909.

Mas, Emile. "La main-d'oeuvre étrangère en France," *Revue politique et parlementaire* 11 (March 1904): 474–500.

Mauco, Georges. *Les étrangers en France*. Paris: A. Colin, 1932.

————"Immigration in France," *International Labour Review* 13 (June 1933): 765–88.

————"Alien Workers in France," *International Labour Review* 16 (Feb. 1936): 185–93.

Maurin, Paul. *La main-d'oeuvre immigré sur la marché du travail en France*. Paris: 1933.

Mayer, Arno. *Politics and Diplomacy of Peacemaking, 1918–1919*. New York: Vintage Books, 1967.

McDonald, James. "Towards a Typology of European Labor Migration," *International Migrations* 7 (1969): 6–24.

Mesnaud de St. Paul, Jean. *De l'émigration étrangère en France, consideré au point de vue économique*. Paris: A. Rousseau, 1902.

Michelis, Guiseppe de. *La corporazione del mondo*. Milano: V. Bompiani, 1934.

Miller, Mark. *Foreign Workers in Western Europe: An Emerging Political Force*. New York: Praeger, 1981.

Millet, Raymond. *Trois millions d'étrangers en France*. Paris: Librairie de Medicis, 1938.

Minces, Juliette. *Les travailleurs étrangers en France*. Paris: Éditions du Seuil, 1973.

Ministère de l'agriculture. *Statistiques de l'immigration, 1918–27*. Paris: Imprimerie nationale, 1928.

————*Enquête sur les étrangers*. Paris: Imprimerie national, 1929.

Molinari, G. "The Decline of the French Population," *Journal of the Royal Statistical Society* (March 1887): 183–97.

Morain, Alfred. *La réconstitution du Nord dévasté au 1er septembre 1923*. Lille: Martin–Mamy, 1923.

Muller, Helmut. *Die Polnische Volksgruppe im Deutcher Reich seit 1871*. Waschau: Rostock, 1941.

Nicolaï, A. *Les remises des émigrants italiens*. Nice: Société générale d'imprimerie, 1935.

Nogoro, B. "L'introduction de la main-d'oeuvre étrangère pendant la guerre," *Revue d'économie politique* 44 (Nov.–Dec. 1920): 718–33.

Nogoro, B., and Lucien Wiel. *La main-d'oeuvre étrangère et coloniale pendant la guerre*. Paris: Presses universitaires de France, 1926.

Oblath, Attilio. "Italian Emigration and Colonization Policy," *International Labour Review* 11 (June 1931): 805–34.

O'Connor, James. *The Fiscal Crisis of the State*. New York: St. Martin's Press, 1973.

Office de reconstitution industrielle. "Comment les industriels peuvent-ils se procurer la main-d'oeuvre dont ils ont besoin?" Paris: Jan. 1919.

————"Régles à suivre par les industriels ayant besoin de main-d'oeuvre." Paris: March 1919.

Offices régionaux, départmentales et municipaux du placement. *Compte rendu analytique de la deuxième conférence.* Marseilles: Jan. 1919.

Ogburn, William. *The Economic Development of Post-War France.* New York: Columbia University Press, 1929.

Opera Bonomelli. *Vadecum dell'emigrant.* Milan: Opera Bonomelli, 1923.

Organski, A. F. K. *The Stages of Political Development.* New York: Knopf. 1965.

Oualid, William. *L'aspect juridique de l'immigration ouvrière.* Paris: F. Alcan, 1923.

————"La France deviendra-t-elle un pays de minorités nationales?" *Le Musée social* 34 (May-June 1927): 125–59.

————"L'immigration ouvrière en France et ses causes," *Revue d'économie politique* 41 (1928): 1455–88.

————"The Occupational Distribution and Status of Workers in France," *International Labour Review* 9 (Aug. 1929): 161–84.

Packowki, Andrzek. "La presse des émigrés polonais en France, 1920–1940," *Revue du Nord* 60 (Jan. 1978): 151–62.

Pairault, André. *L'immigration organisée et l'emploi de la main-d'oeuvre étrangère en France.* Paris: Rieder, 1927.

————"La politique italienne d'émigration," *Revue politique et parlementaire* 10 (October 12, 1927): 459–72.

Paon, Marcel. *L'immigration en France.* Paris: Delagrave, 1926.

Parto communist français. *L'importance de la MOE et les diverses immigrations.* Paris: n.d.

Pasquet, Louis. *Immigration et la main-d'oeuvre étrangère en France.* Paris: Rieder, 1927.

Payen, Edouard. "Les étrangers en France," *Économiste française* 38 (March 19, 1910): 195–203.

Perrin, J. *La main-d'oeuvre étrangère dans les entreprises du bâtiment et les travaux publics en France.* Paris: Presses universitaires de France, 1925.

Perrot, Michel. *Les ouvriers en grève,* Vol. 1. Paris: Mouton, 1974.

Pic, Paul. *Traité élémentaire de législation industrielle.* Paris: A. Rousseau, 1902.

————"Les ouvriers étrangers en France," *Revue économique internationale* 8 (March 1911): 224–63.

Pinot, Françoise. *Travailleurs immigrés dans la lutte de classes.* Paris: Éditions du Cerf, 1973.

Piore, Michael. *Birds of Passage.* Cambridge, Mass.: MIT Press, 1979.

Piore, Michael and Suzanne Berger. *Dualism and Discontinuity in Industry.* Cambridge, Eng.: Cambridge University Press, 1980.

Piou, Gaeton. "La main-d'oeuvre étrangère en France," *Revue socialiste* 51 (May 15, 1912): 410–15.

Poignant, R. "L'immigration polonaise dans le Pas-de-Calais." Memoire. Arras: 1948.

Poszwa, Louis. *L'émigration polonaise agricole en France*. Paris: Gebethner et Wolff, 1930.

Poulantzas, Nicos. *Political Power and Social Classes*. London: Sheed and Ward, 1973.

Prato, Guiseppe. *Le protectionisme ouvrier*. Paris: M. Rivière, 1912.

Prost, Albert. *L'immigration en Franche-Comté*. Paris: A Rousseau, 1929.

Prost, Antoine. "L'immigration en France depuis cent ans," *Esprit* 348 (April 1966): 532–45, 808–24.

Prost, Antoine. *La CGT à l'époque du Front populaire, 1934–1939*. Paris: A. Colin, 1964.

Raflin, Numa. *Le placement et l'immigration des ouvriers agricoles polonais en France*. Paris: Imprimerie nationale, 1911.

Raisin, Charles. *La dépopulation de la France et le Code civil*. Bourg-en-Bresse: Imprimerie du "courrier de l'Ain," 1901.

Raphael, Paul. "Le problème des étrangers en France," *Grande revue* 30 (Aug. 1926): 184–214.

Reardon, Judy. "Belgian Workers in Roubaix, France, in the 19th Century." Ph.D. diss., University of Maryland, 1977.

Remond, Gabriel. *L'immigration italienne dans le sud-ouest de la France*. Paris: Recueil Sirey, 1928.

Reynaud, Georges. "La colonie italienne d'Homecourt," *Le Musée social* 15 (Oct. 1910): 205–41.

Robertson, Esmonde M. *Mussolini as Empire Builder*. New York: Macmillian, 1977.

Ronse, M. "L'émigration saisonnière en Belgique," *Bulletin de l'Association internationale pour la lutte contre le chômage* (Oct.–Dec. 1913).

Ronsin, Francis. "La classe ouvrière et le neo-malthusienisme." *Mouvement sociale* 106 (1979): 85–117.

Rose, Arnold. *Migrants in Europe: Problems of Acceptance and Adjustment*. Minneapolis: University of Minnesota Press, 1969.

Rosoli, G. F. *Un secolo di emigrazione italiana*. Rome: CSER, 1978.

Rossillion, Pierre. *L'invasion étrangère en France en temps de paix*. Paris: La Nation, 1938.

Rozwasowski, Jan. *L'immigration polonaise en France*. Lille: G. Sautai, 1927.

Saposs, David. *The Labor Movement in Post-War France*. New York: Columbia University Press, 1931.

Sauvy, Alfred. *The General Theory of Population*. New York: Basic Books, 1969.

———*Histoire économique de la France entre les deux guerres*. Vols. 1–2. Paris: A. Sauret, 1969.

Scarzanella, E. "L'emigrazione veneta del periodo fascista," *Studi storici* 18 (1977): 171–99.

Schreiber, Thomas. "De la résidence à la naturalisation: Les étrangers dans la vie civique," *Esprit* 348 (April 1966): 808–24.

Sellier, Henri, and Emile Deslandres. *La constitution de l'office départmental du placement et de la statistique du travail de la Seine.* Paris: 1918.

Société générale d'immigration (SGI). *La Société générale d'immigration vous fournira de la main-d'oeuvre étrangère.* Paris: SGI, 1930.

————*Société générale d'immigration, Guide du travailleur étranger.* Paris: SGI, 1938.

Sinicki, Henri-Jean. *Le problème de l'émigration polonaise.* Nancy: Société d'impressions typographiques, 1938.

Skucpol, Theda. *States and Social Revolutions.* Cambridge, Eng.: Cambridge University Press, 1979.

Smith, Denis Mack. *Mussolini's Roman Empire.* New York: Penguin Books, 1977.

Sorre, Maximilien. *Les ressources d'outillage et la production de la région du Nord.* Lille: 1er région économique, 1927.

Souchon, Auguste. *La crise de la main-d'oeuvre agricole en France.* Paris: A. Rousseau, 1914.

Spengler, Joseph. *France Faces Depopulation.* New York: Greenwood Press, 1968.

Stahl, Robert. *L'organisation du relèvement économique dans le Nord libéré: Un an de reconstruction.* Lille: 1920.

Stearns, Peter. *Lives of Labor.* New York: Holmes and Meier, 1975.

Stein, Louis. *Beyond Death and Exile: The Spanish Republicans in France, 1939–55.* Cambridge, Mass.: Harvard University Press, 1979.

Taft, Donald. *Human Migration.* New York: Ronald Press, 1936.

Tapinos, Georges. *L'économie des migrations internationales.* Paris: Foundation nationale des sciences politiques, 1974.

————*L'immigration étrangère en France, 1946–73,* Institut national des études économiques, *Travaux et Documents,* No. 71. Paris: Presses universitaires de France, 1975.

Taylor, Philip. *The Distant Magnet: European Emigration to the U.S.A.* London: Eyre and Spottiswoode, 1971.

Ter-davtian, Léon. *Les étrangers en surnombre dans l'économie nationale.* Paris: Recueil Sirey, 1942.

Thomas, Brinley. *Migration and Economic Growth.* Cambridge, Eng.: Cambridge University Press, 1973.

Thomas, William I. *The Polish Peasant in Europe and America.* New York: Dover Publications, 1958.

Tilly, Charles. et al. *The Rebellious Century, 1830–1930*. Cambridge, Mass.: Harvard University Press, 1975.

Trempé, Rolande. *Les mineurs de Carmeux, 1848–1914*. Paris: Éditions ouvrières, 1971.

Treves, Anna. *Le migrazioni interne dell'Italia fascista*. Turin: Einaudi, 1976.

Tugault, Yves. "L'immigration étrangère en France: Une nouvelle méthode de measure," *Population* 25 (July 1971): 691–708.

Urig-Wehler, Hans. ed. "Die Polen im Ruhrgebiet, bis 1918," *Modern Deutsche Socialgeschichte*. Koln: Berlin Kiepenheur Witsch, 1968.

Valet, Henri. *Les restrictions à l'immigration*. Paris: Recueil Sirey, 1930.

Varlez, Louis. *Les migrations internationales et leur réglementations*. Paris: Recueil des cours, 1929.

————"General Principals of an International Convention on the Conditions and Contracts of Employment of Foreign Workers," *International Labour Review* 9 (March 1929): 317–37.

Varlez, Louis, and Charles Picquenard. *Le placement public à Paris: Situation actuelle et projects de réforme*. Paris: Association française contre le chômage, 1913.

Vidalenc, Jean. "La main-d'oeuvre étrangère en France et la Première Guerre Mondiale (1901–1926)," *Francia* 2 (1974): 524–50.

Vieuguet, André. *Français et immigrés: le combat du CPF*. Paris: Éditions sociales, 1975.

Wallerstein, Immanuel. *The Modern World-System*. I: *Capitalist Agriculture and the Origins of the European World-Economy in the Sixteenth Century;* II: *Mercantilism and the Consolidation of the European World-Economy, 1600–1750*. New York. Academic Press, 1976 and 1980.

Walter, Gérard. *L'évolution de problème de la main-d'oeuvre dans la métallurgie de la Lorraine*. Maçon: J. Buguet-Comptour, 1935.

Weber, Eugen. *Peasants into Frenchmen*. Stanford, Calif.: Stanford University Press, 1976.

Wiel, Lucien. *La main-d'oeuvre étrangère et coloniale pendant la guerre*. Paris: Presses universitaires de France, n.d.

Wilcox, Walter, and Imgre Ferenczi. *International Migrations*, 2 vols. New York: National Bureau of Economic Research, 1929 and 1931.

Willis, Kenneth. *Problems in Migration Analysis*. Lexington, Mass.: Lexington Books, 1974.

Wlocevski, Stephane. *L'installation des italiens en France*. Paris: F. Alcan, 1931.

————"La main-d'oeuvre polonaise in France," *Pologne* 14 Nov. 1933): 45–53.

————"Le scoutisme polonais en France." *Le Pologne* 13 (Nov. 1933): 185–89.

————*Les mineurs polonais en France avant, pendant et après la guerre*. Lens: M. Kwiatkowski, 1935.

————*L'établissement des Polonais en France*. Paris: Librairie Picart, 1936.

————"Y a-t-il trop de travailleurs étrangers en France?" *Revue d'économie politique* 49 (1935): 324–59.

Woog, Claude. *La politique d'émigration de l'Italie*. Paris: Presses universitaires de France, 1930.

Index